THE
BESSIE SMITH
COMPANION

THE
BESSIE SMITH
COMPANION

A Critical and Detailed Appreciation
of the Recordings

by
EDWARD BROOKS

Bayou Press

First published 1982 by
Cavendish Publishing Company

This edition published 1989 by
Bayou Press Ltd
117 High Street
Wheatley
Oxford

British Library Cataloguing in Publication Data
Brooks, Edward
  The Bessie Smith Companion: a critical and
  detailed appreciation of the recordings.
  1. United States. Blues. Singing. Smith, Bessie
  I. Title
  789.9' 136453 ' 00924

ISBN 1–871478–60–X

CONTENTS

To Shirley

I love the blues, they hurt so nice.

Anonymous Blues

... the best pieces of jazz, like any first-rate product of a cultivated art, require and repay study for their own sake.

William W. Austin
Music in the Twentieth Century

ACKNOWLEDGMENTS

I am grateful to Bruce Beavan, Owen Robinson, Brian Sharpe and John Stephan without whose ideas, records and alcohol over the years, this book might never have been.

FOREWORD

At first glance Edward Brooks' project could seem heroic but misplaced; the track by track analysis of 159 recordings of a blues singer who died forty-five years ago, plus alternative takes and the crackling sound-track of her only film, not to mention a careful assessment of those musicians who accompanied her, many of which, by the author's own admission, were at best mediocre.

If one also takes into account that Brooks' approach is technically uncompromising, bristling with 'tonic minor 7th chords', 'pentatonically based melody' and 'glissandi', it may seem that his book's appeal is only to those who have a) an obsessive interest in the oeuvre of Bessie Smith and b) a working musical knowledge; a comparatively rare combination I should have thought.

In practice however, and I write as one whose own grasp of musical theory is rudimentary, this turns out to be a fascinating enterprise. Its principle virtue lies in the author's conviction of his subject's genius and his passionate concern to transmit this belief. The result is no dry academic thesis, but the journal of a love affair set down without bathos, and with full awareness of her occasional failures or inadequacies as well as of her towering and majestic glory, her ability to transmute simple if frequently moving material into statements of universal beauty and significance.

Bessie's life, a self-destructive tragi-comedy in which fact and myth are hopelessly intertwined, is already well-covered; Chris Albertson's book is probably the nearest to the truth that we shall ever reach; but her work has never been examined in such depth. It is Brooks' achievement that, while appearing on the surface to concentrate on what his ear has to tell him, and the practical information as to when, where and with whom each song was recorded, he should gradually build up a solid picture of the singer and the social context in which she lived and worked. He stresses that much of her material was autobiographical. She sang of strong sexual appetite, heavy drinking, joy and remorse. Brooks, so unobtrusively that we are almost unaware of it, equates the singer and the song.

*   *   *   *

It is my long established custom when at home to listen every morning to two or three tracks of Bessie while I am dressing. I am in consequence probably as exposed to her complete work as almost anyone. Since receiving this manuscript I have added a minute or two into my routine by reading his analysis of the songs in question, and have discovered by doing so an added dimension. Bessie's amazing diversity, given the simplicity of her means, has become manifest, her technical armoury described and explained, yet without in anyway blunting what is after all the final test of a work of art, its emotional impact. Not that I am always in agreement with his assessment of individual recordings; he dismisses *Eavesdropper's Blues* as one of her rare failures while I rate it quite highly, but even here I have been forced to listen rather than to yield, as perhaps I have for some years, to the overall familiar spell.

My only carp is of omission. It would be a great help if the words of every song were included or, perhaps more practically, issued as soon as possible in a separate book. Even after all this time, some phrases of Bessie's rich Southern diction escape me, especially on the early pre-electric recordings. For

a novice much of what she is singing must seem impene-
trable. Otherwise this is an estimable work and essential
reading, tonic minor seventh chords and all, for anyone who
has been touched by the Empress of the Blues. A close study
of her work was long overdue. That it has been done without
obvious pedantry, and with such freshness and enthusiasm is
our good luck.

GEORGE MELLY, 1982

INTRODUCTION

One test of an artist's achievement is the numerical one, setting successes against failures over a period long enough to avoid statistical distortion. Bessie Smith (1895–1937),[1] emerges from such an examination as the most consistently successful of the 'classic'[2] blues singers. Out of 159 titles released, perhaps no more than 4 disappoint seriously.[3] This, in spite of the fact that she was often cursed with tawdry material and inadequate accompanists. But whatever criterion is used, Bessie towered above her contemporaries; to have been another blues singer in the 1920's must sometimes have been a discouraging experience. Her aesthetic taste, which seldom faltered, was built upon incomparable technique; the former depends upon subjective opinion but technique is something which can be quantified more precisely. This book sets out to describe the details of her technique and at the same time assess its appropriateness to the material she found herself with. Some considerable space

[1] There is some doubt about her date of birth; it has been variously put as 1894, 1898 and 1900 by others.
[2] Defined by Paul Oliver in 'Bessie Smith', page 4, as one 'who added a conscious artistry to the blues'.
[3] In an art-form where value-judgement deputises for reasoned analysis, few are likely to agree upon either the number of unsatisfactory releases or on their titles. I personally consider such a list should include *Haunted House Blues* and *Eavesdropper's Blues* of 1924, *Looking For My Man*, 1927 and *You Ought To Be Ashamed* of 1928.

will be devoted to an analysis of the performances of her accompanists and as these include some of the best (and worst) jazzmen, it will, to some extent, provide a commentary on the jazz styles of the 1920's and early 1930's.

This is a music which has often been dismissed as too simple to be worthy of serious investigation and its vernacular origins have helped to support such views. It is music with few intellectual pretensions certainly; a long-term musical memory such as is necessary to obtain a proper understanding of the best products of the European classical and romantic periods for instance, is not a prerequisite to full appreciation of Bessie's collaboration with Louis Armstrong on *The St. Louis Blues*. But if the surface of the often exciting streams of sound is penetrated, a fascinating world of borrowings, adaptions and juxtapositions from other musical cultures is revealed and it is irrelevant that the inclusion of these elements by the performers was often unconscious. By European standards, the harmony and structure of this music is simple: rhythm, counterpoint, timbre, and pitch and dynamic manipulation on the other hand, turn out to be too complex for our supposedly comprehensive system of notation to embrace. It is a music in which a tension between the old (folk) and the new (composed-art) ingredients provide its potency, and recognition and understanding of these ingredients will add a new stratum of satisfaction to the listener already prejudiced in its favour.

Whilst a description of the technical reasons for Bessie Smith's greatness form the core of this book, visceral pleasure is in no way disparaged. I include myself amongst those countless people, world-wide, who get a strong gut-derived satisfaction from much early jazz and in particular the songs of Bessie Smith and I would not even argue that this is not the most important factor contributing to the listener's enjoyment. On the other hand there must be reasons why one singer produces such pleasure for so many people whereas another lacks this power. The fact that it may be difficult to identify such reasons and on many occasions will not be possible at all, is no excuse for not trying. Informed listening can only be another element in our delight which, in spite of a widespread myth, will not tarnish our 'natural' joy.

Stravinsky considered a work of art to be something quite separate from its maker, not merely when finished, but apparently whilst it was being produced as well. Of his *Le Sacre du printemps* he said 'I am the vessel through which *Le Sacre* passed'. This would seem to repudiate the value of biographical information in any assessment of an artist's work. But jazz and blues are highly personal forms of self-expression, which the everyday experiences of life inform and throw light upon.[4] They were forms not understood by Stravinsky and many other composers of art-music, whose efforts were detached by comparison. It is true Stravinsky was influenced by jazz in some of his early compositions, but his borrowings came from that pale pastiche that passed for jazz in the Europe of the first two decades of this century. Although in no respect a biography therefore (there are already enough of those), references to the details of Bessie Smith's life will be made when appropriate.

One of the difficulties inherent in the analysis of early jazz and blues is the fact that little, if anything, was ever written down. A musicologist delving into the origins of the symphony say, will examine the manuscripts of Stamitz, Sammartini and others of the Mannheim School. With written notation before him he can dwell for as long as he desires upon the various features he wishes to study. Early jazz and blues have, as their only primary source, the gramophone record, where the sounds reproduced occur in a time continuum and cannot be frozen to facilitate analysis. To add

---

[4] Well over half of Bessie Smith's songs are about love (mainly the unhappy kind) and the rest are mostly concerned with private pain caused by such things as poverty, homesickness, the supernatural, prison, alcohol, death and natural disaster. Problems of the group are rarely dealt with: politics as a theme does not figure at all (political apathy was widespread amongst American Blacks in the 1920's and early 1930's) – racial and social protest (of a mild kind) in only a handful of titles.

to the difficulty, the sound quality resulting from early recording techniques and the passage of time, is usually less than satisfactory. This means that the dissection of a single chord, let alone a passage, will often have to rely upon intuitive, rather than certain, identification of pitches.

It is sad to realise that Bessie Smith's recording years spanned only a quarter of her life and only one-third of her singing career. Even sadder, we shall never know how she sounded as a young woman. She was twenty-eight when her first commercially acceptable recording was cut and her 160 sides confirm that her style was mature by then, relatively little further evolution being evident. Of her rivals, Ma Rainey and Chippie Hill were often Bessie's equal in the sincerity of their work but could not approach her technique. It is true that Clara Smith could get near to Bessie's all-round ability but only on occasion. Of the younger singers with an elemental style, Mahalia Jackson was similarly larger than life but her ornaments were more precise, antiseptic even. Bessie Smith is the main, virtually the only link between the itinerant male rural self-accompanying blues singers of the 1920's and beyond, and the female jazz singers of the 1930's. Ella Fitzgerald and Billie Holiday both owe her a considerable debt whilst at the same time making her style commercially redundant. Bessie Smith is of enormous importance because of her influence on these and other singers but she will never be reduced to merely a historical footnote because of this — her art carries its own unique viability. To adapt a phrase of George Melly quoted by D. Stewart-Baxter,[5] she offered feeling and technique in perfect accord.

Although Bessie's stature was probably not recognised immediately, her first record to be released was certainly what America's increasing urban Black population wanted, judging by the sales figures. Most sources, until 1979 suggested sales in excess of three-quarters of a million for this record, *Down-Hearted Blues*. But perhaps a more realistic

[5] 'Ma Rainey and the Classic Blues Singers', page 7.

xviii THE BESSIE SMITH COMPANION

figure is obtained from the recently unearthed Columbia sales
card showing total sales to September, 1929 (shortly after
which the record was deleted from the catalogue) of 276,796
of which 258,214 were sold in 1923.[6] Even so, quite phenomenal figures for those early days of recording. Earlier records
had been released of blues singers, and singers of ballads and
popular songs who temporarily converted to singing in a
blues style, but few approached these figures. Mamie Smith's
Crazy Blues of August 1920 on Okeh was the seminal recording of the genre but it needed the talent of Bessie Smith (no
relation) to communicate consistently with the mass audience
from the northern Black ghettos.[7]

Some explanation of my perhaps arbitrary descriptions of
structure is necessary. With very few exceptions, Bessie's
output falls neatly into two classes; twelve-bar blues where
the chord sequence, subject to a relatively small number of
variations, is predictable; and popular songs where it is not.[8]
Twelve-bar blues, follow or at least make reference to the
following chord sequence:

Four bars tonic: two bars subdominant:
two bars tonic: two bars dominant: two bars tonic.

Quite often minor-seventh chords will be substituted for
the triad. And sometimes the order of chords in the progression will be altered a little. Usually the basic form will be

---

[6] 'Storyville 83', June-July, 1979. Storyville Publications and Company
Limited. Page 200.
[7] Gunther Schuller in 'Early Jazz', page 226n, quotes the sales figures for
Crazy Blues as 'over a million in the first half-year', but Mamie Smith's total
of released titles was certainly only half that of Bessie Smith.
[8] Whether or not a title contains the word 'blues' is no guarantee of its
structure. The waning selling power of the word can be deduced from the
fact that of Bessie Smith's first eighty titles, fifty-four were called blues and
twenty-six were not: of the last seventy-nine titles, twenty-eight were
called blues and fifty-one were not. The actual twelve-bar blues format was
used more often in the first half of her output too but the rejection of the
form in the second half was not so dramatic as was the avoidance of the word
'blues'.

garnished in a Bessie Smith performance, with an introduction, coda and perhaps a verse. Under the generic description 'popular song form' I mean numbers including chords on other degrees of the scale in addition to tonic, subdominant and dominant and with more complex progressions; further, the number of bars for a chorus can range up to 32.

It should also be mentioned that many of Bessie Smith's melodic lines are modally derived, sometimes almost exclusively so. One of her most used, the pentatonic mode, is the earliest of all scales and is easily found by striking the black notes on the piano in an ascending or descending progression; by retaining the intervals between these black notes, this scale can be transposed to start on any pitch of the chromatic scale. Many folk-songs the world over are based upon the pentatonic[9] or one of the other modes and in employing these scales Bessie is unconsciously following a very old tradition.

It was the gramophone which made Bessie Smith famous and together with radio hastened her decline. It was not merely that 'it brought other more sophisticated musical forms to the remoter districts' as Paul Oliver claims[10] although this was certainly true. There was also the saturation effect resulting from music continually on tap, speeding up the natural evolutionary process of a style which previously might have lasted for several generations with little change. It took nearly one hundred years for the musical culture of southern Black slaves to produce Bessie Smith. Then suddenly, as she appeared on the scene, musical evolution began to follow an exponential curve, a curve her total and unchanging commitment to her material disqualified her from following. During the period of her recording career jazz underwent tremendous changes but Bessie Smith hardly noticed. A dinosaur but a magnificent one.

E.B. 1982

[9] *Auld Lang Syne* for instance has a melody which is exclusively pentatonic.
[10] 'Bessie Smith', pages 56/7.

NOTE

Whilst this book may be seen primarily as a work of reference, if read through concurrently with a reflective playing of the recordings and frequent appeal to the discography, an accumulative empathy with Bessie Smith's achievement may result.

The discography lists the original 78 rpm records issued by Columbia in the U.S.A. but the most convenient way to obtain Bessie's whole output (excluding alternate takes and film soundtrack) is to purchase the five twin-record albums re-issued by CBS in Britain, in 1970/71, the numbers of which are 66258, 66262, 66264, 66273 and 67232. Most of these reissues were still in the catalogue at the time of writing (March, 1982).

ONE

Her first releases

On 16th February, 1923 Bessie Smith cut her first recording to be released, *Down-Hearted Blues.* She was accompanied by Clarence Williams at the piano. But this was not her recording debut; she had cut sides previously for Okeh and Black Swan[1], and, the day before, Columbia. The products of these earlier sessions were all rejected. From this session however, Columbia hesitatingly decided to release the fifth take of *Down-Hearted Blues* with the third take of the only other successful number, *Gulf Coast Blues,* on the two sides of a 78 rpm 10 inch disc.

The choice of *Down-Hearted Blues*, written by Alberta Hunter and Lovie Austin and recorded by Alberta Hunter and others previously, seems an overly cautious way to launch a new singer on record. But it not only proved to be an immediate success but quickly replaced all previous versions as the definitive one.

Listening to the record now with the benefit of over fifty years of electrical recording behind us, requires the exercise of some imagination. The most obvious difference between this accoustic recording and present day electrical recordings is the amorphous nature of the sound. Piano and voice are not as clearly separated as we nowadays expect. The purely musical

[1] There is also some evidence that she recorded for Emerson as early as 1921. John Hammond believes he has Bessie's first recording, released under the name of Rosa Henderson.

I

2 THE BESSIE SMITH COMPANION

differences from her later recordings are almost as obvious. Reputedly she was nervous at this session[2] and whilst a broad, rich, velvet quality of voice shines through the aural fog produced by primitive recording technique and the passing years, the subtle microtonal shadings which are such an impressive feature of her later releases are largely missing.

Although possibly hindsight-assisted, it now seems that Bessie's clear diction which she retained through her career was a significant factor in her popularity. Every word can be heard, (although not necessarily understood by a late twentieth century listener). Clarity of diction is essential for this type of narrative song where the story, like the harmony is unresolved at the end of the verse; few other popular singers of the time could approach Bessie's limpidity however, without the sacrifice of expression.

Any doubts that this was to be something grander than a twelve-bar country blues are dispelled by the 4 bar piano introduction and the 16 bar voice and piano verse which precede the first chorus. Four choruses in the expected twelve-bar blues form follow but the piece finishes with Williams alone adding a neat tonic and dominant coda to round-off the largely strophic structure. The structure of Bessie's performances is usually simple but is always an important factor in musical understanding. Here, as well as

[2] The failure of the previous day's session to produce an acceptable master and the number of takes necessary on 16th February are often used as evidence of her nervousness on this first successful date. The acoustic system of recording was however very primitive, relying upon vibrations carried down a large horn on to a needle which then cut grooves in a wax-like disc: after processing the disc to produce a metal master, from which commercially released pressings were made, the reverse procedure was adopted to reproduce sound. As it was not possible to play back the freshly cut wax disc immediately, several takes were made as a matter of course, irrespective of whether there were defects in performance, since flaws in wax or metal could easily cause an otherwise acceptable performance to be rejected. Furthermore, instead of a motor, the equipment was powered by pulleys which turned a lathe. In cold weather these pulleys could become sluggish as lubrication thickened and this had the effect of increasing playback pitch by a microtone or more.

providing introduction and coda, Williams provides the antiphony endemic to the blues with his linking breaks. Although his playing is disparaged by most observers, it must be admitted that he is sometimes inventive in his responses to Bessie's voice patterns. His style is simple certainly, but he does not try to play beyond his rudimentary technique;[3] more ambitious financially than Bessie, he was content to leave her to dominate their musical performances. He would delineate the main beat with minimal swing[4] and syncopation leaving her to provide between-the-beat accentuation and a more positive swing.

It has been said that the words on this first release which really set her listeners on fire and boosted sales were in the last chorus: 'I've got the world in a jug, the stopper's in my hand.'[5] An extravagant boast, certainly likely to appeal to the imagination of a repressed race.

Paul Oliver[6] complains that the Bessie Smith version was deliberately designed to supersede Alberta Hunter's version of July 1922 and that this megalomanic trait surfaced more than once in Bessie's recording career. But her ability proved to be such that almost anything she recorded was bound to supersede a previous version. It seems perverse therefore to, in effect, suggest that she should avoid numbers previously recorded by others or give such pieces less than her usual full commitment. And in any case, competition is at the heart of show business: the bands of New Orleans, a decade earlier certainly accepted 'cutting' contests as part of every day life in their profession. It is interesting to note that Alberta Hunter who wrote the song and whose own record of it had been a best seller, apparently felt no bitterness. She says that by the

---

[3] It is interesting to note that Williams adopts C major, the pianist's easiest key for this seminal effort with Bessie.

[4] Swing. A tension between the basic pulse and the actual placing of the harmonic and melodic superstructure.

[5] Frank Walker, her recording manager at Columbia in 'Hear Me Talkin' To Ya', page 240.

[6] 'The Story of the Blues', page 96.

time Bessie recorded it, everyone thought its economic potential exhausted. She goes on to acclaim Bessie as 'the greatest of them all'.[7]

Of course she was right. But to prove this we have to look beyond the usual hotchpotch of glossy subjective opinion for more musical reasons. Firstly, although largely self-taught and producing an 'illegitimate' sound by the standards of European composed-art-music, her voice production and projection was of the highest quality. Secondly, a desire to avoid symmetry, a frequent characteristic of twentieth-century musical genius (for example Stravinsky, Bartok, Schoenberg, Louis Armstrong) was the reason for her developing integrity of expression. The cause lies in her breathing. In this record the two-bar regularity of phrasing results from a delivery which mostly follows the superficial sense of the words. But as she became at home in the studio she tended to pause for breath in unconventional places, astonishingly enhancing rather than detracting from the linguistic sense, and at the same time increasing the narrative flow. Even here, there is a line in the verse which illustrates the technique, 'The next man I get has got to promise me, to be mine, all mine'. She takes a main breath after 'has got to' rather than carrying on to take it after 'promise me' where her breath is less deep. This tends to integrate the words 'promise me' with 'to be mine, all mine' where they really belong, thus highlighting the meaning.[8] An augury of what was to come.

Thirdly, her control of intonation is flawless and her work contains a greater abundance and variety of decoration than

[7] 'Hear Me Talkin' To Ya', page 247.
[8] The words of this piece follow the normal twelve-bar blues pattern, the lyrics of the first line being repeated and with the third line drawing together the proposition(s) of the repeated first line. Blues singers however, whilst repeating the sense of the first line in the second, traditionally omit and substitute words there for variation. Bessie Smith's ouvre is full of such modifications but in each of the four choruses of *Down-Hearted Blues* she repeats the words of the first line exactly. Perhaps further evidence that she is feeling her way.

that of her contemporaries. As already pointed out, the full development of this area of her art was yet to come, but even at this early stage pre-echoes of her later sure microtonal control can be found, in the form of the occasional blue note.[9] Mostly however, major- and minor-thirds and sevenths are hit cleanly even where such semitonal intervals occur consecutively.

Fourthly there is her innate sense of swing, a quality not possessed in such abundance by other popular singers of the time. Later, this talent also is developed, but even here she often phrases across the principal accents to build up an agreeable tension against the main pulse.

Finally, there is her total commitment to almost every performance, a quality difficult to pin down but apparent as soon as her voice is heard. The intensity of her commitment was unique at the time and still remains so. It gave her the ability to make the poignant and banal alike, into something deeply meaningful, sometimes, as will be seen later, catching her accompanists unawares in the process. In *Down-Hearted Blues,* Williams' bland piano is almost an uninvolved observer but its detachment fortunately does nothing to detract from her heart-felt cries of unrequited love.

Another plane of tension is set up in the melody of the verse which is almost purely pentatonic in derivation. This causes a satisfying friction with the diatonic harmonies of the accompaniment, but as indicated in the introduction, the use of melodies based upon the pentatonic and other modes is not the preserve of Bessie Smith alone.

Bessie's range in *Down-Hearted Blues* falls almost entirely within the tonic triad, middle C to G. Only in the verse does

[9] Blue Note. A note fluctuating about and between the major- and minor-third and seventh of the scale (and sometimes the fifth). Used extensively by jazz and blues, singers and instrumentalists for expressive purposes. It sets up a false relation with the major (or minor) scale used and is especially noticeable when the piano, with its fixed pitches, incapable of microtones, is used for accompaniment.

she extend to the major-seventh of the scale, B^{10} with an occasional A in the choruses. Whilst she often later uses a wider range than this her melodic line may still revolve largely around one note. Here, as Richard Hadlock[11] points out, it is the dominant, G. However, the impression one is left with from his comments is that this is perhaps a technique she invented herself, whereas it is a strong feature of much folk music (including that of Russia, Eastern Europe, the Balkans, and North Africa). She has merely inherited a tradition. On the other hand the notes she favours are those she naturally endows with the richest harmonics, or as Hadlock puts it, her 'most powerful, ringing tones'.

The idea of the climax is common to both European composed-art and popular music; it is not a very marked feature of the rural blues from which Bessie Smith's songs developed. Quite often in her later performances she will prepare a climax; just as often, as here, she will not. It is tempting to attribute the lack of climax in her first release to an unsophisticated technique but this view does not fit the facts.[12]

Gulf Coast Blues was the only other successful side produced at this session, (*Keeps On A-Raining'* was abandoned after five takes). It is similar in construction to *Down-Hearted Blues* but there are differences. Although it would not be profitable to analyse the structure of all of Bessie's recorded performances it is worth pointing out that almost every one is different. this results in an astonishing number of variations for such a simple music. Here, the structure of the previous number is augmented with a 2 bar verse-anticipation by the piano and varies by dividing the verses into two similar 8 bar sections.

[10] This may be more evidence of nervousness. One would expect a minor, possible blued seventh from the later Bessie. But here she employs the diatonic major-seventh.
[11] 'Jazz Masters of the Twenties', pages 223/4. He calls them centre-tones.
[12] It might of course be argued that the words 'I've got the world in a jug' etc., are sufficiently apocalyptic to need no other climax.

And although there are four twelve-bar blues choruses as before, the third of these is by piano alone.

The vast majority of Bessie's recordings from her early years were speeds below $\quarternote = 91$. *Down-Hearted Blues* at $\quarternote = 80$ has therefore an entirely typical tempo for the period. *Gulf Coast Blues* at $\quarternote = 96$ however does not.[13]

This is another blues of unrequited love and, as in her first release, the words of each second line are identical with those in the first. Again the only sense of climax lies in the words; those of the concluding chorus draw together the complaints of the earlier choruses.

Already, in her second release, Bessie's art is beginning to flower, and the main advance is in pitch manipulation. The acciaccaturas remain but here she introduces a slide (glissando) which changes direction. This is to be made much of later in her career. In the first chorus the first appearance of the word 'town' is sung with a straightforward rising smear[14] but on its repeat the voice slides from the fifth, down below the third degree of the scale and then back up to it (Ex. 1).

Ex. 1

'News' in the second chorus and 'tired' in the last are also given both treatments. It would be naive to suggest that the melisma of Ex. 1 had been developed during the course of one recording session; we must assume that it was within her repertoire when she recorded the earlier piece but that as with

[13] These speeds are approximate and many performances have speeded up by the end.

[14] Smear. A short glissando of less than a tone.

[15] Musical examples are written at actual sounding pitch, i.e. non-transposing.

some other facets of her art, tension perhaps prevented her from using it. [16]

Williams in his middle- or late-twenties displays his fully developed but limited ragtime-based style. His performance is unexceptional and, in fact, in his solo chorus he displays uncertainty over the correct progression of some of his arpeggios. [17] From this distance we can see that his main contribution to jazz was in the field of organisation. He does however use a figure in both releases from this session which, unremarkable in itself, is useful evidence of identity later; [18] at the end of the second, third and last choruses here, he employs an upper mordent based riff over tonic and subdominant harmonies. Ex. 2 describes the version used at the end of the second chorus.

Ex. 2 (top line notation only shown)

[16] As Schuller says, this is her most oft-repeated double-note ornament and is reserved to approach the third of the chord. He is obviously wrong however to suggest on page 232 of 'Early Jazz' that she does not begin to use it until 1925. Bessie, incidentally, was not the only singer to use it; Maggie Jones also used it, for example in *Poor House Blues* of December 1924.
[17] Williams' coda incidentally, makes use of silence in a way rather reminiscent of Jelly Roll Morton.
[18] Specifically on *Need A Little Sugar In My Bowl* of 20th November, 1931.

TWO

April, 1923

With her first and enormously successful recordings behind
her, it might be supposed that Columbia would get Bessie
back to the studio quickly but it was in fact nearly two
months before she returned. The reason was that her first
record had not been issued – its phenomenal success still in
the future. It was not issued until some four months later. On
the 11th April, 1923 therefore, Columbia were still exercis-
ing caution; most of the tunes had previously been recorded
by other singers.

Quantitatively, this session was much more successful
than the previous one. Six sides were released, two with
instrumental trio including Clarence Williams on piano and
four with Williams alone accompanying on piano. Even
'Tain't Nobody's Biz'ness If I Do and Keeps On A-Rainin',
unacceptable in February, were released from this session.

The first two numbers from this session are marred by the
unsubtle clarinet of (probably) Ernest Elliott. There is little
to be said in his favour except perhaps that he had the luck to
be present in Mamie Smith's recording of Crazy Blues on 10th
August, 1920 – the first of the genre. As the only horn on
Aggravatin' Papa, he would have been the natural choice to
provide the antiphony at the end of the vocal lines; fortunately someone's good taste prevailed and we find Bessie
herself providing many of the responses at these points.

9

The chorus is 32 bars long[1] and after Bessie and Clarence Williams have been through it once, it is repeated by the instrumentalists without the singer until the last 8 bars, when Bessie breaks-in over stop chords, providing a climax by musical means rather than a linguistic climax as in the two previous releases.

This is another piece taken at an untypical pace for the period, $\downarrow = 104$. Although Bessie copes well enough, she is forced to restrict her technique. Two-note decorations, although present have to be of less duration and weight. Only her phrase-end downward slides can be imbued with full expression. However, if her technique is restricted, and the lightweight lyrics certainly call for nothing more, she does extend her range at its upper end to touch the C above middle C (on 'down' at the end of the first 16 bars of chorus). Her timbre is perhaps a little thin on this note but she shows no sign of strain on the long-held final high Bb of the performance. It may be that the harmonic rhythm,[2] faster than that of a twelve-bar blues, inspired her to stretch herself.

Her growing confidence in the recording studio is also evidenced in the sure way she handles the stop-time passages. Over stop-chords at the end of the record on 'don't' she even brings off a measured vibrato wide enough to constitute a trill – a relatively rare effect from her 'bag'.

This is a suitable point to mention a truism of early jazz – that the instrumentation both in number (although it should not generally exceed seven) and type, is not of vital importance. This parallels the composed-art-music of the seventeenth- and eighteenth-centuries; Corelli, Vivaldi and even Haydn and Mozart wrote pieces for violin which were easily and often played by flute or oboe. The instrumentation of both jazz and the concerto grosso depends mainly upon what

[1] This is not the AABA construction of what was later to become the thirty-two bar popular song form. Instead of four sections of 8 bars each, the sections here are of 4 bars and progress AABC, ADEA.

[2] Harmonic Rhythm. The rhythmic pattern provided by the changes in harmony. 'Harvard Dictionary of Music', page 369.

is available. What is of vital importance in jazz is the ability of the performers, since anyone may be asked to play a more or less virtuosic solo. Talent was not so important for the performance of a piece by say Corelli, since virtuoso parts were given to few performers. In *Aggravatin' Papa,* whilst the banjo is at least competent and stylistically acceptable, the clarinet seems to come from the world of the dance-band; its improvisations, if that is what they are, are unsubtle and stilted. The superficiality of Elliott's ideas in fact tempt one to argue that the aural breadth of Bessie Smith's voice make anything more than a piano unnecessary.[3]

Bessie's continually increasing confidence comes through again on *Beale Street Mama.* She now touches high D and in her last half-chorus, with harmony on the first word only, bursts back with 'How come you do me like you do'. The pace at $\downarrow = 92$ is a happier one for her, encouraging a majestic delivery extravagant with melisma. A good example is her slightly articulated slide on 'don't' in the verse, which spans a falling major-third, and, when the vowel is repeated in the next bar, a perfect-fourth; in addition, she treats both first notes, Gs, to an ascending smear before beginning the downward slide. On 'cry' at the end of the verse she demonstrates her keen harmonic sense. Like Louis Armstrong, she would often suggest the harmony appropriate to her melodic line; here the melody requires only the dominant-seventh, Bb, but Bessie's fall-off descends to the next lower note in the chord, G.

The quality of the accompaniment is much the same as in the previous piece except that the clarinet's wailing glissandi would be even more at home in one of the novelty records of the period.

For *Baby Won't You Please Come Home,* her second Clarence

---

[3] One of the main factors in her breadth of sound is the rich vibrato with which she invests every note long enough to carry it.

Williams composition[4] and one of his most popular, Bessie chooses a slower pace than is usual today, $\downarrow$ = 82. It allows her to deck out the popular song form as a blues. At the start, for instance, she richly blues the area around and between the major-(E) and minor-seventh (Eb) on the most important words, 'blues' and 'world' and by hitting most of the other notes cleanly achieves increased emphasis. On 'understand', she provides her own harmony with a falling arpeggio of the submediant-minor, clashing satisfyingly with Williams' submediant-major chord. Then, towards the end of the verse, her cry of 'Oh', blueing the third, is pure Expressionism[5] but of a natural, slowly evolving tradition, not the palimpsest of the Second Viennese School.[6] Her adventures with pitch are a delight throughout the piece. Her control is never found wanting and, as Paul Oliver says, 'she seems to enjoy the enunciation of every word'.[7]

In the key of F major, this piece represents a reversal of the range-extending process seen so far; the tessitura is normal and restricted to the perfect-fifth, D to A above middle C with only the last 'please' on high C breaking out of these limits to effect a simple climax. A high C which she now sings without strain incidentally. The reason for this apparent atavism is that the melodic line requires no greater range. Even so her line is still full of contractions and ellipses.

Bessie's breathing pauses are more conventional here. Perhaps at this early stage of her recording career she still needs to limit the number of things she does at once, concentrating here on pitch control.

Oh Daddy Blues is another popular song but one with an unusual structure — the choruses are of 28 bars each. The opening bar from the piano is a little unusual too. To introduce a touch of the Orient (for what reason is not clear)

[4] The first was *Gulf Coast Blues*.
[5] Expressionism. 'A quality of expressive emphasis and distortion which may be found in works of art of any people or period'. 'Expressionism', page 8.
[6] Schoenberg, Berg and Webern.   [7] 'Bessie Smith', page 19.

Williams starts the melody over chords based on the super-
tonic triad (a minor chord) instead of over the dominant-
seventh as might be expected. Much of the melody of the
verse is pentatonic but after the first bar, the oriental flavour
disappears.

At $\downarrow$ = 96 it is one of Bessie Smith's faster performances of
the period but she is still able to make much of her smears,
slides and melisma because of the length of the notes covering
some of the more important words; for example the persistent
sliding around the title words. To counteract this anarchy,
she hits notes exactly on the main beat more often than usual
– note the five tonic notes on 'don't do me no good' in the
verse.

There is a rare linguistic distortion from Bessie in the first
line 'Just like a flower, why I'm fading away', where '(flo)wer,
why I'm' suggests a cornet with plunger-mute. But it makes
perfect musical sense.

This time Williams' piano is less florid, perhaps also
an attempt to introduce discipline into a performance
threatened by Bessie's freer melodic line.

The words of *'Tain't Nobody's Biz'ness If I Do'* reflect a facet of
Bessie's own character. The theme of all her previous releases
is unrequited love. Here she makes a fierce demand for the
right to be unconventional.

Her vocal line offers an extreme example of Hadlock's
so-called 'centre-tone' effect. She constantly returns to G, the
third of the key (Eb), adjusting the melodic line to achieve
this. This G is in fact not central but, with one exception, the
highest note of the piece.[8] Ex. 3 showing her melodic line at

Ex. 3

If I,   should take a no-tion,   to jump in,   to the   ocean,

[8] Hadlock states the key for this piece to be D but on the early 1970's
Columbia reissue of her complete output, the key is Eb.

the start of the first chorus illustrates something of her obsession with the note.[9]

At this stage in her career, Bessie sometimes felt it necessary to exercise on-the-job control over the speed of a number, her authority deriving from a growing confidence. Here Clarence Williams starts off at ♩ = 96 but Bessie soon pulls him back to a steady ♩ = 82. The slower pace allows her to make full use of her skill in microtonal variety (although extended portamento is absent) and to display a magnificent vibrato on some of the longer notes. There is also, for the first time, a trace of roughness around the edges of her voice; perhaps a sign of her now very busy stage career.

The three choruses are each 16 bars long, split into two similar halves of 8 bars. At the end of these half-choruses, Bessie completes the antiphony herself but surprisingly, her ending of each matching half is similar throughout with only the last 'if I do' differing in being sung on the same note. Then there is really no marked sense of climax in the last chorus; the final note is the tonic, Eb above middle C but as she had already hit high D in *Beale Street Mama,* a real enthusiasm for the song might have urged her to extend her range upwards a further semitone to high Eb. Perhaps the performers had been through the song too many times to be other than merely relieved when it finished – this was the tenth take, the previous nine having been cut and rejected on 15th February, 1923.

But Bessie's professionalism prevents this from being in any sense a failure. She instinctively breaks up the symmetry of the short phrases: note for example the first words of Ex. 3. Orthodox phrasing would require a breath to be taken after 'should', instead it comes after a long held 'I', leaving four words to be squeezed into the next bar. Her proclivity for between-the-beat accentuation is very evident too – in the verse particularly, she contrasts phrases in which notes are

[9] European staff notation offers only an approximation of the music. Although it has now become very elaborate, even for composed-art-music it is incomplete and imperfect.

rarely hit on the beat, with others where the beat is firmly stated.

Taken at $\quad = 72$, *Keeps On A-Rainin' (Papa, He Can't Make No Time)* the only number attempted on 26th April, 1923, is the slowest so far. Neither Clarence Williams nor Bessie seem comfortable with the pace however. Williams, perhaps understandably, has difficulty keeping time but mistakes also occur in his harmony; in bar seven of the verse for example, and in his antiphonal bridge at the end of the first chorus he repeats a wrong chord three times. His mistakes may account for the ten takes over three sessions[10] and the over-familarity thus engendered, the reason for the lack-lustre result. Perhaps part of the blame though can be attributed to the tune itself. Bars five and six of the chorus form a particularly feeble progression that, for once, even Bessie Smith cannot overcome.

After eight sides each involving Clarence Williams, on 30th April, 1923 Bessie Smith changed her pianist. For the next eight releases she is accompanied by bandleader and arranger, Fletcher Henderson. These have been largely ignored by writers. Henderson, a chemistry graduate of Atlanta University later proved to be a better pianist than Williams but on the two sides released from this session he gives little sign that this might be. He is rigid in the extreme, particularly when completing the responses at the end of vocal lines.[11]

[10] These comments apply to the tenth take. The ninth take cut on 11th April was also released: Columbia issued both under A-3898.
[11] Brian Rust, in 'Jazz Records 1897–1942', page 1524, shows Henderson as the pianist but in a footnote states that Clarence Williams is shown in the Columbia files. Paul Oliver in 'Bessie Smith' goes further; he claims that the label of the original release is in error and that Williams should be shown as pianist. Albertson on the other hand, in 'Bessie, Empress of the Blues', tells us that Bessie's dispute with Clarence Williams over money dates from mid-April, 1923 and this alone, if correct, would tend to confirm that the pianist must be different.

The structure of *Mama's Got The Blues* is the simplest so far, being merely four choruses of twelve-bar blues with a 4 bar introduction and 2 bar coda tacked on. It is its simplicity perhaps which stimulated Bessie to introduce the riff[12] of the fourth chorus, a very unusual device for her. As can be seen from Ex. 4, the first four repetitions are virtually identical with the last two being modified versions:

Ex. 4

I got a man in At-landa,   two in Al-a-bam-a,   three in Chatt-a-nooga,

four in Cin-cinn-ada,   five in Mi-ssi-ssi-ppi,   six in Mem-phis Tenn-e-ssee.

Eb   Bb

The slow pace allows Bessie to employ a broad vibrato to good effect and in aiming for the third degree of the scale she makes extensive use of a version of the double-note ornament of Ex. 1 (In Ex. 4 it is indicated by an asterisk).

Another narrative referring to unrequited love, Bessie, as usual eschews sentimentality. Her biographers all remark upon her keen sense of colour classification and the words of the third chorus confirm her prejudice against light-skinned men (and women): 'Brown skin's deceitful but a yellow man is worse' (twice). 'I'm goin' to get myself a black-man and play safety first'.

[12] Riff. An integral structural device with a strong rhythmic element found in much country blues and, especially in the 1930's, jazz. As here, it is usually played over changing harmony. A form of ostinato, it is derived from the call-and-response (antiphony) format of African and Afro-American folk-music. Bessie uses it here to heighten the tension of the last chorus.

The first two choruses of *Outside Of That* are each 16 bars in length but then, strangely, the third and last chorus is of only 15 bars, bringing the performance to an abrupt end. This could be a reference to an earlier tradition. Itinerant male blues singers of the rural South were often erratic over the number of bars used in each chorus. In a nominal twelve-bar blues, it might be 10½ bars or perhaps 14 bars. This was sometimes for musical effect and sometimes to give the singer time to remember or think of the words of the next line. In this piece however, there are indications that it was the intention for only two choruses to be performed since the first ends on a dominant chord and the second on the tonic. This would have been the normal harmonic resolution of the piece but on this record a third chorus is played, also ending on the tonic chord. By this stage the engineers must have been running out of wax-cutting surface and it is possible therefore that it was a signal from one of them which brought the proceedings to their sudden close a bar too early.

Bessie's overall range is not extended in this number; it runs from the Bb below to the Bb above middle C and her slight strain on the higher note produces a beauty which briefly elevates the performance to something above her average.

There is little effort by either performer to reach a climax in the last chorus. Stop-time is used in the second and third choruses but without any real constructive effect and although Bessie does use the high Bb in the third chorus, it occurs too early to have any climactic consequence. All that can be said is that her first use of speech on record during the last chorus does produce a certain finality. Perhaps conscious of the pedestrian nature of the performance and feeling that something extra is necessary to spice it up, Bessie introduces a variation of the wide vibrato-cum-trill of *Aggravatin' Papa*; she uses it on 'right', a key-word at the end of the second and third choruses. Her oscillations this time are less regular than before.

Henderson may be marginally less plodding than on the

previous track but as if to atone for any slight improvement in this direction, he finishes the introduction and the first and second choruses with what must have been a clichéd perfect-cadence even in 1923.

The words, about the pleasure to be found in a sadistic lover, carry a wry humour and Bessie's use of speech in the last chorus heightens the comedy.

Albertson reports the Chicago Defender as saying that this number was the greatest hit of a broadcast Bessie Smith made later in the year.[13] This shows how important the backing can be; Henderson is not yet able to inspire her.

[13] 'Bessie, Empress of the Blues', page 42. On the broadcast she was apparently accompanied by an orchestra.

THREE

June and September, 1923

Bleeding Hearted Blues of 14th June starting at ♩ = 66 is the slowest number so far (although it later speeds up to ♩ = 72). However it does not really seem as slow as this since much of the piano and some of the vocal is performed in ♫.rhythm. This rhythm helps Henderson to keep better time but soon becomes irritating. He also tends to follow the vocal line rather too closely for a satisfactory accompaniment.[1]

After the verse this is a twelve-bar blues. The words about loneliness are trite but in spite of this and Henderson's dispiriting piano, Bessie invests them with desolation and manages to better the version previously recorded by Alberta Hunter as well as one soon to be made by Edna Hicks. But she does display a rare uncertainty over the choice of notes in her fourth bar where the word 'blue' is commenced on the minor-third. It seems for a fraction of a second as if this is to be the beginning of a smear up to the major-third but at the last moment she decides to fall down to the second degree of the scale, thus anticipating the first note of the next phrase.

[1] Henderson's biggest failing at this time was the stolid nature of his bass. His right-hand does occasionally achieve a modicum of swing but even there, his patterns are usually obtrusive, drawing attention from, rather than complimenting and supporting the singer. His playing lacks grace with a constant dynamic level throughout and no suggestion of light and shade. He was a 'classically' trained pianist (by his mother) and from a middle-class Black family; this may account for his initial lack of empathy with the blues.

Both choices are perfectly admissible, in fact the one she makes avoids the cliché of the alternative. But the decision seems to have been rushed.

To add to the awkwardness, the modulation to the dominant key at the end of the verse is clumsy, this presumably the fault of the composer, Lovie Austin.

In *Lady Luck Blues* from the same session Bessie employs her widest range of pitches in one number so far, from the A below, to the C an octave above middle C. But again, Henderson fails to inspire her. He does show some improvement; although still stilted, he is not so obtrusive. This may be partly due to better recording balance, but even so his left-hand is lighter and his right-hand patterns more attractive. He seems to enjoy the tune which has a chordal progression more likely to appeal to him than that of a twelve-bar blues. A clear trace of his 'classical' training appears behind the word 'sympathy' which occurs in both choruses. With a slightly different rhythm each time, his accompaniment consists of a bar of falling parallel chords, something new to jazz in 1923 but which had already become a cliché in the composed-art-music of the period.[2]

The words, dealing with a plea to fate and including some of the invocations used to appease it, were likely to appeal to the Black population of America at that time – black magic was still a very real force in the lives of many of them.

Yodling Blues, the last number from this session, is Bessie's most lyrically intense performance so far. She makes the most of a majestic melodic line in a tune which although basically a twelve-bar blues is assisted by having the harmony of the second bar, unusually, based on subdominant and dominant

[2] Parallel harmony. The same, or nearly the same chord follows the melody (or in this case the antiphony) up and down. Used here for decoration and/or to create a mood, in longer passages it also has the effect of destroying functional harmony.

chords, instead of tonic.[3] Her blueing of 'seems' on the
seventh degree of the scale and the additional catch in her
voice when the melody is repeated on 'happiness' in the first
chorus are auguries of a deeply-felt performance. Inspired, a
genuine climax begins to be built up when she touches the
high Bb of the last chorus[4] and then again holds that pitch as
a long last note, a last note she seems perfectly secure upon
and the effect of which is marred only by Fletcher Henderson's hackneyed tonic minor-seventh chord. This apart, the
piano is unexceptional in a performance carried almost
entirely by the singer.

The words are simple in the extreme: the significance of
the title upon the narrator's problems is passingly referred to
in the second chorus when Bessie sings of her man going 'out
without a call'.

An unusual rallentando coda completes the number.

Having ended the last piece with a cliché, Henderson employs another to start *Midnight Blues,* the next day. The five
bars of his introduction are presumably intended to evoke
oriental night, the other-worldliness being effected by chords
of parallel harmony in typically gapped pentatonic pattern.

As in *Yodling Blues* the twelve-bar form is interestingly
varied harmonically, encouraging another good performance
from Bessie. The simple words about desertion are sung
without sentimentality or self-pity and another satisfying
climax is reached at the beginning of the last chorus as she

[3] Clarence Williams is credited as one of the composers. Although at this
time his relations with Bessie were strained, he still managed to use his
influence with the studio to ensure that she performed some of his compositions.

[4] In spite of the title, Bessie Smith does not actually produce a yodel
throughout the performance. She does offer a simulation however in the last
chorus, an astonishingly graceful phrase during which she momentarily
touches high C. The reason she does not attempt this device is presumably
stylistic; that she is more than competent in the falsetto range is clear from
the A she hits in *Soft Pedal Blues* of May 1925, an A which is a major-sixth
above the top C of this performance.

soars up to high Bb, cutting free from the accompaniment.

Henderson, gradually showing more sensitivity, displays his first real touch of imagination in backing the first two bars of the second verse with chime-like discords which on 'midnight', give a sudden evocation of despair: a rare example of musical onomatopoeia from him and one that for once does not sound hackneyed.

On 21st June 1923, Bessie was accompanied again by Henderson in the popular song, *If You Don't, I Know Who Will*. It is started at what she feels is too fast a pace and she pulls him back from $\downarrow = 92$ to $\downarrow = 80$. The melody is based very largely around two similar rising phrases, the second starting a tone higher than the first.

The words, evidencing sexual self-confidence are identical in both choruses except that in the coda to the last chorus Bessie is more specific about 'who will'. The sense of climax relies entirely upon this revelation. The words call for no great depth of feeling but, as so often, Bessie appropriates them, investing them in the process with a profundity transcending their triviality. The opening 'Daddy'[5], for instance, a glissando of a major-sixth from top A down to middle C, is a rousing call for attention, giving notice that she will be endowing the material with her full commitment. It is, incidentally, interesting to note in the verse, her pronunciation of 'aeroplane' as 'aeroplan'. She might have been expected to use the American 'airplane' but the British 'aeroplane' is certainly more suitable musically since it has the extra syllable necessary to match the following 'motor cars'. But there seems no explanation for the mispronounciation unless it was caused by unfamiliarity.

Although it is certain that Bessie's art had been almost fully evolved by the time she started recording, it was not completely so. Her talent with dynamic shading is equal to

---

[5] Bessie's vehemence on this word causes Henderson to make an error in accompaniment.

her pitch control in later years but at this stage she had hardly begun to develop it.

Nobody In Town Can Bake A Sweet Jelly Roll Like Mine of 22nd June, 1923 demonstrates the adaptions which may have to be made to a popular song format to squeeze it into the temporal limitation of a 78 rpm ten-inch disc; the first 16 bar chorus ends on the dominant chord and the second on the tonic and a repetition of these progressions would have presented a balanced structure. Unfortunately, there is not room and the third and last chorus finishes on the tonic too. The twelve-bar blues format does not present this problem since each unit is shorter.

The words of course are obsessively sexually allusive (a jelly roll is a swiss roll made with jelly instead of jam but here is used as a phallic euphemism). In previous compositions Bessie has been refreshingly explicit about such things but here the whole piece is a prolonged double-entendre and aesthetically, from a poetic viewpoint at least, we reach the nadir of her output so far. It has been said that she disliked such hypocrisy and this may well be true since she also displayed throughout her life an equal dislike of sham.[6] Frank Walker of Columbia however, firmly controlled the direction of her recording career and it seems she often had little choice herself over the type of material. Still, once again, she transcends the material and gives the subject-matter a full, serious treatment instead of the sidelong sniggers which could have been expected from some of her contemporaries. As Paul Oliver says, 'Bessie sings the bragging lines with a sadness, a poignancy of mood which seems to express a deep regret that the ability to love passionately is gone to waste.'[7] The vocal line in this piece is interesting in being based upon the tonic triad with added-sixth and added-second (plus appoggiaturas). Jazz was just beginning to explore the possi-

[6] There is some evidence that on stage she was far less inhibited in her language than on record.

[7] 'Bessie Smith', page 20.

bilities of added-note chords at this time.

Fletcher Henderson who is getting better and better, here plays with assurance and comfortably within his limitations.[8] Some of the antiphony is repetitive and pentatonically based (this last presumably intended to evoke the Orient – perhaps a Chinese baker, although the protagonist is a Miss Mandy Jenkins) but it is mostly complementary to the voice and his phrasing overall particularly, has improved; it is now more flowing and sympathetic, less rigid and heavy-handed. He displays a structural sense too in repeating his adroit 'oriental' perfect cadence from the end of the introduction, at the close of the performance.

The words of *Jailhouse Blues* which Bessie recorded in September, 1923 seem at first as if they might be to do with social protest but then some unconnected phrases from the common-stock destroy the narrative and change the mood in the last two choruses. There is no musical climax built-into the performance but the heightening of mood produced by the wry despair of the words of the last chorus do have the effect of rounding it off:

> Good mornin' blues; blues how do you do? how do you do?
> Good mornin' blues; blues how do you do?
> Say I jess come here to have a few words with you.

As Schuller points out, in this record 'we can hear the embellishment traits that form the essence of Bessie's style'.[9] Perhaps because this is almost a folk-blues referring to her earlier repertoire, most of her basic ornaments are included and for a careful analysis in some detail the reader should refer

[8] With the exception of the introduction and verse anticipation where his timing and choice of notes is wayward – the four bar introduction for instance carries a crotchet beat too many.

[9] 'Early Jazz', page 231. Incidentally, on page 232, Schuller claims Clarence Williams to be the pianist but the general consensus (see Rust for example) is that it is Irving Johns and certainly aural evidence confirms we are listening to this much more imaginative musician.

to the appropriate pages in Schuller's book.[10] (The main omission is her favourite double-note third-seeker — it is not appropriate to the melody, the third, G, being the top note of the melody and therefore impossible to approach from above). More than half the words are adorned in one way or another and her unorthodox breathing pauses are a major factor in the unity of each chorus. Generally, her voice in these late 1923 sides is harsher and more authoritative: her spoken introductions on this number and on *Sam Jones Blues* are handled with great aplomb.

Perhaps her authority stems at least partly from the stimulus of a new and more talented pianist. Irving Johns' introduction is in two parts; the second is conventional enough but the rubato call-to-attention first section manages to suggest the boogie-woogie piano of a house-rent party which Bessie says is about to be raided, and at the same time carries more than a trace of Gershwin's *Rhapsody in Blue*.[11] The measured time commences at ♩ = 96 but Bessie quickly pulls Johns back to ♩ = 80: a better pianist than either Clarence Williams or Fletcher Henderson, he responds immediately. His superiority is evident at various other points in the performance: his greater sense of swing:[12] his varied accompaniment including tremolos, and the trills and caressing arpeggios behind Bessie's 'tickling me under my chin' of the third chorus: the suggestion of a 'primitive' boogie behind the last chorus which as mentioned above begins 'Good mornin' blues', probably the most 'primitive' line yet sung by Bessie.

In spite of the unsettling effect of the lyrics most commentators agree that this is one of the best performances from this early period.

St. Louis Gal cut on the 24th September, 1923, is the only record by Bessie Smith to be released on which she is accom-

[10] 'Early Jazz', pages 230/232.　[11] Orchestrated that year by Ferde Grofé.
[12] Johns like James P. Johnson derives much of his swing from the use of broken tenths in the bass.

panied by two pianos; Irving Johns is joined by Jimmy Jones.[13]

There at first seems to be little sense of a climax being developed apart from Bessie's high B on 'Louis' in the last eight bars. But this turns out to be not the whole story. She presents another factor, integrated with the overall structure: each of the seven appearances of 'St. Louis' is given a different treatment by her but only in the first and last appearances does she emphasise its titular importance by taking an unexpected breath between the two words. (She also treats us to a rare, fully articulated quaver triplet on 'shake in your (shoes)' in the thirteenth bar of the first chorus).

The presence of two pianos does add a fullness of texture to the performance but it is difficult to believe that this choice was deliberate. Such a relatively subtle improvement would have been lost upon the average listener of the time and presumably Columbia would not have deliberately sought to pay two pianists. Their presence in the studio together must have been fortuitous.

The texture is made doubly rich by the tremolos, sometimes combined with portamento with which one of the pianists (persumably Johns, since Jones' tremolos tend to be more tentative) infuses the piece. These devices also have the effect of imparting a fine solidity to the performance. The tremolos strengthen the performance in a more subtle way too − they exactly match the speed of Bessie's vibrato. And the solid beat encourages her to stress between-the-beat accentuation; see particularly 'You stole my pal' at the end of the second 16 bar chorus.

Although the pianists achieve considerable rapport they do commit a rare error in the fourteenth bar of the first chorus; behind Bessie's 'hear what I say' they take a different harmonic road from hers. They quickly recover in the next bar however.

[13] Albertson in his sleeve notes to the early 1970's reissues, claims the existence of an alternate take with Irving Johns alone on piano.

Sam Jones Blues, cut the same day, is the first of Bessie's records to have a chorus which approaches AABA form. The fact that only one chorus is possible illustrates again the difficulty record producers had in fitting more than a token chorus of the larger popular song structures on to a 10 inch, 78 rpm disc, with a singer like Bessie Smith who preferred slow tempos, (at least during her early recording career). Here, at the beginning of the verse, she makes an attempt to reduce the speed ($\quartnote = 88$) but this time Johns does not yield.

Bessie seems to enjoy this song. Possibly she identified with 'Miss Wilson' but the satisfying chord sequence and fast harmonic rhythm must have pleased her too. For the first time she introduces an extra-musical effect (door-knocking) and a speech falsetto on 'pew', both at the beginning of the record. Once again she divides phrases to achieve emphasis: whereas on the two appearances of 'Mrs Jones' she links the two words normally, the more important 'Miss Wilson' is separated by a breath. A climax is prepared in the bridge[14] where Bessie speaks over stop chords and is achieved in the last 8 bars when she breaks into song again.

Johns enjoys himself — he swings beautifully.

Graveyard Dream Blues, cut two days later, has Bessie accompanied by Jimmy Jones alone; he reveals his playing to be considerably inferior to that of Irving Johns. Although managing to impart a little swing, (admittedly not easy at this tempo of $\quartnote = 76$) he completely misreads Bessie's mood. Whilst she imbues her performance with a slightly detatched, but real grief, Jones is flippant, particularly in his antiphony. His introduction (at a faster pace than the rest) is lighthearted but he fails to learn and at the end of the performance, his double-time and tonic minor-seventh chord are as inappropriate as his beginning. And he is guilty of a jarring error in the ninth bar of the third chorus; instead of

[14] Bridge. The B section in the AABA thirty-two bar popular song construction.

the required dominant harmony, he plays a subdominant chord. To his credit though, he recovers to sound the correct harmony, and then tries to justify his mistake as being an intentional choice by repeating it immediately, almost convincing the listener in the process.

Bessie's range is restricted almost entirely to the pentachord Bb below middle C to the F natural above. Her main departure from this range occurs in the last chorus of this twelve-bar blues when she ventures up to the G natural and Ab above middle C as a climax; Jones attempts to assist her here by playing some responses to the vocal line without a bass.

At 2 minutes, 40 seconds, this is the shortest performance so far. At first sight this is strange in view of the fact that it is a twelve-bar blues – certainly one more chorus and possibly two could have been fitted in; the answer of course lies in the fact that this song by Ida Cox presents a narrative complete in itself.

Cemetery Blues is another in the twelve-bar format and although Bessie's overall range is the widest employed for over three months (From the Bb below, to the C an octave above middle C), she manipulates the pentatonically based chorus melody to produce one of her most economical lines. She keeps mainly within the tonic minor-third interval, Eb to Gb, subjecting this Gb to a variety of treatments ranging from hitting it exactly on pitch, including it as part of a two-note ornament, to applying orthodox blueing.

The words, about Cemetery Lize who preferred a ghost as a lover, could not be given too weighty a treatment, but Bessie allows hardly a hint of humour – perhaps she is wrong in this (especially as the ghost's name is Jones). Even so, since it is her vehicle, she is entitled to a compatible accompaniment and Jones fails to give her this. His flippancy may be justified by the lyrics but is certainly not by Bessie's mood. He is too obtrusive, providing a series of irrelevant responses rather than seeking to compliment the vocal line. Again he fails to catch-on: his lugubrious cinema-piano opening is matched by a coda that is just as inappropriate. Overall his ideas are too fragmentary, his main concession to structural unity being wildly inapposite references to Gershwin. Timekeeping is not Jones' strong point either on this record. After a rubato introduction he strikes a tempo of $\downarrow = 68$ but by the end, after a series of erratic variations it has reached $\downarrow = 88$.

It seems that the penultimate chorus was originally intended as the final one, Bessie touching her highest note there. But presumably receiving a signal from the engineer, another chorus is tacked on. This is possible, since unlike the words of *Graveyard Dream Blues,* here they do not form a rounded whole.

FOUR

October and December, 1923

The vast majority of Bessie Smith's performances were presented on stage and her importance was such that she need not, and did not, tolerate any other blues singer in the show. It is strange then that she should record with one. In *Far Away Blues,* Clara Smith (no relation) joins her with Fletcher Henderson as accompanist. Albertson[1] suggests that although on stage, Clara's physical appearance could have been a threat to her, on record she posed no problem in view of the disparity in the quality of their voices. However, this is a view which does not square with the facts since here an off-form Bessie offers little improvement over Clara. In fact, Clara Smith, who was slow to develop, proved in a session at which they both performed two years later, that she could, on occasion, be almost the equal of an on-form Bessie[2]. Presumably therefore, the session came about at the insistence of Frank Walker – Clara was at that time Columbia's second rating blues star behind Bessie and it must have seemed a logical development to him.

Bessie restricts her range almost entirely to a perfect-fifth whereas Clara's extends to a minor-seventh, overlapping Bessie by only a minor-third. But with two similarly sounding voices this is not enough to achieve the effect of a duet. To

[1] 'Bessie, Empress of the Blues', page 45.
[2] *My Man Blues.* 1st September, 1925.

try to get the necessary separation, Bessie, providing the antiphony, employs generally shorter note-values than Clara. This gives rise to a rigid format with Bessie sounding like a not very imaginative cornet. In the presence of another singer who has been given an equally important melodic role, she is often shrill and sounds uncomfortable, unable to use breathing pauses to illuminate the words; boxed in by her rigidly prescribed function. When she does attempt to impose some individual mark on the proceedings, the result is the triplet á la Gracie Fields of the second chorus. Even her slides and swoops are made for effect only, an effect which has no cause.[3] Clara Smith, a more technically limited singer has no compulsion towards this form of display.

But it is not all dross. There are some moments of delight, particularly at the end of each chorus where they sing a third apart.

Henderson is called upon here to do no more than thump out a slow four-beat rhythm.

In the previous release from this session, Clara Smith was the challenger[4] but on *I'm Going Back To My Used To Be* their roles are less rigidly defined and artistically the performance is more successful.

Clara's voice timbre is often represented as thin. On this evidence that is hardly an adequate description; her voice is actually quite full but rather more penetrating than Bessie's. But certainly the ornaments in Clara's 'bag' are not as extensive as those at Bessie's command and she is never in such complete control of pitch. A study of their vibratos reveals Bessie's to be completely under her domination whilst Clara's often seems to be on the point of disintegrating.

Although Bessie is not at her best on this record, it does have the almost unique merit of juxtaposing good perform-

[3] A comment once made by Wagner about another composer's music.
[4] In his generally excellent book, 'Early Jazz', Gunther Schuller, on pages 239/40 claims that it is Clara who replies in *Far Away Blues*. He is clearly in error on that point.

ances by the foremost 'classic' blues singers and providing comparisons in near-laboratory conditions. Clara's melody is never as well articulated as Bessie's: Clara uses portamento for longer periods, making for a less well-defined line. Ex. 5 shows a similar phrase based upon the tonic triad with added-sixth, as treated by each singer:

Ex. 5

Whereas Clara slurs her pitches and blues the F sharp and E natural, Bessie's treatment is more sharply defined and complex. Sometimes simplicity may be meritorious but here Bessie needed to elaborate after Clara's straightforward arpeggio and had the technique to do so.

Whilst Clara sings of her nostalgia for a previous love, Bessie responds with comments which become increasingly impudent. Only in one area is Clara allowed to exert more influence than Bessie – Clara's presence is evidently the reason for the very slow tempos; her preference was for a pace even more pedestrian than that of Bessie.[5]

Henderson's technique is still improving: here his short bursts of double-time are quite impressive but aesthetically they jar and the reason for the success of this performance lies entirely with the singers. Instead of the artificial limitations imposed on them in *Far Away Blues,* here they are allowed to find their own level and their disparate talents result in a true duet.[6]

Whoa, Tillie, Take Your Time, from Bessie's 15th October, 1923 session[7] has words which are not suitable for any serious treatment. They are about an over-exuberant dancer. But Bessie does her best with them, coming to grief only over 'you don't know what to shake' where the harmony becomes static for four bars. Later in her career she was able to cope with such dead spots but here she lapses into repetition.

Bessie is again burdened with an insensitive clarinet. Some discographies are uncertain about the identity of this clarinet: it certainly sounds the same as that on the 11th April, 1923 session and Albertson[8] suggests Ernest Elliott as possible (although it is not certain that Elliott was present on the earlier session). Rust[9] however, comes down firmly in favour of George Baquet. Its solo is well recorded which is a pity as it has little to say, engaging mostly in meaningless note-spinning. Although behind Bessie it keeps mainly an octave above her (frequently clashing with the piano pitches), it stays too close to the melody and its antiphony is fatiguing. It would be disappointing to learn positively that it was Baquet in view of Jelly Roll Morton's statement that 'George Baquet

[5] *Far Away Blues* ♩ = 72. *I'm Going Back To My Used To Be* ♩ = 66.
[6] Both singers use the full range from the A below to the A above middle C.
[7] Both selections from this session were previously recorded with the same instrumentation and possibly the same personnel on 27th September, 1923 but all takes were rejected.
[8] Sleeve notes to the early 1970's Columbia reissues.
[9] 'Jazz Records, 1897–1942', page 1525.

was the earliest *jazz* clarinettist':[10] he seems an unlikely candidate however. The bookkeeping at these early sessions was often lax and matters were sometimes confused by the participants themselves (Bessie once claimed that the cornet on her sides with Louis Armstrong was in fact Joe Smith). The firmest piece of evidence indicating that it is not Baquet on these sessions is that the break in register, peculiar to the accoustical properties of the clarinet, is transversed only once in a phrase; and this excursion down to the chalumeau register offers only the simplest possible figure. This hardly squares with the technique of a 'classically' trained, near-legendary figure from the early days of New Orleans jazz. It might be argued that passages in the chalumeau register would clash with those of Bessie's voice but a musician of Baquet's reputed talents could easily have avoided duplication.

The identity of the pianist is even more uncertain. It seems to be a choice between Jimmy Jones or Fletcher Henderson. If it is Jones, then his ego is not very much to the fore and it seems much more likely to be the reticent Henderson. Whoever it is, he engenders a quite engaging swing.

The second release from the 15th October, 1923 session, *My Sweetie Went Away,* offers interesting proof of Bessie's ability to manipulate a melodic line. Whilst in a lot of her work it is hard to be sure what the original melodic line is because of the present-day difficulty in obtaining published scores of these relatively obscure tunes, this song is still well-known today. Her line in this performance, although spanning the full compass of the melody, adjusts the contours and tends to gather in a general pitch area for a bar or two until the original melody moves too far away, when she will shift to another pitch area. At each 'resting' area she levels out the undulations of the original melody.

[10] 'Mister Jelly Roll', page 124 (Morton's italics). Morton is here differentiating Baquet from the ragtime musicians of the early part of this century.

The chorus is in AABA, thirty-two bar form with the A sections very much more similar than in *Sam Jones Blues* of three weeks earlier. And this time with the faster tempo of ♩ = 96 the final B and A sections can be repeated; a satisfactory structural compromise.

The words, although still trite, carry perhaps a little more emotional content than those of *Whoa, Tillie,* but they would be rather better suited to a singer with a more lightweight style. Still, Bessie awards them her full commitment.

The clarinet and piano offer no improvement over their performances on the previous release.

On *Any Woman's Blues* cut the next day, Bessie gives one of her most artistically successful performances, in spite of the slightly distracting piano. The record is full of her own brand of Expressionism; the first line of her first chorus for instance "cause, I love my man, better than I love myself', seems to reach out straight from her nerve-ends. and she transforms the melodic line into something more dramatic to stress the importance of the word 'love' in its context, as shown in Ex. 6.

Ex. 6

ORIGINAL MELODIC LINE

I love my man

BESSIE'S TRANSFORMATION

I love my man

In the second chorus, she breaks the flow of her line, 'my man's got teeth like a lighthouse on the sea' in a different way each time and for different reasons. The first time she takes a breath after 'like', thereby building some suspense as to what is to follow. The second time with the need for surprise gone, she highlights the importance of 'teeth' by placing a more equal stress on both 'teeth' and 'like'. Then in the first line of the last chorus, she treats the word 'chimes' to her favourite two-note ornament, the third-seeker of Ex. 1.

Throughout the performance, her smears and slides are in full array, imparting a heavy, tragic quality invested with more than a hint of pain. But none of her effects impairs the narrative continuity.

Henderson's contribution is particularly noticeable since he employs a rather obvious unifying idea; the runs with which the piano part abounds. He introduces the first in the third and fourth bars, a series of falling parallel chords from the tenth to the first degree of the scale over tonic harmony. In the eleventh bar he uses a similar series but this time describing an arpeggio based upon the tonic triad with added-sixth and second. At the twenty-first bar, the brief descending run describes the dominant triad with added-sixth, again in parallel chords. Henderson is becoming more technically proficient, and, perhaps unhappily, more knowingly sophisticated. His new-found self-assertion may have been why the climax was left entirely to him; a series of 'chimes' in the last chorus after Bessie's repeat of 'organ kind'.

Hadlock attributes the choice of B major as the key for this piece to Bessie;[11] however, it seems more likely that provided her range could be accommodated she would not be fussy about the key nor even aware of what key she was in.[12]

The earlier two takes of this number cut at this session included an 18 year-old Coleman Hawkins on tenor saxo-

[11] 'Jazz Masters of the Twenties', page 224.
[12] The choice of B major with its five sharps is an unusual one. It is further evidence of Henderson's growing competence.

phone but both were rejected in favour of the third take with Henderson alone as accompanist.

The records issued from the session of 4th December, 1923 were, according to Paul Oliver, 'the rage of the day'.[13] The words of *Chicago Bound Blues* must have been at least partially responsible; many a southern Black woman's man was forced to the North to better his lot. And Bessie's delivery conveys the appropriate will-sapping misery suggested by the words which treat tongue and feet as having lives of their own, not under the narrator's control.

In the first line of the third chorus we hear something new from Bessie. She produces an unusually thin timbre on 'mean (old fireman)' the first time round – how unusual it is, can be heard by comparing it with her second and more conventional treatment of the word in the next line. The sound is quite deliberate and very appropriate – we get an instant picture of the object of her vilification. Another effect is less agreeable – her hackneyed catch on 'engineer', again in the first line of this chorus. It appears to have been culled from some vaudeville singer of the day. Fortunately it does not become a regular part of her technique. And she makes amends with her elongated pronunciation of 'cruel (old engineer)' in the next line, again providing a vivid image.

Redman's stiffly phrased and repetitive clarinet does nothing to enhance this performance. He has little empathy with Bessie's mood. In fairness however, it should be said that his best instrument was the alto saxophone.[14] Little sense of climax emerges in the last chorus – what there is, is suggested by Redman's syncopated patterns which temporarily replace his ubiquitous triplet chromatic runs.

Henderson needs to do little other than provide the chord

[13] 'Bessie Smith', page 26.
[14] Redman's greatest fame came later as arranger to Fletcher Henderson's Orchestra (and others including Louis Armstrong's and Paul Whiteman's), whose 'modern' music was to some extent responsible for Bessie Smith's decline.

progressions, since Redman provides the antiphony.

The other side released from the 4th December, 1923 session, *Mistreatin' Daddy,* with the exception of two new
effects, has Bessie singing, for her, in a very straightforward
manner. Her phrases are quite symmetrical and she rarely
makes use of unconventional breathing pauses. It is true that
the words are humourous but this did not stop her treating
some earlier numbers of a similar type to a more extensive
range of effects. One of the features she introduces, is often
used from now on in her more jocular songs – a rasp such as
might be produced by a playful New Orleans trombone. She
uses it here at the end of the first 16 bar chorus on 'all' in the
line 'I can cut you all to pieces like I would a piece of meat'.
At the end of this line she also affects an arch, half-spoken
delivery.

Redman is as uninspired as on the previous release but
Henderson offers an interesting development of a motif
which he briefly introduced there. This time his short chromatic runs are expanded into a fully-fledged structurally
unifying device and on occasion he even employs them as
stop-chords.

FIVE

January, 1924

Chris Albertson[1] has made some interesting speculations about *Frosty Mornin' Blues* released from Bessie's session of 8th January, 1924. He suggests tiredness and lack of spirit and goes on to say she sounds 'unusually high-pitched, and she is unable to sustain a note'. But on even a casual listening, many sustained notes can be detected and to my ears at least, there is no lack of spirit. As for 'tiredness' whilst she is restrained, this is probably because of Reser's plaintive, lagging guitar and the mood of desolation suggested by the words about deserted love. Albertson's other complaint perhaps has more substance. Certainly Bessie's voice has a different timbre, a lighter sound. But she is singing no higher than before – in fact she reaches farther down (by a semitone) than in any previous piece and at the top falls a considerable way short of her so far highest recorded note. The different sound may be merely the result of an accoustical change in the studio. Or it could be, as Albertson says 'some blues scholars' suggest, that the voice belongs to another singer. His comments refer only to *Frosty Mornin' Blues* and the number recorded on 10th January, *Easy Come, Easy Go Blues,* but if there is some doubt over these recordings, there must also, in my opinion, be doubt about the intervening session, (9th January, 1924). If it is another singer, the most likely candidate is Clara Smith. One of the tunes cut by Bessie the next day was *Eavesdropper's Blues* and her timbre there is very

[1] 'Bessie, Empress of the Blues', page 52.

39

similar to that on some of Clara's releases; Clara's phrase in the first chorus of her *Broken, Busted Blues* (7th January, 1925) carrying the words 'Everyone knows', for instance. Then there is the fact that Clara was in the Columbia New York studio on 11th January, 1924 and her releases from that day have the next matrix number (14006–D). Further, on 10th January, 1924, in addition to the released *Easy Come, Easy Go Blues,* the discographies show Bessie as having cut four takes each, of two other unreleased titles with her 'Jazz Band' the personnel of which is unknown. Clara's two released sides of 11th January, 1924 are by her 'Jazz Band', most of whose personnel are also unknown. Could the band and singer be the same? In spite of the circumstantial evidence it seems unlikely – Albertson dismisses the possibility saying 'Only the phrasing can convince the listener that the voice is Bessie's'. Bessie, although showing similarities to Clara's style, is still more like herself than anyone else. What similarities there are between them are probably the result of an unconscious assimilation by each singer of a portion of the others style following their duets of October, 1923, the proximity of Clara to this present session, (possibly rehearsing while Bessie was recording) and the fact that they must have often heard each other around the studio anyway. And of course Bessie's slightly emaciated tone-colour could all be due to torpid recording equipment, this is after all, January in New York. Whatever the truth, it is a glorious performance climaxed by the singer's extraordinarily decorated last note, which in gracefully florid curves, descends the octave from top Ab.

The guitarist, Harry Reser, is white, This is unusual for 1923 when white and Black musicians were still following parallel courses with little mixing. It is true that white musicians would listen to Black groups and sometimes a Bix Beiderbecke would be allowed to sit in for a chorus or two; and Jelly Roll Morton recorded some sides with the New Orleans Rhythm Kings in July 1923. But these would be isolated incidents in a prevailing atmosphere of segregation.

It was not until the later 1920's that mixed 'jam sessions' began to occur, with mixed recording even later still.

The white 'country' flavour of this twelve-bar blues is due partly to the guitar style but also to the shape of the melody carrying the first line of chorus; a tonic first inversion arpeggio with added-sixth. It comes straight out of the repertoire of the white country-blues singer, Jimmy Rodgers. His *Nobody Knows But Me* of 25th November 1929 is based upon a similar chord, rhythm and melodic shape.

Compared to the piano, the guitar is over-recorded and allows Jimmy Jones little say in the proceedings. Only occasionally can the piano be heard clearly, when it is playing an octave above the guitar. The guitar plays in the same octave as Bessie and also an octave below her. Voice and instrument sound quite separate however even when sharing pitches, due to their different pitch attack and decay patterns, and timbres.

The session on 9th January, 1924 produced Bessie Smith's most unsatisfactory releases so far. We have become used to hearing even on worn dubbings[2] a clear differentiation between the performers. Here the sound is amorphous and fuzzy. On the first release, *Haunted House Blues*, there is present a musically-extraneous siren which further muddies the texture. But it is not the hokum which turns this into delinquency, the main problem seems to be the recording balance and the fact that Redman's clarinet is often doubling Bessie's pitches. Then Bessie seems to find the tempo too fast ($\downarrow$ = 96) and uncertain whether to treat the piece with the levity the hokum suggests or to commit herself fully, as she would normally in a twelve-bar blues. She struggles hard to bring some credibility to the proceedings but in the last analysis they lack conviction.

But then it is not a twelve-bar blues. An additional bar, (always played by clarinet and piano) has been slipped in after

[2] Dubbing. A recording reproduced from a commercially issued pressing rather than an original master.

the first eight bars and this has an unsettling effect upon the whole performance. No doubt this was intentional in view of the lyrics but it turns out to be another element contributing to the failure. As previously mentioned, country blues singers often truncate or lengthen a song's choruses but theirs is a spontaneous manipulation of structure and as such, perfectly acceptable; here, the additional bar is planned and quite unnecessary. Moreover, the minor key[3] is employed for much of the subdominant harmony, presumably to facilitate the 'ghostly' mood, (this is the first time on a released track that Bessie has sung in other than a major key).

The result of all this is that by the end of the record Bessie has lost interest. Her 'blue' in the second line of the fourth chorus is symptomatic; she treats it to a facile descending glissando, quite meaningless in the context.

Henderson's piano is purposeless and Redman's arch and watery clarinet at its most oppresive and superficial.

The key of the original 78 rpm release is Bb but the Columbia reissue of the early 1970's slows it down to A. Unfortunately the transposition has been imperfectly effected and pitch fluctuates throughout the record.

In *Eavesdropper's Blues* from the same session, Bessie sounds even more like Clara Smith, especially in her loosely constructed phrasing in the seventh bar of the verse. But it is still almost certainly Bessie, and, by her standards, a failure, for much the same reasons as was *Haunted House Blues*. Minor improvements result from the absence of the siren and the fact that Redman's extreme archness is mitigated, although this merely reveals the underlying insipidness of his playing.

Again, Columbia on their 1970's reissue have tampered with the speed resulting in the original key of Ab being lowered to a slightly sharp G. They have done this to improve the fidelity of the sound but it was really a waste of time on this record.

[3] Often a superfluous mood intensifier in a musical form rich in microtones.

The words of *Easy Come, Easy Go Blues*, cut the next day, 10th January, 1924 are a celebration of the narrator's sunny character and Bessie imparts to them a serene authenticity. In keeping with the mood, her decorations are kept down to a minimum and phrases are mainly symmetrical, unbroken by unexpected breath.

Although linked by Albertson in his remarks with *Frosty Mornin' Blues*[4] there is really little evidence here either that she is unable to sustain a note. It is true that her voice seems to give out on 'happiest' in the fifteenth bar of the verse—an accident maybe, but if so an example of a delightful serendipity, adding to the hint of pathos informing the piece.[5] Many of the words require short note values but many also can be and are, fully sustained. The last word of the piece, 'blue', for example is held by Bessie for nearly six crotchets.

Like *Frosty Morning' Blues*, this is fine, restrained, satisfying performance helped enormously by Reger's bare guitar. Again suggestions of other singers can be found, especially Clara Smith, but this is unmistakably Bessie. Much of her melody revolves around the top four notes of the scale, E, F sharp, G sharp and A, a folk-song borrowing which is particularly appropriate for this piece with its 'country' flavour. Jimmy Jones' piano makes little impact again.

[4] 'Bessie, Empress of the Blues', page 52.
[5] Bessie Smith in most of her tragic blues usually manages to impart suggestions of optimism, even triumph. Here she treats words which seem to call for a lighthearted approach, with great seriousness hinting at some underlying tragedy.

SIX

April, 1924

In *Sorrowful Blues* of 4th April, 1924, Bessie Smith moves even more deeply into the rural blues genre. Robert Robbins' slippery double-stop phrases on violin[1] added to John Griffin's guitar[2] evoke a strong flavour of itinerant Blacks on Southern dirt roads. Bessie is temporarily moving away from her more usual material at this time (no doubt on the commercial instructions of Frank Walker), towards more 'primitive' music and on the whole she does so successfully if not quite authentically. Robbins' antiphony at vocal phrase-ends, like most of the words, comes from the common, near-hillbilly stock.

This is no narrative-poems. The words are a hotchpotch. They offer comments on inherited kleptomania, sexual popu-

[1] The whole position of the violin in jazz (like that of flute and the double reed instruments, e.g. oboe and bassoon) is still the subject of debate, with those who complain that the tone of these instruments is too thin for jazz and in any event they were never part of the standard New Orleans instrumentation, (not entirely true), lined up against those who maintain that jazz should be able to accept any instrument and the only criterion is the standard of performance. It is a large subject for which I have no space here; but it does seem likely that trumpet/cornet, trombone and clarinet were originally chosen as the melodic triumverate producing sounds nearest to the 'open' quality of Black speech timbre and in preference to the thinner sounding instruments which seem more appropriate to the music of the Indo-Arabic cultures, the most obvious feature of which, to European ears, is the whining tone evidenced by the ubiquitous double-reeded shawm.
[2] Schuller, in 'Early Jazz', page 239, claims it to be Reser again.

44

larity, racism, the difficulties of husband-stealing and end
with a horticulturally based sexual metaphor. But, in spite
of, or possibly because of, the commonplace words, Bessie
still seeks to avoid the musical clichés of her contemporary
blues and ballad singers.[3] On the first two appearances of
'nineteen' in the second verse for instance, instead of following the speech-rhythm stressing the second syllable, she
instead stresses 'nine'; none of the linguistic sense is lost and
she manages to introduce an element of extra musical interest
by doing this. (The unusual scat opening however is borrowed from Gertrude Saunders who later borrowed Bessie's
husband, Jack Gee.[4] The penultimate chorus therefore carries
a prophetic irony).

In seeking the third of the scale, Bessie often decorates her
line with the double-note ornament of Ex. 1, frequently
varying it quite subtly.[5] She uses one such variation to
provide the climax: in the fifth chorus, at the end of the first
line, she adopts the ornament's usual contours but at the end
of the second line effects an uncommon and remarkable
variation as shown in Ex. 7:

Ex. 7

vines

BECOMES

vines

[3] Bessie's version so impressed Trixie Smith that she recorded a close copy
the following month with a group from Fletcher Henderson's Band.
[4] 'Bessie, Empress of the Blues', pages 57/8.
[5] This ornament never features in her numbers with a popular song
structure.

Two takes of a version of this number with Bessie accompanied by Robbins' violin and Irving Johns' piano were also cut at this session but rejected.

The second successful number from the 4th April, 1924 session was *Pinchbacks, Take 'Em Away*, a tune closely based upon *It's A Long Way To Tipperary*. Starting at $\quartnote = 120$ the tempo has increased by the end to $\quartnote = 132$ Bessie's fastest number so far, enabling her to complete two full thirty-two bar choruses in addition to an introduction, verse and coda. The choruses are not in AABA form however but follow *Tipperary* with AAAB.

Because of the pace and generally boisterous mood, Bessie adopts a more 'shouting' style still incorporating plenty of smears and glissandi but with less of her more elaborate ornaments in evidence.

With such a well-known melody as the basis, it is easy to identify Bessie's manipulations. Her range is exactly the same as that of *Tipperary* (excluding the anacrusis[6]), but within that range of a minor-seventh she adjusts and moulds the melody to her own ends.

The reiterated words give advice to girls to marry a working-man rather than the superficially more attractive sweet man, the pinchback.[7] There is little sense of a musical climax but the parody of *Tipperary* comes closer with the line near the end, 'It's a long way to Oklahoma', and the admission of the plagiarism resolves a certain literary tension.[8]

In the middle of the first chorus Johns performs one of these breaks for which Jelly Roll Morton was renowned but although the tone of the piano is quite similar to that obtained by Morton, the timing and choice of notes has none of the beauty of his model. It makes one wonder, tantalisingly, how Bessie would have sounded performing with

[6] Anacrusis. Upbeat.   [7] Pinchback. Counterfeit, sham.
[8] Bessie and Johns are shown as composers presumably of words and music respectively. The joint composers of *Tipperary* were Harry J. Williams and Jack Judge.

Morton. Johns' strongly ragtime-flavoured piano played in double-time is in fact considerably less accomplished than it has been in the past; he continually rushes the tempo. Fortunately however, he fails to disturb the sense of inevitability achieved by Bessie. She probably holds him back from worse excesses as the most glaring example of his precipitancy occurs in the coda which he performs alone.

The overall emotional structure of the choruses of the last successful release from the 4th April, 1924 session, *Rocking Chair Blues*, is in the form of an arch with the third chorus constituting the keystone. In this chorus Bessie opens up the melody and touches top C. The harmony here is also slightly different; the chords of bar two being subdominant rather than the tonic of the other choruses. To add further distinction to this chorus Bessie treats 'away' to her infrequently used measured vibrato around the blue-third of the scale.

The piece is full of references to other recordings. The third chorus for example refers to the 'easy rider'[9] of *Yellow Dog Blues* which Bessie was to record later in her career. It also uses fragments of that number's melodic phrases. The amended harmony already mentioned, also comes from *Yellow Dog Blues*. Then the first chorus carries echoes of *Backwater Blues* and *Empty Bed Blues*, two other numbers she was to record later.

Many of the phrases sung by Bessie come from the common-stock, for example, 'I'm goin' to the river' and 'Blues jumped a Rabbit', but the form of the choruses is not always traditional as shown below:

First chorus: Normal. (i.e. the first line is
                   repeated and the third line new).

Second chorus: All three lines are different.

[9] Easy Rider. In Southern Black slang, a guitar or a particularly sweet lover. Or perhaps a man who lives from the immoral earnings of a woman; a pimp.

Third chorus: The second and third lines are
                  the same but the first is different.

Fourth chorus: Normal.

Fifth chorus: Normal.

Robbins' violin achieves a notable trombone imitation in the first chorus with slurs on a single string at the bottom of his register. Irving Johns' piano, largely relieved of its melodic duties, is able to concentrate on the harmony. This simplification helps him to keep much better time than on *Pinchbacks* even though *Rocking Chair Blues* is considerably slower ($\downarrow$ = 84).

There is little sense of climax and the last verse ends rather abruptly as if sliced off by the engineer.

Bessie was accompanied by the same musicians the next day when the only title attempted was *Ticket Agent, Ease Your Window Down*. The words of the first chorus are a plea by the singer to the ticket-agent not to give her man a railroad-ticket—she wants him to stay with her. The rest of the choruses justify the reasons for her demand. In a sincere performance she applies consistent and varied forms of blue-ing to the minor-third, Gb[10] together with slurs down to the second degree of the scale, F natural. She applies a fine control in shading 'ease' in the first chorus, one of the words carried by Gb. The melodic line is very economical, mostly restricted to the minor-third interval Eb to Gb. As Hadlock points out, she 'could fashion a compelling solo from an absolute mini-mum of musical raw material',[11] and the material she uses here are those pitches she naturally endows with her richest tone-colours.

The responses to Bessie's melodic line are shared more equally here between violin and piano. But they are no more inventive than before. The violin responds in a particularly

[10] The key is Eb.
[11] 'Jazz Masters of the Twenties', page 224.

threadbare fashion often with decorated arpeggios. Schuller finds Robbins' double-stops in the second chorus 'a fine compliment to Bessie's pleading blues',[12] but to me they are inadequate, operating on a much lower emotional level. His imitation of tears behind Bessie's last line of the second chorus is arch and obvious and his chromatic descending run (with piano) behind the repeat of 'he stole my money, he pawned my clothes' in the fourth chorus, is especially embarrasing.

Boweavil Blues recorded on 7th April, 1924 is one of Bessie's most simple and sparse blues. The bollweevil attacks cotton, and Southern Blacks had long sung songs in which they identified with it as the cotton-grower's implacable enemy. Perhaps, as Blesh says, in some versions of *Boweavil Blues*, the beetle has become a symbol of deliverance.[13] The words here do not, on the surface, comprise a continuous narrative and the sense is somewhat diffused, however there does seem to be more than an element of psychological transference contained in the words of the first and second choruses.

Hadlock complains of a weakness in the words of the last line which are a repeat, (as opposed to Ma Rainey's version which avoids repetition).[14] He is technically correct but Bessie's version makes up for poetic deficiency with a superbly extended and rising 'tired' upon the repetition, balancing the earlier inexorable climactic riffs of the chorus.

Bessie's restriction of the melodic compass to a perfect-fifth, middle C to G, seems appropriate respect for such a traditional subject.

Although a little over-recorded, the piano on the whole plays an adequate accompaniment with its responses adding enough interest without distracting attention from the singer.

[12] 'Early Jazz', page 238.
[13] 'Shining Trumpets', pages 83/84.
[14] 'Jazz Masters of the Twenties', pages 226/7.

The structure of *Hateful Blues* cut the next day, presents an unusual amalgam;[15] after a 4 bar introduction, two choruses of twelve-bar blues are followed by 24 bars in a popular song form. It is also a number in which Bessie obsessively attacks a particular pitch; this time it is her top Ab which astonishingly, she hits over one hundred times during the performance.

Her deployment of the words at the beginning of the second chorus, 'I cried last night and I cried all night before', provide a neat summary of her art; replete with a variety of ornaments, she also breaks the flow on 'all' by treating it to a more extended ornament than the rest — an interruption which, as so often, and paradoxically, binds the phrase together making it a poignant statement of misery, one it is hard to imagine being bettered. But in unsentimental mood, hope shines through as she sings about her love gone cold.

In contrast, Robbins' work is steeped in sentimentality. His comments behind the stop-chords of the last 16 bars are still too glib and he crowns bad taste with his awful aping of crying for a coda.

Frankie Blues, recorded the next day, is also unusual in structure; after a 4 bar introduction and 16 bar verse, a chorus of twelve-bar blues is followed by 20 bars in a popular song form, the last 12 bars of which is repeated.

Without it being exceptional, Bessie gives another good performance: this of course means that it still transcends anything done by her rivals at this time. And there is one particularly wonderful moment — her glissando on 'mad' towards the end of the verse: describing the second inversion of the dominant chord, her blueing around the major- and minor-third is magnificent.

The lyrics make use of more phrases from the common stock; the first words of the first chorus for example are lifted directly from the traditional *Worried Man Blues*.

[15] Unusual for Bessie Smith, but Duke Ellington for instance combined the two forms (blues and popular songs) in many recordings.

Robbins' playing is not so irrelevant in this, his last accompaniment for Bessie. His low-register backing at the beginning of the twelve-bar blues chorus and also at the beginning of the last 12 bars is particularly sumptuous, sounding like another voice. His double-stopping at the end helps to build-up the climax; its other element being, as so often these days, Bessie's voice over stop-chords.

The piano again is no more than adequate.

Moonshine Blues cut on 9th April, 1924 is another juxta-position of twelve-bar blues and popular song forms, the words describing the less than perfect palliative effect of moonshine[16] upon unhappiness.

As in *Hateful Blues*, the tonic (this time G) figures strongly in Bessie's line, particularly in the third of the twelve-bar blues choruses where it sounds over 35 times.

Irving Johns, alone as accompanist here, provides a reliable progression of harmony and antiphony but without impart-ing any swing or lightness of touch. Bessie surmounts her prosaic backing though and treats us to a wide selection of the facets of her art.

[16] Moonshine. Illicitly distilled liquor. The manufacture, sale or carriage of alcoholic drinks was prohibited in the USA from January 1920 to December 1933 by the 18th Amendment to the Constitution. It was a law which was widely evaded with clandestine stills springing up everywhere. Bessie Smith allegedly preferred home-made liquor to satisfy an im-moderate appetite.

SEVEN

July, August and September, 1924

On 22nd July, 1924, Don Redman, alto saxophone and Fletcher Henderson, piano, joined Bessie in two numbers, the first of which was *Lou'siana Low Down Blues*, in essence a twelve-bar blues.

Albertson believes Bessie's voice had matured by this session, 'it had become richer and deeper'.[1] He may be right, but it is difficult to be sure as so much depends upon recording balance and accoustical conditions in the studio. Certainly she extends her favourite third-seeker of Ex. 1; on the repeat of 'wide' in the first chorus she describes the pattern roughly outlined in Ex. 8:

Ex. 8

Henderson's technique has improved further since he last accompanied Bessie in January but Redman's phrasing is just as inappropriate as before even though the clarinet has been

---

[1] 'Bessie, Empress of the Blues', page 64.

discarded in favour of his preferred instrument; still, the broader tones of the alto saxophone when in its lower register, are at least less obtrusive. Both however show their usual disregard for the mood of Bessie's song of unleavened despair; a particularly blatant example of this lack of sensitivity is the brief, arranged, double-time riff, antiphonal passage in the second chorus which has no place in a piece of this emotional intensity.

Mountain Top Blues, the second release from 22nd July, 1924, extends the mood of the last number and, unusually, hope has now vanished and suicide contemplated.

Redman's alto is as flippant as ever. His quote from Chopin's funeral march in the first 2 bars is unsubtle and as Bessie's temper grows darker, his jejune phrasing is thrown into greater relief.

In both releases from this session, Fletcher Henderson adopts a dotted quaver/semiquaver rhythm but although it is one often used by boogie-woogie players, here there is no real feeling of that more basic form; Henderson's approach is too detached and lightweight. Evidence of Redman's arranging ambitions appear in the over-pretty phrases in thirds he and Henderson perform throughout the piece.

At last in *Work House Blues* cut the next day, Bessie gets a horn-player of the quality she deserves. Charlie Green's growling, muted trombone, offering occasional wa-wa effects, inspires even Fletcher Henderson to provide a more insistent beat. Whilst not born in the South, (he came from Omaha, Nebraska), Green had absorbed the Southern Black idiom of trombone playing and although he was working regularly with Fletcher Henderson's band at this time, the smoother (white) influences he must have felt there, did not affect his style very much. Here, at twenty-three, he provides the first of many superb 'accompaniments' to Bessie. I have put the word in quotations as Green's trombone is more of an equal partner with the voice, the piano being left to provide the real accompaniment. Green's expressive, improvised responses, drive Bessie on to perform at her best. She provides a perfect example of classicism in the blues, a model of restraint, order and understatement.

In the penultimate chorus Green changes from mainly antiphonal passages to continuous harmony behind the voice. Then in the last chorus he stimulates a feeling of climax by reverting to antiphony again, finishing on the G near the top of his range. It is a chorus full of tension, with Bessie hitting high C for the first time in the number.

The words form a not very continuous narrative about the uncongenial nature of the work-house and the necessity of escape. Again the common-stock has been raided – particularly effective is 'long old lonesome road', from the second chorus where Bessie makes the most of its onomatopoeic Os to suggest despair.

From the same session, *House Rent Blues* has words about eviction for non-payment of rent which are strangely prophetic of Charlie Green's death. At the age of 36, unable to get in one night, he froze to death on his own doorstep.[2] Bessie's dilute timbre on the first line of the first chorus 'On a cold, dark and stormy night', suggests a biting wind and produces a distinct frisson.

Henderson here has picked up a cadential phrase from the common-stock. It is a figure reminiscent of the itinerant boogie-woogie pianists of the time; Clarence Lofton comes immediately to mind – he often used a similar unaccented

[2] I am grateful to George Melly and John Chilton for the following information: in an interview, Coleman Hawkins described how jealous of his wife Charlie Green was. If on tour he called her up and she was not there, he would quit and return home to check-up on her. Melly feels therefore that it is more likely that Green died on his doorstep because his wife was either out or would not let him in, rather than because he was broke and homeless.

quaver-rhythm too. It first appears in the second bar of the instrumental introduction as shown in Ex. 9:

Ex. 9

Modified, the phrase is used at the end of the first chorus. On both occasions it is picked up by Green who plays his own version of it. At the end of the second chorus Henderson plays another modification and Bessie now picks it up, refining it and making it entirely her own. Although Henderson displays none of the improvisational imagination of Bessie and Charlie Green, he does elevate the phrase to the status of a motif, its overriding purpose being structural not melodic, helping to bind the piece together.

When in two of Bessie's early pieces with her Down Home Boys,[3] an instrumental only chorus was included, the mediocrity of the performers ensured that the result would be lifeless. Here, in spite of Henderson's inflexible piano, the result is vastly different. Green's 'dirty' tone is exciting and his improvisations a delight. Whereas the other horn men to record with Bessie, Elliott and Redman, and Robbins on violin, offer a form of improvisation, a lot of their phrases are really learnt from constant repetition. They are afraid to depart from what they know. Many of Green's phrases are also no doubt learnt but many are not; and even when a phrase is dug up from previous performance, he has the knack like Bessie of making it sound fresh. This is partly the result of the various tone-colours he produces but also because he alter-

[3] *Aggravatin' Papa* and *Beale Street Blues*, 11th April, 1923.

nates phrases where notes are hit on the beat, with others where the accentuation is between-the-beat.

Bessie's accompanists of the previous session were with her again on 31st July, 1924 when they cut *Salt Water Blues*. It is a song full of animal imagery and seems to be expressing a dislike of water with a high saline content. Some research into the argot of the period however may well reveal other meanings. Composition is attributed to G. Brooks, a pseudonym for Fletcher Henderson. It is not known whether he wrote the words too but the awkward construction of the line in the fourth chorus 'worried in both heart and soul' suggests that he might have done. Had Bessie for instance been responsible, she would probably have dispensed with 'both'.

To analyse Bessie's and Charlie Green's performances in detail would merely repeat much that was said about their two previous records together but it is clear that there is a symbiotic relationship between them which spurs them to greater heights than can the relatively intellectual support provided by Henderson. Green seems to dislike staying for long at the centre of any particular note, preferring to slide around it. Bessie on the other hand, needs the discipline provided by hitting the higher proportion of her notes on the nose. This lends her a dignity which Green does not quite approach.

Henderson's unobtrusiveness is exemplary; he fully accepts his purely accompanimental role here.

The words of *Rainy Weather Blues* released from the session of 8th August, 1924 hardly sound like an authentic plea from an oppressed race. Credited to G. Brooks, it is again not certain that Henderson was responsible for the lyrics although presumably the composer of the music. But it is tempting to find him guilty because of their trivial nature. He could have had little personal knowledge of the hardships of Southern Blacks and the words reflect this. The rain in this piece is inconvenient but not the possible cause of a disastrous flood; the mention of death in the last line is quite inappropriate, an unlikely over-reaction.

Fortunately, Bessie ignores the insignificance of the lyrics and treats the number to the full range of her microtonal shading techniques.

Green is as expressive as ever, his simple solo in the third chorus as vocal as Bessie's voice is instrumental.

Henderson is again content to leave the creative work to others.

On September, 26th, 1924, inspired by her backing, Bessie Smith gives one of her most poignant performances. The words of *Weeping Willow Blues*[4] about deserted love seem to come directly from her own experience.

For the first time a cornet is added to her backing. Joe Smith (no relation) joins Charlie Green and Fletcher Henderson in the most structurally complex number recorded by Bessie to date. A 4 bar instrumental introduction leads into three choruses[5] with vocal, each of the first two followed by a 4 bar instrumental interlude. Then follow 16 bars of riffs and a final 4 bars of chorus by all four performers. The key is Ab (but with a temporary modulation to B minor in each chorus) until the riff passage when it modulates to the subdominant, Db (as in the trio section of much ragtime). The key of Db is retained to the end and the last 4 bars of chorus, although derived from previous material in Ab, now has the new key. Such modulation, although simple, is quite unusual in a Bessie Smith performance.

A climax is effected from the tension created by the static harmony of the 16 bars of modulated riff passage. Bessie's line is rhythmic rather than melodic and so are the lines of cornet and trombone. But as can be seen from the first four bars of this passage shown in Ex. 10 (excluding the piano part),

[4] Some information on this title is drawn from the Open University course, 'The Rise of Modernism in Music, 1890–1935', Units 25–27, pages 52/55.

[5] Of 12 bars each but not in twelve-bar blues form.

cornet and trombone play riffs of roughly similar shape and
similar rhythm whilst Bessie sings a figure which is quite
different melodically and rhythmically from theirs. The
instrumental riff falls into a 3 + 3 + 2 pattern which collides
with Bessie's basically regular quavers, setting up a restless
tension which is continued until the last 4 bars of the number
when it is deliciously resolved with a repeat of the end of the
chorus.

Ex. 10 [6]

(* = BLUE NOTE)

When you're broken hearted and your man is   out of town,

go to the riv-er,   take the chair and then sit down;   and

[6] Drawn from the Open University course, 'The Rise of Modernism in
Music, 1890–1935', Scores 8, page 26.

The 22 year old Joe Smith had been recording with Henderson since 1921 and was soon to become a regular member of the band. He combines with Charlie Green to produce here a developed form of New Orleans style backing (although Smith was actually born in Ripley, Ohio, not in the South). One of the delights of their performance is the beautiful precision of their muted riffs in the passage commencing with the 4 bars of Ex. 10, a result no doubt of their work in the Henderson band.

Both horns blow in a heavily vocalised manner, almost talking to Bessie Smith. Joe Smith's tone is wide and in his liking for the middle register and his lyricism, he has been suggested as a Black equivalent to Bix Beiderbecke (white cornet player, 1903–1931). His style is certainly lyrical but he carries a trifle more 'edge' to his tone than Beiderbecke. Buster Bailey, (later to appear at several of Bessie's recording sessions) is quoted as saying that Joe Smith 'was pretty in the middle register – he didn't go above high C'.[7] Patently his range was greater than this – here he sometimes reaches up to high G. Leora Henderson, Fletcher's wife, said that Joe Smith 'had such a big, soft, beautiful tone'[8] and this can clearly be heard in his introduction to this number. But sometimes, when he is rising perhaps a little higher than his preferred range, he can produce a vitreous, slippery sound.

Joe Smith and Charlie Green were said to be Bessie's favourite cornet and trombone; interestingly she preferred Joe to Louis Armstrong who recorded nine selections with her in 1925. Part of this preference may have derived from her unconscious recognition that they all three used a vibrato with much the same speed of oscillation. And Joe Smith in particular always had a special sensitivity to what she was doing – note his high, muted stabs behind her 'I went up on the mountain', in the second verse.

7 'Hear Me Talkin' To Ya', page 214.
8 'Hear Me Talkin' to Ya', page 222.

The other number from the 26th September session, *The Bye Bye Blues* had Bessie evoking a mood of satisfaction verging upon triumph; the words describe the end of an emotional conflict out of which, unusually, she comes off best. Whilst dominating the proceedings with her perfect control of on- and off-pitch phrasing, the quality and number of her collaborators does slightly diminish the importance of the voice which tends to become more of an ensemble instrument – a definite shift of emphasis from her earlier records.

A sympathy between Green and Joe Smith is apparent throughout – Green's chattering cornet-like phrase at the end of the first four bars, picked up and commented upon several times in the verse by the cornet, is but one example. And there are many other good things to be heard: note the early muted sounds of Joe Smith (again often well above high C) contrasting with his fat, saxophone-like sounds of the last 18 bars: then there are his beautifully controlled explosive rip-ups in these bars which were pre-echoed by the less dynamic stabs of the first chorus.

Henderson concentrates on the harmony again and on providing a steady, if pedestrian beat (unusually the tempo has hardly increased at all by the end).

EIGHT

December, 1924

In *Sing Sing Prison Blues* recorded on 6th December, 1924, Bessie Smith employs one of her smallest pitch-spans. She ranges over-all from middle C to the G above, a perfect-fifth but this G is reached only once, in the last chorus and apart from that she stays within the major-third, C to E. A very restricted range therefore which few other singers could accept or in fact do very much with, but Bessie's clever control of pitch manages to avoid monotony. The other unusual feature is the modulation in and out of the relative minor key – the harmony constantly alternates between C major and A minor. These factors produce an oppressive mood which is only relieved by the G Bessie touches in the last chorus as a climax.

This session is a culmination of the sessions of the two previous days with Fred Longshaw on piano, to the second of which Buster Bailey and Don Redman on clarinets were added. All five tunes from these previous sessions were rejected, eighteen takes in all and we are lucky that Columbia persisted since Longshaw and Bailey at least, were later to become two of Bessie's more dependable accompanists. Even here, although Longshaw stays in the background, his rhythm is clearly more springy than that of Fletcher Henderson.

The piece is spoilt by the totally arranged clarinet lines, starting with their one-bar trill between E natural and Eb, a rather obvious augury of the pitches to be emphasised by the voice. This is particularly disappointing because Buster Bailey is actually a fine, imaginative player in the New Orleans tradition (although he was initially classically trained and later in his career did occasional symphony work). Bailey was in the Henderson band at this time and Redman, who was also with Henderson no doubt perpetrated the arrangement. Redman was later to become famous for 'inventing' the three-clarinet chorus used in many of Henderson's band recordings. In the big-band context these often have merit – here a two-clarinet version only detracts from the performance. From time to time, the clarinets play percussive slap-tongued notes but these fail to relieve the tedium, merely presenting another aspect of it.

Five days later, in *Follow The Deal On Down,* we can hear Longshaw properly for the first time. He lays down a rock-steady beat, yet with a certain unassuming delicacy in his right-hand trills, tremolos and glissandi. Truly the Gerald Moore of early jazz piano, preferring to encourage the singer's performance rather than indulge his own ego.

Bessie responds with a relaxed performance of great charm assisted also by the chord-sequence, progress to the resolution of which is satisfyingly inevitable. One of the ornaments she has been using for some time now is the fall from a phrase-end note. As Schuller says, mostly effected on the tonic, she sometimes used it on the third and fifth of the scale as well.[1] Here for example, on 'go' in the fifth bar of the last chorus, she drops from the fifth to the third as shown in Ex. 11:

Ex. 11

[1] 'Early Jazz', page 232.

This clearly does not fall into her usual category of ornaments where the decorated pitches enrich her path to an intended target note. Here the ornament is tacked on afterwards, a sort of dying-fall.

The other release from the 11th December, 1924 session, *Sinful Blues,* has Bessie Smith, for the only time on record, playing an 'instrument'. In the last chorus she hums away at the kazoo, in the process losing the rich timbres of her voice. We are left with an impoverished sound, only the rhythm of which is stamped as hers. The impression we get from her attacking phrases however, is that had she taken up trumpet or cornet, she would have been very good.

Apart from the kazoo chorus, a rich joy pervades her performance even in the third and fourth choruses where suicide and shooting are threatened. This may have been because of the fast tempo ($\downarrow = 108$) forcing her to discard her more significant ornaments, or because this is another number with a particularly satisfying chord-sequence.[2] But her main stimulus was most likely to have been Longshaw's performance. He is even better at this pace. A fragile rhythm is augmented with telling musical ornaments, only one of which resorts to cliché (the arch, 'cinematic' tremolos at the start of the fourth chorus may be appropriate to the half-spoken words about shooting but do not match Bessie's actual mood). His occasional stop-chords reveal a real mastery of timing.

Buster Bailey and Don Redman were back with Bessie and Fred Longshaw on 12th December, 1924 with *Woman's Trouble Blues.* As on *Sing Sing Prison Blues,* their clarinets are hamstrung with a dispiriting arrangement (by Redman?). Longshaw tries to open up the rhythm at the start of each of the last two choruses, but they overwhelm him with the

---

[2] This number is in fact very similar in construction, melody and harmony to *Follow The Deal On Down* from the same session.

deadly rigidity of their phrases. Again they try their meaningless slap-tongued effect and in the second chorus, introduce a habanera[3] rhythm, the Spanish import of which has no
special relevance to the words or mood. Their worst offence
however occurs in the fourth chorus where an imitation of
sobbing cries is produced—about the most synthetic comment
to have appeared from any of Bessie's accompanists so far.

Fortunately Bessie transcends it all, singing the words
about the consequences of a prison sentence, with a monu-
mental disdain for her backing.

The words of *Love Me Daddy Blues,* the second number from
the 12th December, 1924 session are rather limited. Another
set about deserted love, the lyrics of the last two choruses are
virtually identical. Bessie however uses the piece as the
vehicle for another highly professional performance in spite of
this duplication. Melodic symmetry is still her enemy,
throughout she adjusts her phrases to avoid regularity. An
example is the remarkable downward four-note portamento
from high Bb on 'blue' starting in the first bar of the first
chorus. This word is held for five crotchet beats which means
she has to crush the preceeding 'now I'm' into about a one
crotchet anacrusis, and the following 'and lonesome' into
about two-and-a-half crotchet beats. A less imaginative
singer would have spread the whole phrase out more evenly
and probably started it in the first bar of the chorus rather
than the last bar of the verse.

The first chorus contains a rare mistake by Bessie; on 'try'
in bar fourteen she looses her way harmonically. She overlooks the fact that the chorus at this point is moving towards
the dominant, the only one of the three to do so. But she soon
recovers.

The reason for the addition of the two clarinets at the
beginning and end of the performance only, is hard to

---

[3] Habanera. A Cuban dance of Spanish origin. In duple time with dotted
rhythm. The pianist Jimmy Yancey was noted for his extensive use of this
rhythm.

comprehend. But it is quite a relief to discover that their arranged wailing is limited to four bars only.

Longshaw's piano sounds much fuller than in any of his other performances. This is because of his not unattractive, ubiquitous tremolos – they sometimes make him sound like two pianists. And occasionally he somehow produces the plucked sound of a guitar or banjo but this may be caused by a faulty damping pedal. From time to time his texture becomes thinner and it is during one of these spells that he executes a beautifully imaginative touch – the descending F natural semiquaver/dotted quaver octave leaps at the end of the first chorus after 'my man, he left today'. It is true that he has used this device before on record with Bessie but never with such relevance.

Dying Gambler's Blues, the last number from 12th December, 1924 session, is attributed to Jack Gee, Bessie's second husband. But this is probably Bessie's own tune, the credit to Jack being a gesture of generosity. As Jack had no musical talent, it could of course be argued that the very odd construction is evidence that he did write it himself; the four choruses are of ten, eight, nine and eight bars respectively.[4] However, it really hangs together too well in spite of its asymmetry, to be the work of a musical illiterate.

The words, although ostensibly about a legendary gambler, are really about the death of a lover. Perhaps the most powerful line, 'My best friend, he's died today' at the end of the first verse, scores principally because of its tragic understatement. And a perfect example of Bessie's upgrading of otherwise trite lyrics comes at the start of the ten bar chorus, 'Oh me, Oh me'. The first 'Oh' is elongated to the point at which chaos threatens, but it is exactly what she intends and the whole phrase, including the second 'Oh me' in more conventional form, enchants. In this piece Bessie also

---

[4] The four choruses follow a trombone and piano introduction of 4 bars, two verses of 8 bars each with Bessie Smith added, and a 4 bar interlude again by all three performers.

simulates Charlie Green's trombone slides. On 'heard', at the start of the 4 bar interlude, she manipulates the pitch carrying the word exactly as Green would, and in fact does, in his responses.

The substitution of Green's trombone for the awful clarinets of the other two releases from this session tends to make any criticism of his playing seem churlish but it has to be said that on this piece, in spite of the admiration of some observers, in trying to walk a tightrope between sublimity and absurdity he is sometimes guilty of pure bathos.

Longshaw's piano provides a wealth of interesting background arabesques without going too far beyond an accompanimental role.

NINE

January, 1925

The St. Louis Blues on which Bessie and Fred Longshaw are joined by Louis Armstrong was cut on 14th January, 1925 at a session which marks the start of the most important phase in her early career. The artistic level of her work with Armstrong, whilst being not entirely without flaw, easily transcends all that has gone before. The tune was not new, having been published by W. C. Handy in 1914 but during those three minutes in 1925 she and Louis made it the definitive version. We are fortunate that this should have happened as Bessie was reputed to have preferred accompaniment from less flamboyant performers and to have initially disapproved of Armstrong's presence: Armstrong himself later said he preferred his recordings with Maggie Jones, (a singer of far less talent). Perhaps it was this conflict which enabled them to produce some of the best music either of them was to put on record. The most important thing about this piece is the perfect rapport between Louis's open cornet and Bessie's voice; in transcribing the vocal line from single-note piano approximation, I found myself constantly continuing with the cornet response after a phrase by Bessie had finished, so homogeneous were the two lines.[1] Confirmation of this rapport is found in the low number of takes required to produce each acceptable master. Out of nine titles on which

[1] Humphrey Lyttelton has also noticed the extraordinary rapport between the vocal and cornet lines. 'The Best of Jazz', page 77.

they were both present, not one was completely rejected and two was the maximum number of takes per title needed. Five first takes were released including this one. (It is true that a third attempt at *Nashville Woman's Blues* was cut in May, 1925 but both this and the second take were released under the same Columbia record number.) This is a much better average than at her sessions with other musicians.[2]

Handy's composition, never an authentic blues in the first place, has been further modified for this performance. Here, a one-bar introduction by cornet and harmonium leads into two choruses of twelve-bar blues followed by a 16 bar verse; the piece is completed by another twelve-bar blues chorus. In the original the verse comes at the beginning and here Louis Armstrong makes a brief reference to this with his long held Bb first note — Bb being not only the fifth of the scale of the choruses (Eb) but the (minor) third of the scale of the verse (the relative minor, G minor). The verse is in tango time (derived from the habanera) a deliberate move by Handy to make his composition more commercial. The words about deserted love, at this distance in time at least and perhaps because of familiarity, sound reasonably authentic, at least in the twelve-bar sections. Like much of Handy's work, this piece has elements taken from the common-stock[3] synthesised by him into a whole for publication. He was the leader of a brass and concert band and also a trumpet player. Whilst some of his later recordings feature well-known jazz names, his early releases and his own trumpet work reveal a ragtime-like stiffness rather than jazz fluidity. His title, 'The Father of the Blues', is certainly a misnomer and he has even less to do with jazz. It is fair to point out however that this was not a title which he sought himself, and whatever his performing shortcomings, his compositions form ideal vehicles for jazz interpretation. In *The St. Louis Blues,* Handy's own instru-

[2] Presumably also, a growing refinement in recording techniques made this possible.
[3] Blesh, in 'Shining Trumpets', page 146, identifies its origin except for the tango section, as *Jogo Blues.*

ment is revealed in the choice of melodic line at the start of each of the twelve-bar choruses – it is based upon the fourth, fifth and sixth pitches in the harmonic series of an Eb fundamental. A phrase, which once the correct harmonic series has been located (by valve depression), can be played by lip pressure alone.

Bessie's penchant for unorthodox pauses, regrouping melodic lines into new, more imaginative patterns, is well displayed in this performance as pointed out by Humphrey Lyttelton.[4] Blue notes abound – her treatment of 'sun' in the first chorus is exceptional even by her standards; on the flat-third (Gb) of the key, she moves above and below the note in perfect control, as if testing the limits of the pitch, outside of which it is called something else.

Louis Armstrong, at twenty-four, was not yet widely known to the general public but he had already won respect amongst musicians who were beginning to use his phrases in their own work (and not only trumpeters and cornettists). Two years later he was to reach the peak of his innovatory powers and become the foremost influence in jazz, his ideas affecting the music down to the present day. But in January, 1925, the Hot Fives were ten months in the future and the even better Hot Sevens, over two years away. In spite of this he had obviously made sufficient mark upon the jazz world to cause Bessie some uneasiness.

To adapt C. Northcote Parkinson's Law, melody expands so as to fill the time available for its completion. This is often true with Armstrong and to a lesser extent, Bessie Smith. Bessie however at twenty-nine, had a fully mature style which was not to develop very much more during the rest of her career. In her faster pieces it has been noticeable that the only way she could cope with the melody was by cutting ornaments to the bone. In slower pieces she certainly allows

[4] 'The Best of Jazz', pages 61/85. Lyttelton's chapter on Bessie Smith provides an interesting analysis of this performance. And Winthrop Sargeant in 'Jazz, Hot and Hybrid', pages 181/2, gives a detailed comparison between Handy's published first line and Bessie's metamorphosis.

them to flower but she rarely seeks innovation for its own sake. Armstrong however, was still a year or two away from his peak and with his immense energy was pushing against boundaries in every direction; he would often suggest the harmony and even the antiphony to his melodic line. Whereas Bessie found tempos around $\lrcorner = 84$ and below [5] just right for the full display of her art, Armstrong, used to the faster tempos of instrumental pieces, found time heavy on his hands. In his performances with Bessie Smith the slow pace was sometimes too much of a temptation and his elaborations could lead to the brink of chaos. In the last chorus for instance, he courts disaster in his ambitious phrase following Bessie's 'just as blue as I can be'. Bessie was fairly clear as to the limitations of her art but Armstrong either could not, or would not recognise boundaries, at least until 1929. [6] Certainly then, enthusiasm led him into occasional errors of judgement but it is this enthusiasm which made him greater than all other jazz musicians of this time, only Earl Hines (piano) approaching the lofty realms he inhabited. *The St. Louis Blues* at once makes all this clear. His choice of notes, timing, and most obvious of all, his timbre, are quite unique. This latter feature in particular, is full of swinging life – with vibrato alone he can often produce a surging drive. His dynamic approach, whilst perhaps not quite so unique, is still exceptional; he proves that even at this early stage of his career when his technique was relatively untamed, it is not all forte dynamics and brilliance – often it will subside to provide a quiet, rich harmony behind the voice. And on these sides with Bessie, his technique whilst formidable, is still basically within the New Orleans tradition. Later, as his skill developed, he was to be a considerable contributor to the downfall of that seminal style.

[5] The tempo here is $\lrcorner = 70$.

[6] In 1929, Louis Armstrong made a deliberate decision to reduce the innovatory aspect of his work and produce a more commercially acceptable product. As will be seen, Bessie Smith who did not change her style, began to find her career on the slide about this time whereas Armstrong went on to new fame.

There is not much to be said about Longshaw's harmonium except, as Humphrey Lyttelton points out, 'its
sound has become woven into the very atmosphere of the
piece'.[7] With a cornet and voice as rhythmically aware as
those of Armstrong and Bessie Smith, Longshaw needs only
to produce the harmony, which he does competently.
Because of the limitation of the instrument (the delay between key-pressure and resulting sound), he is not able to
produce a vestige of rhythmic drive.

However, in spite of the drawbacks of the somewhat
artificial construction, the out of place harmonium and the
acoustic recording,[8] the result is still a small masterpiece, the
listener's awareness being heightened by the sheer beauty of
conception.

The second number from the 14th January, 1925 session,
Reckless Blues, is an even more satisfying work of art than the
first. The contrivance of the more famous blues is missing and
we are left with elemental statements about the misery of the
human condition from voice and cornet. It is an object lesson
in what inventiveness can be applied above a 'primitive' chord
progression without in any way descending into banality by
attempting more than the vehicle is capable of carrying.

It is another twelve-bar blues and because each of Bessie's
chorus lines ends on the third of the scale, the way is open for
her to make considerable use of her favourite third-seeker.
And she does, using it ten times in all, three times in each of
the first three choruses and managing to fit it in four times in
the last. Many of these repetitions are subtly varied. Mellors
calls it incremental repetition;[9] certainly the cumulative
effect is stunning but even in the first chorus, her clashes
against the fixed pitches of the harmonium are exciting.

By now, Bessie had become largely set in her technique

[7] 'The Best of Jazz', page 76.
[8] Bessie Smith cut her last acoustic recording at this session. From 5th
May, 1925, she was electrically recorded.
[9] 'Man and His Music, Part Four', page 201.

but here, under stress of competition, she pushes it a little further. In the first line of the second chorus on 'Now I', she echoes part of the rhythm of Armstrong's antiphony from the end of the first chorus, producing a new and one of her most tortuous decorations to date. It is outlined in Ex. 12.

Ex. 12

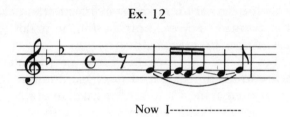

Now I------------------

Often, she seems to be challenging Louis to match her control and feeling, and as he is not only a brilliant jazz exponent but also unrivalled as a player of the blues (not at all necessarily the same thing), he responds to her every nuance immediately. Using wa wa muted effects and at a slightly faster pace this time, he makes few mistakes – neither expressively nor in the aggregate are the bounds of good taste exceeded.[10] He judiciously mixes passages full of short note-values with others comprised of crying wails. And whereas most cornettists and trumpeters phrase in two- and four-bar periods, Louis' phrases are irregular, seeking motivic unity rather than symmetry. Repetition is to be avoided too and as a result a constant and enthusiastic stream of new phrases is produced.

Much of the emotional pleasure from this performance derives from Louis' complete understanding of what Bessie is doing. His long blue flat-third after her repeat of 'My Daddy says I'm wild', in the third chorus, with its shading away from and around the pitch, is an exact translation of her technique to the cornet.

[10] Throughout his career, Louis Armstrong used the mute sparingly.

The role of Longshaw in this number is exactly the same as in *The St. Louis Blues*: the harmonium precludes him from doing anything other than provide a basic harmony.

Sobbin' Hearted Blues, the third number cut on 14th January, 1925, is another elemental twelve-bar blues with some ingredients drawn from the common-stock; the lines of the first chorus for example, 'The sun's gonna shine in my back-door some day', comes from the eight-bar blues *Trouble In Mind* published by Richard M. Jones in 1926 but with roots which reach back into the nineteenth century.

Bessie, again making use of her third-seeker of Ex. 1, does not seem quite so commited this time. Her mood is more intense than that of Louis Armstrong but her heart is not entirely in the performance. Louis' lyricism may be to blame.

But perhaps relaxed would be a better word to describe his approach. Although coruscating through some faster passages, the record is notable for the rich warmth of his open tone on the longer note-values, a tone mainly derived from an incandescent vibrato but partly from his instrument. He was still using a cornet[11] at this time, an instrument with a naturally velvet-textured timbre. The trumpet which he took up in 1926, well after his last record with Bessie, would have given him a more brilliant, heroic sound, presumably at variance with his intentions and even more with those of the singer. But with Louis Armstrong, vibrato is more than just a question of enriching a note. As Schuller points out, 'he

[11] According to Jones and Chilton in 'Louis', page 106, his instrument at this time was a Harry B. Jay model trumpet-cornet. The tone resembles that of the conventional short cornet however. Philip Bate in 'The Trumpet and Trombone', page 253, suggests snobbery as the reason for the long cornet (trumpet-cornet) – it was especially made to resemble the orchestral trumpet. (Although superficially the two instruments look similar and it is relatively easy for a cornet-player to transfer to the trumpet, their ancestry and until recently their history are quite separate. The trumpet's ancestor was a cylindrical reed whilst the cornet is derived from a conical animal's horn. Even today, the trumpet is largely cylindrical in bore with the cornet being mainly conical).

recognised early that vibrato could be an essential ingredient in giving rhythmic momentum to his playing'.[12] On this release, its rhythmic purpose is not quite so necessary and he uses it mainly to add body — his notes sound fat — and to burnish the sound. Later in his career and in pieces which require a higher emotional temperature, he adds the shake[13] and the terminal vibrato.[14]

Back on piano now, Longshaw is able to contribute to the rhythm. It may be that this easing of the rhythmic burden from Louis encouraged his relaxed approach but in truth, Longshaw's contribution in this area is quite minimal.

Bessie's unorthodox pauses for breath are prominent in the fourth number from 14th January, 1925, *Cold In Hand Blues*. In the last chorus for example, on the repeat of 'I'm gon-na find myself another man', she divides 'myself' with a breath,[15] adding variety and interest to the line.

A small point, but curious just the same, is Bessie's pronunciation of 'treats' in the second chorus; she pronounces it 'tweats' although on the three previous singular and plural occurrences of the word she made no error. It is tempting to think that Armstrong's preceding extended wa wa phrase was responsible.

Apart from the last chorus, and an occasional excessive accumulation of duck-like muted sounds, Armstrong's work here is exemplary, his antiphony full of originality. Unfortunately his last chorus work is quite at variance with Bessie's mood (an offence he compounds in his next recording with her). It sounds as if he has suddenly become tired of the heavy misery with which she saturates this piece about her improvident man, and is seeking to spice it up, or perhaps he feels a

[12] 'Early Jazz', page 97.
[13] Shake. In effect, a wide trill. Usually produced by shaking the instrument against the lips, using notes of the harmonic series.
[14] Terminal vibrato. A vibrato which, starting with a narrow oscillation, expands exponentially until it becomes a shake. Used on a long note.
[15] As pointed out by Schuller in 'Early Jazz', page 233.

climax is called for. Whatever the reason, his plaintive chattering is inappropriate.

Longshaw, again on piano, is better at this faster pace and contributes a quite swinging accompaniment but one which falls some way short of infection. In the penultimate chorus, which he performs with Armstrong alone, he does introduce agreeably precise passages of double-time but in the end they merely remind us how much better were Earl Hines and Buck Washington at this sort of thing.

You've Been A Good Ole Wagon, the last release from 14th January, 1925 is a flawed work, not to be compared with the other four in spite of some good things, mainly from Bessie.

The words of this vaudeville tune about a worn-out lover, are usually handled with wry humour. But Bessie decides to treat them as a regretful but respectful dismissal. Unfortunately Louis Armstrong fails to recognise this until too late and his 'pretty' contributions become increasingly irrelevant culminating in the flurry of mocking 'crying' of the last chorus. (Only his work in the third chorus can be excluded from this criticism; there his *piano* phrases are almost perfect in construction and taste). No doubt his intention was to provide a climax but in the event he should have left this to the poignant words to effect alone. Later in his career Louis said that he did not listen to his accompaniment – this was in reference to the very variable and sometimes downright inferior quality of his fellow band musicians. The habit was already forming here. In a band he was usually the star and could set the mood himself – his lack of close attention to whatever else was going on would not greatly detract from the performance. With a singer in a small group such in-attention can damage a performance since the accompanists, however good, should defer to her mood. There may be some excuse however; he played with a lot of blues singers, many of only average ability and in these circumstances his own obvious talent forestalls complaints of inapposite accompaniment. With Bessie it was different – her sovereign talent demanded his full attention and deference, something he was not used to bestowing consistently. In May 1925 however, on his last sides with Bessie, he had learned and his genius became more responsive to her needs.

TEN

May, 1925 –
The first half

On 5th May, 1925, the Columbia recording studio went electric. According to Albertson the new Western Electric system, at a stroke, allowed a large band to back Bessie Smith without drowning her.[1] Certainly in *Cakewalkin' Babies* the recording balance is good, being characterised by the discreteness of each voice and we are left with the impression that a layer of aural gauze has been removed. Whilst coping well with the band however[2] this still relatively primitive system does have some problems with Bessie's voice. For obvious reasons her microphonic technique must have been minimal at this time and she may well have been too close to the instrument; whatever the cause though there is often a considerable over-spill, resulting in distortion. But here, for the first time, she is clearly a jazz singer. She belts out the words in fine style and neither she, nor the band slacken the high intensity of their performances throughout. The words, about some legendary dancers, have little personal emotional content and consequently sound well with the simple

[1] 'Bessie, Empress of the Blues', page 75. Albertson's argument, although attractive, is damaged when it is noted that the Clarence Williams' Blue Five recording of *Cakewalkin' Babies* of January, 1925 was made on acoustic equipment and without the singer, Eva Taylor, being swamped in any way. This earlier recording carried much the same instrumentation but without brass bass. Its instrumental texture however is decidedly muddy.
[2] With the exception of Coleman Hawkins who makes little mark upon the proceedings.

delivery she adopts. Even here though, she does manage to produce a number of long notes allowing some microtonal prospecting. Bessie's influence on Ella Fitzgerald is easy to recognise from this recording. In her early records, for example *Melancholy Baby,* Ella's voice, although smoother than Bessie's, even echoes a lot of her sheer exaltation.

As almost every commentator has pointed out, this release features a notable alteration of the words by Bessie to suit her musical intentions. 'The only way to win is to cheat 'em' of the first chorus becomes in the third, 'The only way is to win is to cheat 'em'. Linguistic sense is weakened but this is amply compensated for by the improvement in melodic line which becomes significantly more rhythmic.

One odd thing about this session[3] is the style adopted by the band. They were all members of Fletcher Henderson's big band, a band which played in a very arranged, chordal style (with occasional improvised solos by Louis Armstrong) but here we have the loosely organised contrapuntal sound of New Orleans. It is only necessary to play some of Fletcher Henderson's band recordings of the time (for example *Swannee Butterfly* of 31st January, 1925 and *Poplar Street Blues* of 4th February, 1925) to appreciate the anomaly (or for Henderson, the anachronism). However, it is a wonderful sound. The front line is not quite the classic one of cornet, trombone and clarinet since a tenor saxophone is also included but as previously noted, this is not obtrusive. Joe Smith plays a solid lead cornet stating the melody clearly and at the same time managing some imaginative improvisation: his high spot comes in the eighth bar of the instrumental chorus where he constructs a perfectly conceived falling break of some complexity and outstanding beauty. Buster Bailey's clarinet is in fine form, weaving intricate arabesques above whilst Charlie Green's trombone pushes the group forward with appropriate stabbing harmonies.

Although the performance is quite propulsive, this is

---

[3] And the session on 2nd March, 1927.

mainly due to the work of the front line instruments and voice; the rhythm section is rather slack and a trifle insipid. The record is in fact a very good negative illustration of the superiority of the plucked string bass over its brass counterpart. Here we have a brass bass which does nothing for the rhythm, merely providing harmonic pitches which are, or could be, played by the trombone. Notes played by a plucked string bass on the other hand, have an attack and decay pattern which is the epitomy of swing. And at faster tempos, a continuous four notes to the bar present no problem to the string bass. Here, Escudero has breath for mostly no more than two.

This first electric recording allowed Bessie to depart considerably from the style of her previous work (this may be why the record was not released until 1940) and the result was a happy, boisterous masterpiece.[4]

The second selection from 5th May, 1925, *The Yellow Dog Blues,* (Matrix 140586–2) has Bessie singing with the same group. In what, after an eight bar instrumental introduction is basically a twelve-bar blues,[5] she is in fine growling form but perhaps even more negligent of the original words. Even her first word is incorrect; it should be 'ever' but for no apparent reason she changes it to 'every'. And as Paul Oliver points out,[6] in the second chorus W. C. Handy's line '. . . everywhere that Uncle Sam has even a rural delivery' is changed to '. . . everywhere that Uncle Sam is the ruler of

[4] Although 5th May, 1925 was the first day on which the new electric system was used by Columbia, Bessie Smith was not the first singer to benefit from it. This same band (excluding Hawkins), had recorded with Maggie Jones immediately prior to Bessie's session. Bessie's incidentally was the legendary occasion when a cloth tent was erected inside the studio by an engineer who felt it necessary to contain the sound. It cut short the session by collapsing on musicians and engineers immediately after the second take of her second selection of the day, *Yellow Dog Blues.*
[5] Uncharacteristically, the third chorus incorporates a modulation to the dominant key.
[6] 'Bessie Smith', page 36.

delivery'; but at least this makes a sort of sense and improves the stilted phrasing of the original.

The words are in fact another Handy pastiche and refer to the search for a runaway lover which leads to a meadow outside Morehead, Mississippi where the lines of the 'Southern' (Southern Railway) cross the 'Yellow Dog' (Yazoo Delta Line).

The instrumental texture this time is a little denser. The brass bass sounds some richly satisfying longer notes (the slower pace making no rhythmic demands upon it) and the tenor saxophone is a little more in evidence. There is also a trace of these musicians' big band work in the clarinet riff which appears in the third chorus. Joe Smith, as usual, proves to be the best musician, playing thoughtful phrases in his lyrical style and even Henderson responds to the railroad connotations with some passages of boogie-woogie. The whole band in fact is in perfect accord with Bessie's mood which treats the mock-serious words more solemnly than is customary and whilst one would not wish to miss any of the vocal, the absence of an instrumental chorus is an undeniable loss.

Columbia issued the other take of *Yellow Dog Blues* from this session (Matrix 140586–1) under the same record number (14075–D) and this tends to confirm that the incorrect words of the second take had been part of her performance for some time – they are exactly the same in this first take. Further, apart from the fact that her range is truncated here by a minor third[7] her phrasing is often similar. The band, on the other hand, give a quite different performance: the clarinet riffs of the third chorus for instance are missing and Joe Smith's breaks, whilst not so well constructed are more exciting – one of his most highly charged contributions is his impatient antiphony to Bessie's first line of the third chorus which he

[7]   In the second take dealt with previously, her range was from the B natural below to the Bb above middle C; here it is from the D natural to the Bb next above middle C.

bases upon the harmonic series. Joe Smith on the whole plays with greater composure and blues feeling in the better known second take but there fails to achieve the emotional impact of this first take.

The greater tension of this take is reflected in the sense of climax engendered in the last chorus, largely missing from the second take. It is a climax almost entirely created by Bessie's attack upon the upper end of her tessitura, especially the Bb.

In *Soft Pedal Blues* (Matrix 140601–2) cut on 14th May, 1925, Bessie mixes a shouting, strident style with her more subtle approach of slides and simple decoration. Her performance is entertaining but not a complete success. Firstly, the chord progressions, whilst sectionally simple, when combined to form this vaudeville song's verse and chorus, become quite complex. This results in Bessie, more than once sounding uncertain about the direction of a particular sequence; the first 8 bars of the verse are a case in point. Then there is the question of tempo. The number begins at ♩ = 84 but Bessie overtly pulls it back to the speed she wants which turns out to be ♩ = 72; eventually a compromise is reached between her and her accompanists and the song proceeds at about ♩ = 80. Another detracting feature is Bessie's series of unsettling falsetto yells[8] the last of which causes all the performers to lose the time and nearly come to grief.

The words are about a lady who runs a buffet flat[9] and a party which is just getting under way when time runs out; the party is continued on the understanding that the band and guests apply the 'soft pedal'. Charlie Green, in what is therefore an emotionally bland piece, has little opportunity to display his more expressive noises and offers mainly

[8] These yells start on the A natural a thirteenth above middle C and are the highest pitches produced by Bessie in any of her released recordings.
[9] Buffet flat. A private, illegal, sporting house offering gambling and bizarre sexual entertainment. Bessie Smith was said to sometimes frequent such establishments.

straightforward harmony and antiphony. But unlike Bessie, he at least never mistakes the direction of the progressions. Henderson is competent enough without doing much more than lay down the chords; it is a performance which suffers from an over-recording of his bass register — it tends to boom out and sound as if the sustaining pedal has been permanently applied (ironic in view of the title).

The first take of *Soft Pedal Blues*[10] has Bessie in more imperious form; symptomatic of her change of mood is her final falsetto yell which is even wilder than that on the second take dealt with previously. These takes vary in less obvious detail too; in the second take, Bessie, on the first vowel of 'early' for instance, the first word of the final 13 bar section, describes a smear up to A natural on which she remains through the whole of the vowel — in this first take, after a similar smear she turns the rest of the vowel into a vehicle for a two-pitch melisma. Then Charlie Green is more subtle — this can be heard by comparing his antiphony in the second-half of the main chorus[11] for instance; on the second take his responses are repetitive whereas here they are more varied, and introduce a slow trill at different pitches.

Overall a more satisfying performance: even the tempo, which at the start is faster, is brought under control within two bars (as if Green and Henderson were being glared at by a silent Bessie) and remains at ♩ = 76 thereafter.

Dixie Flyer Blues, cut the next day has the performers of *Soft Pedal Blues* joined by Buster Bailey, clarinet and James T. Wilson, miscellaneous effects. The theme is homesickness and the words are about a train which goes back South. James Wilson's extra-musical effects are ponderously employed to evoke this train but he cannot be entirely blamed for the

[10] Also cut on 14th May, 1925 and issued by Columbia under the same record number, 14075–D.
[11] The 22 bar chorus which immediately follows the 24 bar verse. The verse is preceeded by a 4 bar instrumental only introduction.

lack-lustre performance; the instrumentalists too, perversely connive to produce a synthetic atmosphere. The passages of piano boogie carry none of that form's vitality and the riffs of the clarinet and trombone quickly become oppressive; the clarinet has all the enchantment of a squeaky axle and, apart from the final cadence, the trombone sound is amorphous.

The reason for all this hokum was the sure-fire appeal of such nostalgia, something it is easy to overlook 50 years later.[12] Crude-sounding to us now, it must have struck a rich chord in the hearts of many an unhappy Black in an alien land. All we are left to admire is some fine, pentatonically based singing by Bessie, constantly seeking the third of the scale.

[12] In view of its appeal, it is strange that homesickness is the theme of such a small amount of Bessie Smith's work. On not more than five numbers does it form the main theme.

ELEVEN

May, 1925 –
The second half

On 26th May, 1925, Louis Armstrong, Charlie Green and Fletcher Henderson joined Bessie Smith on *Nashville Woman's Blues* (Matrix 140625–2). Schuller, commenting upon the transcendental quality of the May, 1925 sides with Armstrong, of which this was the first, says 'in *Nashville Woman's Blues* Bessie's expansive phrasing and rich tone seem to be beyond metric or rhythmic confinement. Her vocal lines float in a manner that sounds improvised, but probably was not'. Later he goes on, 'The two horns of Armstrong and Green offer sensitively placed counterlines and responses, with Longshaw providing strong harmonic backing'.[1] As a succinct description this is difficult to improve upon.[2]

The words tell of the self-assured dancing of women in Nashville, Tennessee and it is the depth of respect with which Bessie handles them that give rise to the only cavil one can make about the performance. The reason for this uncalled for respect is that unusually, for a number with relatively trivial lyrics, a substantial portion is in twelve-bar blues form, a form which she is temperamentally unable to treat lightly.[3]

---

[1] 'Early Jazz', page 238. The most popular opinion, supported by Rust's Discography is that Fletcher Henderson is the pianist on these four May 1925 sides with Armstrong.
[2] But see the alternate concerning the degree of Bessie's improvisation.
[3] She almost inevitably makes use of her favourite third-seeker of Ex. 1; this ornament alone adds considerable gravity to the performance.

Schuller[4] also notes a harder, more biting quality in Bessie's voice from this session which he attributes to the influence of Armstrong's singing. The new electric recording system may bear some responsibility but there is no doubt that her voice had been suffering from wear and tear for some months; nearing the peak of her fame now, part of the cause was no doubt her proliferating theatre engagements.

Armstrong's contribution is relaxed. He makes no attempt to dominate the performance, perhaps a sign of growing maturity.[5] It is noticeable also that in spite of the slow tempo, (at $\int$ = 68 for most of the piece this is one of Bessie's slowest), he shows no inclination to indulge in uncontrolled flights of fancy. An exquisite example of his inventive but structurally logical melodic line is shown in Ex. 13 below. It comes from the end of the interlude[6] and its structural logic arises from the fact that Louis has given us one or two brief hints of it previously in the piece. The first phrase, before the quaver rest, unusually has a similar shape to the following, balancing phrase. This unaccustomed symmetry is another facet of his less ascendant mood.

This performance provides a clear illustration of Louis Armstrong's unchallenged superiority over the other horn

Ex. 13

...choose,   I have got those,   Nashville

---

[4] 'Early Jazz', page 237.
[5] This is not surely because of the addition of the trombone. When he felt that a performance could be so improved, he would have no compunction over dominating much larger ensembles.
[6] This piece is constructed from a 4 bar instrumental introduction, after which Bessie Smith joins them for a 16 bar verse, a twelve-bar blues chorus, a 12 bar interlude, a further twelve-bar blues chorus and a 5 bar coda.

players of this time: consistently good though Charlie Green
is there is a vast gulf between his advanced-tailgate[7] phrases
and Armstrong's inventions. In the use of the mute, to take
one aspect, the disparity is immense; Green using mute
throughout, achieves virtually all of his expressiveness from
the 'oo–ah' sounds produced – Louis, fitting a mute only in
the last chorus, uses it as merely one item in an armoury of
expressive techniques.

In dealing with the third take of *Nashville Woman's Blues*,
(Matrix 140625–3) cut the same day and released by Columbia under the same record number 14090–D, it is perhaps
time to consider the oft-repeated opinion that alternate takes
of Bessie's performances are always very similar. From the
alternates dealt with already it is clear that the instrumental
accompaniment is often considerably different and it must
now be conceded that her vocals can differ too, although not
so drastically. It has been assumed that because of Bessie's
well-known tendency to take pains in the preparation of her
performances, this must have resulted in the elimination of
improvisation; this, together with the fact that her general
mood on released alternates is usually much the same, seems
to have dissuaded commentators from comparing the detail.
    This performance reveals many differences in the vocal
from that on the second take. As just one example, she treats
'down' in the fifth bar of the first chorus of the second take as a
descending ornament on four different pitches whereas on
this third take, she turns it into a four-note arching figure
using G natural and Bb only.
    At this faster pace ($\quad$ = 80), Louis Armstrong is less
composed, more nervously agitated but he does retain the
phrases of Ex. 13 almost intact no doubt remembering their
perfection in that position from the previous take. A bonus is

---

[7] Tailgate. A simple harmonic style of trombone playing stressing the first
and third beats from the early days of New Orleans Jazz, and which
embraces much use of glissando.

his lovely sobbing cries of the last two bars – the second take contains a trace of them but here they are more intense.

W. C. Handy's *Careless Love Blues* (Matrix 140626–1) cut the same day, has a 16 bar chord sequence which falls somewhere between a blues and a popular song but Bessie Smith has no hesitation in treating it as a blues. The words regard 'careless love' as an object to be complained to and Handy has dug deeply into the public domain for his material; they carry considerable power in themselves, giving Bessie a vehicle worthy of her talents. In spite of Blesh's assertion, this is not a narrative of 'unforgotten love, faintly and warmly sweet'[8] but a collection of passionate, visceral statements about the pain of tragic love. Bessie delivers them without a trace of self-pity, limiting her technique to slides, simple decorations and note-end fall-offs, all pervaded with a finely controlled vibrato. Her cavalier way with words is again evident; for example, the third line of the first chorus should presumably be 'You wrecked the life of many a poor gal'. She however, reverses the order of 'many' and 'a' to create a new and more appropriate metre. Throughout, she seeks to smooth out the melodic line and manages to avoid entirely the low A and G of the published version: then, to create a climax in the last 4 bars, she simplifies the melody further, and acknowledging the low A she has been avoiding, presents a high A in substitution. Her already fervent delivery, has, by this climax become quite vehement.

Louis Armstrong is in an altogether different mood from that of *Nashville Woman's Blues*. Here, confident to the point of brashness, he provides magnificent responses to Bessie's lines, constructing intricate improvisations, every one of which has a perfect integrity. Sometimes it is true, he seems about to become inextricably entangled in the texture he weaves, but always emerges, to leave behind a triumphant

---

[8] 'Shining Trumpets', page 131.

suggestion of inevitability. And he is quietly busy behind the vocal line, providing a complex melodic web, full of harmonic suggestions.

Compared to the high emotional intensity of Bessie and the dazzling technique of Armstrong, Charlie Green's thrusting, sliding, blue harmony notes seem ingenuous in the extreme. But he provides the essential foundation over which they can exercise their genius. Henderson, sensibly in such inspired company, confines himself to keeping time and stating harmonies.

The second take of *Careless Love Blues* (Matrix 140626–2) cut the same day, was also issued by Columbia under the same record number as the first (14083–D). This time Bessie sings in remarkably similar fashion on both takes. And, as we have come to expect, the wrong words of the third line of the first chorus have become fixed in performance. Above all, the air of hope, hinting at triumph shines through again.

The instrumental differences are more marked and result in this take being decidedly inferior to the first. For a start, the introduction is almost a disaster; Green strikes an incorrect harmony between bars one and two – Henderson is thrown and stops momentarily. Only Armstrong is unfazed. In addition, Green throughout has trouble with his intonation, sometimes sounding flat. Louis, moreover is occasionally guilty of an obvious phrase – take for example his first antiphony in the fourth chorus where he tacks a bugle call to the end of an otherwise worthy phrase; it is perfectly executed but, by his standards, aesthetically disappointing.

In the last chorus, Henderson introduces a gently rocking boogie bass, not present in the first take – this assisting propulsion, constitutes one of the few improvements.

J. C. Holmes Blues cut by the same personnel the next day, is that quite rare construction, an eight-bar blues. The chords are derived almost entirely from tonic and dominant triads with only one bar of subdominant harmony and perhaps this is why Bessie treats the pentatonically based melodic line to less manipulation than usual for a blues format. The words tell of a legendary but mistreated railroad engineer and their structural unity assist Bessie's dramatic performance. It is a performance of no great emotional intensity however; but there is a stirring moment in each chorus when the strain of reaching up to top D natural adds a trenchant beauty to her timbre.[9]

The accompaniment is again exceptional but at this slow pace ($\quad = 72$), another measure of the gulf between Louis Armstrong and the other instrumentalists becomes apparent. Whereas Green and Henderson are basically thinking in 4/4 time, Armstrong assumes 12/16 in which to construct his astonishing phrases.

The second title cut on 27th May, 1925, *I Ain't Goin' To Play No Second Fiddle,* proved to be Bessie Smith's last collaboration with Louis Armstrong. The words by Perry Bradford, a demand for emotional status, contain a grain or two of oblique humour but Bessie decided to sing them straight. Her decorations are spare and she somehow manages to produce a self-assured ultimatum which at the same time contains more than a hint of misery. Particularly resonant is her climactic top C on the penultimate word.

Louis Armstrong is again at his intuitive best, never committing the obvious phrase and continuing as Charles Fox says, to create 'a vocabulary of jazz improvisation'.[10] For example, his clarion call in bar twenty-three of the 32 bar chorus,[11] after Bessie's 'heed', is a phrase which has been copied and adapted, again and again by jazz musicians even to

[9] With the exception of the falsetto yells on *Soft Pedal Blues,* this is Bessie's highest note so far and has been used by her on only one previous release, *Beale Street Mama* two years earlier.

[10] 'Jazz in Perspective', page 34.

[11] This number is comprised of a 4 bar instrumental introduction, a 16 bar verse, a 32 bar chorus (not AABA format) a further 16 bars of chorus finishing with an instrumental 2 bar coda.

the present day. It is interesting to compare his relatively subdued and economical accompanimental playing here with his performance of the same tune recorded some five months later by Perry Bradford's Jazz Phools. On the latter he is wild and profligate with his notes, only the superlative technique linking the two performances.

Henderson's piano and Charlie Green's muted trombone stabs and glissandi do little more than thicken the texture but they do provide a reliable platform from which Louis can play some of his most majestic cornet. His sheer authority raises the performance above that of a mere jazz recording, transforming it into surpassing music of classic proportions; his sense of order and restraint are exemplary.

With their last recording together an attempt might be made to assess the relative importance of Bessie Smith and Louis Armstrong. Bessie, it must be admitted, was a singer with a limited style (her later decline through its ossification shows that), but no one in jazz has approached the intensity of emotion she projected. Louis, therefore was not in the same class emotionally but in every other area of jazz musicianship he was the greater artist. And in addition, for a time, he influenced the course of jazz more than any other musician, spontaneously creating schools of copyists even to the end of his life in 1971. Bessie's influence was much more limited, proving to be inspirational rather than technical. She has spawned not one copyist of note and chose to confine her art entirely to the elemental blues genre. Louis Armstrong broke through the frontiers of jazz as it was known in the 1920's to produce something else again. During his handful of sessions with Bessie Smith, he curbed his burgeoning soloistic ambitions and accepted second place; but the role of accompanist to an urban blues (occasional jazz) singer was too circumscribed for him and he never recorded with her again.

TWELVE

June, 1925 – to the end of the year

Blesh's reference to Bessie's 'sad, unhurried, implacable and strangely triumphant phrases'[1] is particularly apposite to her performance on *He's Gone Blues* of 23rd June, 1925. She treats the words about deserted love, which she wrote herself, with reverence, imparting an awesome resignation to the last repeated line, 'Oh well, I guess he's gone', which is deeply moving. Her always disturbing quality of voice has a thinner, more strident timbre here – this may be a recording fault[2] but could arise from the key employed. She adopts the fifth of the scale as the pitch around which to construct her melody and as the key is C sharp finds herself with a fulcrum (G sharp) which is rather higher than usual, bringing different overtones into play more often.

Longshaw generates little swing and unfortunately seems intent on elevating what should be merely a texture-thickening device, his omnipresent tremolos, to obtrusive foreground ornamental status.

Some of the words and melody of Clarence Williams's *Nobody's Blues But Mine* cut on 19th August, 1925 are reminiscent of *'Tain't Nobody's Biz'ness If I Do,*[3] but whereas

[1] 'Shining Trumpets', page 112.
[2] The balance between voice and piano is certainly faulty, Longshaw being over-recorded.
[3] By Porter Grainge and E. Robbins.

that, unusually, was a cry for self-determination, here we are back to the familiar ground of lover's complaint.

Bessie Smith is better treated by the recording engineers this time but as she is often in the higher reaches of her range (the key is again C sharp), her voice once more displays unusual resonances especially when, as a climax, she twice stretches up to high C sharp at the beginning of the penultimate 8 bar chorus. Although the lyrics are suitable blues material, this number is actually in a popular song form and Bessie accordingly limits herself to simple ornamentation.

The sleeve notes and Rust[4] give Fuller as playing clarinet and alto saxophone on both sides from this session, but repeated listening suggests that he uses clarinet here, reserving the alto for *I Ain't Got Nobody*. The confusion arises because he somehow manages to eliminate most of the clarinet's characteristic mellowness from his playing, instead imparting a brass-like vibrato. Whilst he takes himself seriously, little genuine feeling for the blues comes through his overpowering wails, and the double-time arranged passage at the end of the instrumental introduction exemplifies a poverty of invention.

If the engineers treat Bessie more generously, they are unfair to both banjo and piano; the former is over-recorded and the latter almost inaudible. But it hardly matters, neither rhythm instrument generates even a modicum of swing.

This is one of Bessie's few second-rate releases. The rest of the group sound like dance band hacks.[5]

I Ain't Got Nobody from the same session is notable for being one of the few released recordings on which Bessie fails to

[4] 'Jazz Records 1897–1942', page 1528.
[5] Although Elmer Snowden (banjo) at least, has impressive credentials, having led or played in bands including many of the best jazzmen of the 1920's on, including Count Basie, Claude Hopkins, Jimmy Lunceford, Bubber Miley, Frankie Newton, 'Tricky Sam' Nanton, Chick Webb and Benny Carter.

have her way with the tempo. The instrumental introduction starts at $\downarrow = 120$ and when she begins to sing she attempts her familiar tempo-reducing efforts, managing to bring it down to $\downarrow = 108$; but she fails to hold the group and they are all soon back to the original speed.

The theme is summed up in the title and Bessie's mood of elation could be considered a flagrant disregard of the composers' intentions. But as so often, there is a sadness there which tempers the triumph. A popular song[6] and very fast by her standards, she performs in the attenuated style we have come to expect in such circumstances. She compensates however with a shouting expressionism, which is particularly powerful on her jubilant re-entry to the last 16 bars of chorus. The excitement she generates is no doubt largely inspired by the satisfying chord sequence, a sequence which has ensured the composition's popularity down to the present day.

Mercifully, Fuller's bleating alto saxophone[7] when playing with Bessie in the choruses at least, abandons antiphony and provides either a wide-toned legato backing or single stop-time notes. The banjo[8] again submerges the piano and what could have been an interesting structural experiment, the intermittent Charleston rhythm, turns out in the end to be too disruptive, fragmenting rather than unifying the performance.

Another flawed work therefore but one we would not be without if only for Bessie's superbly defiant singing.

On 1st September, 1925, Clara Smith joined Bessie for the third[9] and last time on *My Man Blues,* written by Bessie herself. It is basically an eight bar blues in C major with Clara

[6] In thirty-two bar AABA format.
[7] See comments regarding the identity of this instrument in the analysis of the previous release.
[8] According to Feather ('Encyclopaedia of Jazz', page 427), of his own recordings, this was one of the three which Snowden liked best.
[9] Their previous collaborations were *Far Away Blues* and *I'm Going Back To My Used To Be* of 4th October, 1923.

ranging over the octave from middle C whilst Bessie remains largely within the major-third Eb to G natural, an attempt to differentiate between two similar voices which is not wholly successful. The words form a humorous argument over each singer's claim to 'Charlie Grey', Bessie taking the first four bars of each chorus and Clara answering the challenge in the last four.

Nearly two years have passed since their previous duets and although Clara is now stronger and her tone richer, there is still a patent difference between their relative talents. Bessie is regal in her authority over the melody — she is quite capable of producing a satisfying line even whilst restricting her compass drastically; Clara ranges more widely but her melody is not the more attractive for that. Bessie's supremacy comes from her tight control over inflection – her favourite two-note third-seeker of Ex. 1 is used frequently and its exact form often varied. The two occasions on which she uses it in the fourth chorus form good examples of its subtle variety; on 'man', the Eb is treated as a semiquaver and the E natural as a dotted-quaver but on 'own', the Eb becomes an acciaccatura onto the E natural which is extended to a minim.

Both singers blue notes and employ a fine collection of smears and slides but Clara Smith uses far fewer articulated ornaments than Bessie and her lines therefore tend to be more amorphous. The last chorus (which is of twelve-bars) is most instructive in this respect. Clara, superficially, sounds more like Bessie than ever before but only in tone-colour. They each sing a similar melodic line for the first time but whilst Bessie seeks the third degree (E natural) with her meaningful and familiar ornament, Clara sings the note straight, unable to copy or improve upon Bessie's version. On the other hand when hitting high C, whilst Bessie's 'to' is almost undecorated, Clara in her version tries a ballad singer's catch which proves to be completely out of place.

The pianist's (Stanley Miller) contribution is plodding and whilst this may be partly excused by the slow tempo ($\quad =$ 72) it cannot pardon his lack of sensitivity.

Another performance falling some way short of perfection then but still a fascinating document and one incidentally, which completely dispels the doubts of some commentators about Bessie Smith's supremacy over her nearest rival.

Bessie had made up her quarrel with Clarence Williams by November, 1925 and on 17th of that month joined him for a new version of his *Gulf Coast Blues* which they had recorded two years and nine months earlier. The original words were quite clearly about unrequited love but those of *New Gulf Coast Blues* are more ambiguous; seemingly about leaving the South and the 'woes' endemic to it, it is not until the last line 'because my skin is dark, don't mean my heart ain't right', that we realise the song is more specifically a protest against racial segregation. It was a problem rarely referred to in songs at the time – Louis Armstrong's *Black And Blue* of July, 1929 is the only other recording of the 1920's which comes to mind.

Bessie, at the peak of her career, offers a considerably more mature performance than on the earlier version; there is a greater range of expression – note the second line of the last verse for instance, in which the unusually thin timbre she applies to 'teeth' links with her similar timbre on 'mean' in the third line. And she manipulates the melodic line to a much greater extent.

Playing more slowly[10] this time, Williams finds it difficult to achieve even the mild swing of the earlier version. But this does not deter him from stamping his signature on the performance with a version of the upper mordent based riff of Ex. 2 when leading up to the final cadence.

Florida Bound Blues from the same session is another Clarence Williams composition. The words tell of a longing to leave the cold North for the warm South and specifically Florida

[10] At $\quad = 72$ only three choruses of twelve-bar blues can be included; the original at $\quad = 96$ allowed four.

which was in the throes of a land boom at the time. The penultimate verse refers to this;

> I got a letter from my Daddy, he bought me a sweet piece of land;
> I got a letter from my Daddy, he bought me a small piece of ground;
> You can't blame me for leavin', Lawd, I mean I'm Florida boun'.

The last line contains a warning which turned out to be unnecessary;

> My Papa tol' me, my Mama tol' me too;
> My Papa tol' me, my Mama tol' me too;
> Don't let them bell-bottom breeches, make a fool out of you.

'Them bell-bottom breeches' were yachting-suit wearing whites who might defraud Blacks of their money knowing they would not be allowed into the area because of segregation. As it happened, coincidentally with the release of this record in February, 1926, the bubble burst and vast fortunes were lost although they were almost entirely white fortunes.[11]

That Bessie enjoys this number is reflected in the various effects she introduces, from her ultra-simplicity in the first two lines, her shouts of 'Hey' in the third chorus and her delicious, climactic glissando up to 'fool' in the last line. Her euphoria is even undisturbed by the fact that Williams manages to insert two additional bars in the first chorus.[12]

Again William's swing is minimal but paradoxically, his solid timekeeping with sometimes only four chords to the bar, seems to inspire Bessie. He once more includes the upper mordent based riff of Ex. 2 this time at the end of the second chorus and with a further suggestion at the end of the piece.

[11] This information about the Florida land boom of the mid-twenties has been culled from 'Bessie, Empress of the Blues', page 92.
[12] Otherwise in twelve-bar blues format, the first chorus is 14 bars long.

At The Christmas Ball from Bessie's 18th November, 1925 session, was an attempt by Frank Walker to cash-in on the forthcoming festivities at a time when the number of issued copies of her titles was just beginning to decline. As it happened, the record was not actually released until many years later; Paul Oliver suggests that this was because of an off-form Joe Smith[13] but any deterioration in his playing is hard to detect.

Threadbare though the sentiments of this 16 bar popular song[14] are, Bessie sings with an easy, attractive warmth.

For such a small group, a remarkably dense sound-texture is created; they achieve this, quite simply by playing continuously, both behind the voice as well as at phrase-endings. Charlie Green takes a mainly supporting role to Joe Smith's lyrical and symmetrical phrases and Fletcher Henderson, more inspired than usual, helps to thicken the texture, keep time and indicate harmony all whilst swinging in a light, effortless manner. Two features of Joe Smith's cornet are worth mentioning; firstly his remarkable muted tone in the instrumental chorus which is fuller than that of the muted trombone: secondly the brief evidence of Armstrong's influence which occurs at the start of the second half of this chorus when he translates one of Louis' calls-to-attention into his own milder language.

The music of *I've Been Mistreated And I Don't Like It* is similar to that of its session-mate, *At The Christmas Ball;*[15] both are popular songs but the words of the former, the theme of which is summarised by the title, stimulate Bessie to imbue it with much more blues feeling. Her embellishments are more complex, sometimes involving three or four articulated

[13] 'Bessie Smith', page 39.
[14] The record starts with some hokum from cornet and trombone sounding like discordant squeakers and toy horns and with spoken greetings between a male voice and Bessie. Then follow 2 bars of verse anticipation and a 20 bar verse after which three choruses of 16 bars each, complete the performance. The middle chorus is purely instrumental.
[15] Both are by Fred Longshaw.

pitches in their execution whereas those of *At The Christmas Ball* hardly ever embrace more than two. Her phrases in the more superficial *At The Christmas Ball* tend to be symmetrical too; here, to celebrate and reinforce her deeper commitment, she revises the rhythmic shape of her lines to avoid regular 2 and 4 bar phrases. Interestingly, she contrives this mainly by lengthening and shortening note-values rather than by taking pause for breath.

The instrumentalists, recognising this as entirely Bessie's vehicle, play more quietly behind her this time. Joe Smith's contribution is up to its usual high quality although his tone is more penetrating.[16] Charlie Green, still muted, plays a more prominent and growling part. Both releases from this session have backing of a class which Bessie deserves but all too seldom gets.

Columbia pressed 27, 675 copies of this record in January, 1926 – a long cry from *Down-Hearted Blues,* her first release, the pressings of which were ten times greater. But a Clara Smith title also released in January, 1926 only justified 12,200 copies.[17]

Two days after her last session, Bessie Smith cut *Red Mountain Blues* with Don Redman on clarinet and Fletcher Henderson's piano. It is basically a sixteen-bar blues but before the last chorus, carries a 16 bar interlude based mainly upon subdominant harmony. It is an interlude which has a similar climactic purpose to that in *Weeping Willow Blues* of 26th September, 1924, i.e. the static harmony creates a tension which is only resolved upon the return to the original chord sequence in the last chorus. Bessie's pentatonic ostinato of the interlude is perfectly in keeping with the folk-like character of the words which recommend the voodoo talisman, snakeroot, as a cure for an unsatisfactory lover.

[16] In the instrumental chorus of *At The Christmas Ball,* Joe Smith is probably using a bucket mute; here his mute is one which filters out the lower overtones.
[17] 'Bessie, Empress of the Blues', page 107 (note).

She adopts two quite separate approaches to this blues. The choruses are treated plastically, some phrases extended, others compressed, and her most frequent decoration is unusually, the long note fall-off which here, sometimes goes on to develop into a more complicated ornament; they are fall-offs which are not only employed at the end of phrases, but applied to any note long enough to carry them. Her other approach occurs in the interlude where she sings with minimal decoration, thereby setting up a further contrast to be resolved in the last chorus.

In view of the careful construction of the piece,[18] it is a pity that Joe Smith and Charlie Green are not present to display some of their precise riffs during the interlude. Redman's work is unsatisfactory for several reasons. His cadences at the end of the first two choruses for instance are abysmally unimaginative whilst at the same time being very similar. Then in the interlude, he 'discovers' fluttertonguing and does it to death. But these defects pale in comparison with his delinquent tone – it is too pure, coloured with none of the 'dirtyness' required by the genre.

The second title from the 20th November, 1925 session, *Golden Rule Blues* has Bessie for the first time making significant use of dynamic gradation as an expressive device; the entire performance is peppered with examples of her new approach to volume – 'ago' at the end of the first chorus[19] line for instance, starts powerfully but is then subjected to a rapid paring of sound. It is the only area of her technique which has markedly changed since her recordings began and it is surprising that she should suddenly present it fully developed. But this is what she does, adding instantly a new dimension to her art.

The theme of the man who is 'cold in hand' is one which Bessie would understand from experience and this composi-

---

[18] Composed by H. Troy.
[19] The number is constructed from a 4 bar instrumental introduction, an 8 bar verse and four choruses of twelve-bar blues.

tion is therefore an entirely suitable vehicle for this important extension to her technique. Unfortunately the full impact is diminished by the incongruous alto saxophone playing of Don Redman; he takes detachment to the point of complete disinterest in what she is doing as can be heard from his experiments in repeating exactly some of Henderson's right hand figures.

Bessie Smith's words for *Lonesome Desert Blues,* the only release from the session on 9th December, 1925[20] form a disparate collection of metaphors about that familiar figure of Black American folk-lore, the 'mistreatin' man'. Their relationship with the desert of the title is tenuous and tends to be further weakened by the 'row boat out on the stormy sea' image. However, in the end, some integrity is achieved when Bessie links her emotions to the burning sands of that desert.

Bessie, in her element with this type of material, turns in a good performance but her voice does show occasional signs of wear. When straining to high notes earlier an added beauty was often the outcome but here, her high A and B on 'lawd' in the climactic stop-time passage at the start of the last 14 bars, exposes a crumbling control. And there is little evidence of her new-found dynamic authority of *Golden Rule Blues.*

Shelton Hemphill's cornet whilst fascinating to listen to, does unfortunately prompt a disparaging comparison with Louis Armstrong. He is of course copying Armstrong's muted style of *Cold In Hand Blues* without the refinement of his vibrato and certainly without Louis' genius for picking the right notes from which to construct an elegant phrase. He also tends to finish his notes too early, failing to carry them right through, lacks Armstrong's command of dynamic

[20] Two other numbers were attempted at this session, one of which was *At The Christmas Ball;* all three takes of this were rejected however, in favour of the Joe Smith/Charlie Green version of 18th November, 1925 previously discussed. The other number was *Squeeze Me* and the three takes of this were also rejected, this time in favour of the Clarence Williams' version to come (5th March, 1926).

gradation and above all cannot approach his sense of timing. But few, if any, musicians measured up to Armstrong's standards of this time and in spite of apparent shortcomings on this record, Hemphill went on to build a reputation as a fine cornet player – his later work with hands such as those of Chick Webb, Benny Carter, Mills Blue Rhythm and Duke Ellington confirm this. Even here he can be heard to be a sensitive musician, merely lacking judgement in his choice of mentor.

The pace is too slow for Longshaw to shine but he does provide a creditable accompaniment, satisfying in its varying textures.

THIRTEEN

March, 1926

The most patent defect of *Them 'Has Been' Blues* from the 5th March, 1926 session with Clarence Williams, lies in the lyrics about deserted love. Not only are the sentiments shallow but the words are repetitious — the first half of the first chorus[1] carries similar words to the matching half of the last chorus and the composers[2] completely dry up in the verse with its reiterations of 'know why I'm blue' and 'it might happen to you'. But Bessie Smith manages to find sufficient inspiration to introduce dynamic manipulation again as a significant part of her technique; in the first chorus for instance her 'up' and 'rise' in the first line are shaded down from mf to pppp with adroit control. And in the last chorus, following the tension-raising interlude, she combines a generally more raucous tone with dynamic shading on some phrase-end notes.

Clarence Williams' accompaniment is often stiffer and less artful than that of some of Bessie's other pianists but occasionally an antiphonal phrase can be quite delightful — the right-hand passage linking the two halves of the last chorus for example, where although his touch could never be mistaken for that of Jelly Roll Morton, the phrase itself might.

[1] This number is constructed from a 4 bar piano introduction, a 16 bar verse and two 16 bar choruses in a popular song form placed either side of a 16 bar interlude of more limited harmonic change.
[2] W. E. Skidmore and M. Walker.

The words of *Squeeze Me*[3] celebrate for once a satisfactory emotional relationship and the chord sequence is sufficiently stimulating to induce Bessie to float around the original melodic line in a fine heterophony, employing most of her existing 'bag' of ornaments (although as this piece is in a popular song form her favourite third-seeker is missing) and inventing new ones for the occasion.[4] In particular, her convoluted melisma on 'cry' in the first chorus [5] with its slight variation in the second, is marvellous. Ex. 14 shows the first chorus phrase;

Ex. 14

cry----------------------------

That the number's chord progressions carry some inherent fascination is endorsed by its continued popularity today.

Williams, too, is inspired to produce some of his most agreeable accompaniment. His chromatic opening phrase constructed from parallel chords is not only pleasing in itself but also a little surprising from a self-taught musician.

With *Squeeze Me* we are halfway through Bessie Smith's released titles. Evidence of a lessening demand for her product becomes apparent at this point – it emerges from

[3] The composition is credited to Clarence Williams and Fats Waller but is based upon an old bawdy house song. Bessie sings the same words in both choruses.

[4] And her mastery of dynamic manipulation is again in evidence.

[5] The number is constructed from a 4 bar introduction and 4 bar verse anticipation by piano, a 12 bar verse and two 16 bar choruses in a popular song form.

comparing the time during which she produced her first eighty releases, three years and one month, with that of the last seventy-nine, seven years and eight months.

The third release from the 5th March, 1926 session, *What's The Matter Now?* has words which are less directly sexually allusive than usual; more jokely euphemistic, they were no doubt instigated by Frank Walker to bolster a career beginning to show signs of slipping. Bessie sings them with gusto and some humour however, and although very fast for her ($\downarrow$ = 120) she manages to attach a surprising number of ornaments to the pentatonically based melody. This may be a first indication that she was becoming more comfortable at faster tempos, although she does try to reduce the speed soon after her entry (only succeeding temporarily).

For the first time with Bessie, Clarence Williams is allowed a full chorus solo and it is probable that the fast pace was chosen to assist him in this. His performance in fact is one of his best, again occasionally reminiscent of Morton but without the touch and inventiveness of that master. In his solo and his final coda, Williams even manages a spell of habanera rhythm, adding the 'Spanish tinge' beloved of Morton.

I Want Ev'ry Bit Of It, the last release from the 5th March, 1926 session, has Bessie, even at a relatively gentle pace ($\downarrow$ = 84) eschewing her more articulated ornaments in favour of portamento; she slips and glides her way through the pentatonic melodic line. Once in the verse however, she varies this treatment on the words ''cause you been acting quite too bold', projecting them through the gap dividing speech from song in a manner which would have interested Schoenberg,[6] (even though he would have rejected the medium).

A small aural mystery attaches to the performance. On

---

[6] Because of his use of sprechgesang notably in Pierrot lunaire (1912).

most occurrences of the words 'I want', Bessie appears to be joined by another voice. If it is a voice, presumably it is Clarence Williams who often sang on his own recordings (with adenoidal timbre).

The words of *Jazzbo Brown From Memphis Town* from Bessie's session with Buster Bailey and Fletcher Henderson on 18th March, 1926 make an interesting comment upon the musical taste of one member of the British Royal Family of the time: they tell of a legendary non-reading clarinet player with unparalleled power to make people dance and 'good enough for the Prince of Wales'. Bessie restricts her compass mainly to the perfect fourth, Eb to Ab and at times even more narrowly – this is unusual in a popular song. It is another number taken at a very fast pace ($\downarrow$ = 120) but unlike *What's The Matter Now?* here she employs mainly note-end fall-offs as decoration, although she does garnish a number of notes with her growl, thus underlining the jazz, that is instrumental, nature of the material. In a blues, she would tend towards subtler techniques. Further, as Schuller points out, here she employs 'consonants and syllabic articulation in order to swing'.[7]

Opinion as to the identity of the clarinettist whom Paul Oliver says has been 'variously identified as Buster Bailey, Lorenzo Wardell and Garvin Bushell'[8] seems now to have come down in favour of Bailey. He certainly displays the slightly sour sound (caused by playing a little off pitch-centre) one associates with Bailey; 'a fluent technique, a thin tone and a style sometimes called cold but always highly personal' as Feather says.[9] Here, he varies his style to produce playing which is sometimes jokey and sometimes more serious; when he discards the hokum he 'weaves some exceedingly beautiful obbligatos in and out between voice and piano' to quote Schuller again.[10] My own feeling about

[7] 'Early Jazz', page 235.   [8] 'Bessie Smith', page 42.
[9] 'The Encyclopaedia of Jazz', page 108.   [10] 'Early Jazz', page 235.

Bailey's playing is that, like that of so many musicians from the Henderson orchestra, his style is too detached, lacking a deeply-felt blues sound: perhaps not so damaging with superficial material such as this but sometimes quite corrosive on Bessie's more sober sides. Having said this, he certainly plays well in his 16 bars of solo but he is of course tracing only one thread of the rich texture that is New Orleans jazz – it is like isolating a single line of J. S. Bach counterpoint, a lot of the meaning disappears without the other parts. To hear him in his true element, the reader should refer to Bessie's *Cakewalkin' Babies* of 5th May, 1925.

The other release from the session on 18th March, 1926, *The Gin House Blues* has the most primitive construction so far, being simply five choruses of twelve-bar blues without introduction or coda. The words are concerned with gin-addiction and traditionally have been considered autobiographical – certainly Bessie honours them with her complete commitment. Imbued with a deep sorrow, it has a simple and repetitive melodic line, building up a cumulative tension which is left painfully in the air on the last word, the instrumental perfect cadence on to the tonic minor-seventh chord being a deliberately inadequate resolution. It is another performance she colours with rapid dynamic changes especially at phrase ends; otherwise her decorations are kept simple, with portamento the main technique employed.

   Henderson's playing is unexceptional but Buster Bailey's lack of 'vocal' timbre and blues feeling is particularly noticeable in a piece of such elemental cast.

FOURTEEN

May, 1926 –
to the end of the year

At the session on 4th May, 1926, Bessie is accompanied by
Joe Smith's cornet and Fletcher Henderson's piano, the first
time on record with her that Joe Smith has been the only
horn. The first release from this session was *Money Blues,* a
number in a popular song form on the 'cold-in-hand' theme.
Bessie's mood is lighter here however than in her earlier
treatments; there is a greater philosophical acceptance of the
situation and this time it is the man's life which is made 'full
of misery'. Sounding inspired, no doubt responding to the
brilliant support given by Joe Smith, she mostly avoids
complex ornaments, tending on the one hand towards a
slippery portamento replete with microtonal shading and
note fall-offs, and on the other, towards notes hit cleanly on
the nose.

Joe Smith, playing continuously and agile as a clarinet, is
at his most lyrical. Often, when in the low register, he fills
the air with a huge lustrous sound which could be that of a
slide trombone were it not for the slight articulation imparted by the valves. He is quite unusual amongst cornettists
in his considerable use of this register which requires almost
as much control as the flashier effects obtained from the other
end. For a brief moment in the verse,[1] his whole-tone trills

[1] The number is constructed from an instrumental 4 bar introduction and
2 bar verse anticipation followed by a 16 bar verse and two 20 bar choruses
each with a 2 bar codetta/coda.

behind Bessie's 'Samuel Brown', he does seem about to give
way to a syrupy, commercial vacuity but fortunately it proves
an isolated transgression. Sometimes his mood varies from
supporting Bessie's exultation to puncturing it with stabs of
assertiveness; for example he contrasts his phrase gently
encouraging her into the codetta of the first chorus with a
rip-up at the end of that codetta.

Henderson too is better than usual, achieving a nicely
dragging rhythm and in particular, striking a seam of rich
bass notes which give the impression at times that a bowed
bass has been added to the group.

This is one of Bessie's most perfectly reproduced recordings; the texture sounds thicker than could possibly be
produced by three instruments, without in any way sacrifi-
cing the discreteness of the separate lines. It is fortuitous that
the engineers should have devoted such care to such exciting
music.

The second release from 4th May, 1926, *Baby Doll,* is a cry
for emotional security; as Avakian says in his sleeve notes to
the 1950's reissues, 'another tragic study of hope-without-
hope'.

Slightly slower in tempo,[2] Bessie defines the gapped pentatonic shapes of the chorus[3] melody with ornaments which
are more articulated than those on *Money Blues.* In that earlier
piece her glissandi tended to be smooth; here, previously
inferred passing-notes often take on firm shape.

Although as well recorded as *Money Blues,* it does not
possess the inspirational quality of that performance, a
deficiency which cannot be entirely attributed to the different
mood. Joe Smith's shimmering tone is less rich and Hender-

[2] Tempos. *Money Blues* ♩ = 84. *Baby Doll* ♩ = 80.
[3] The number is constructed from an instrumental 4 bar introduction and
2 bar verse anticipation followed by a 16 bar verse and two 16 bar choruses
each with a 2 bar codetta/coda. The first 8 bars of the second chorus are by
cornet and piano alone. Interestingly, the choruses are in AABA format but
of course with only 4 bars to each section.

son's deep, ringing bass notes are missing. The instrumental half-chorus is pleasing but hardly exceptional. Joe Smith's avoidance of the cornet's higher ranges, here results in a rather bland, unvaried diet of warm sounds.

Falling short of perfection therefore but still an above average performance.

Hard Driving Papa, the third release from the session on 4th May, 1926, has words[4] which are mostly a complaint against a cruel husband but with the last line a celebration of masochism. Blesh describes the piece as 'bitterly despairing',[5] ignoring the wry twist to its tail, 'because I love him, 'cause there's no one can beat me like he do'. Bessie turns in another satisfyingly melancholy performance using mainly unarticulated glissandi and achieving extra emphasis when required by lengthening words. Her rarely used low Ab is sounded clearly and without difficulty throughout.

Joe Smith's performance is one of his most disappointing and not merely of this session. He starts well in broad middle-register trombone-like tones and goes on to show that the top register is not beyond him reaching up to Ab (and even Bb), an octave above Bessie's highest note, but his repetitive antiphonal phrases echoing Bessie's descending line, soon becomes tiresome. In the last two choruses, wrong notes begin to creep in.

Henderson sounds uninterested in spite of claiming the composition as his own.

The last title from the 4th May, 1926 session, *Lost Your Head Blues* has Bessie treating the pentatonically based melody to a fine display of timbral distortion and although mostly eschewing articulated ornament, she does 'invent' a remark-

[4] The composition is credited to G. Brooks (Fletcher Henderson) but it is basically a twelve-bar blues with some lines drawn from the common-stock. Unusually, the two middle choruses (of four), have first and second lines which are different, a subtle structurally unifying device.

[5] 'Shining Trumpets', page 130.

able new one at the end of the second chorus[6] on 'gal'; it is a
descending articulated glissando describing the five[7] pitches
of the dominant-seventh chord in root position. Then, as
Paul Oliver points out, every verse has its melody subtly
remodelled;[8] she never repeats herself melodically.

Joe Smith is back in fine form here, wild and rasping and
with a narrow 'mean' timbre matching Bessie's resigned
despair over the man who has left her now he has money.
Playing with open cornet in the introduction, he fits a mute
for the rest of his performance; as Schuller says 'In terms of
purely sonoric identification, Joe Smith and Charlie Green
were undoubtedly the closest to her of the many 'horn' players
that accompanied her'.[9]
Fletcher Henderson's contribution is a pallid boogie-woogie,
not in the least authentic, lacking the driving attack of the
real thing. But at least it does not seem to perturb the two
Smiths.

Bessie's next session was on the 25th October, 1926 at which
she cut two titles, the first being *Hard Time Blues.* It is a
strange structure[10] seemingly cobbled together from several
other songs and disturbingly full of unexpected turns. For
instance it is unsettling to come across a chorus of twelve-bar
blues in a popular song; then again in the fifteenth bar of the
verse, Bessie takes an unanticipated melodic course up to top
C, employing an odd timbre without obvious cause. She
adopts mainly her articulated ornamental style but without
conviction, eventually fazing herself upon a particularly intricate melismatic 'gone' (the first one) in the last few bars.

The only predictable thing about the performance is

[6] The number is constructed from a 4 bar instrumental introduction
followed by five choruses of twelve-bar blues.
[7] The root notes an octave apart being repeated.
[8] 'Bessie Smith', page 45.
[9] 'Early Jazz', page 235.
[10] The number is constructed from a 4 bar piano introduction, a 22 bar
verse, a chorus of twelve-bar blues, 16 bars of chorus in a popular song form
and finally, a 3 bar coda.

Henderson's uninspiring, watery piano. For all his faults however, his chord progressions are usually secure but here, even he loses his way in the tenth bar of the verse after Bessie's 'Lettin' him know'.

Honey Man Blues, the other title from the 25th October, 1926 session, has words on the familiar theme of the 'mistreating man' but unusually, the last two choruses carry threats of retribution instead of the customary resigned acceptance. Although basically a twelve-bar blues, the melody is more like that of a popular song; Bessie progressively flattens its contours after the first chorus whilst at the same time treating its phrases to constantly varying rhythmic shape by syllabic accentuation and by taking pause for breath in unorthodox places. A good example of her mastery of syllabic accentuation occurs in the second chorus on the word 'ocean'; in the first line she stresses the second syllable but in the next line it is the first she accents, in the process completely altering the line's rhythmic shape.

Henderson's piano at this session had probably never been better recorded; it is full of the overtones normally only heard on much more modern recording and at live performance. Unfortunately this tends to stress the inappropriateness of his night-club harmonies and his lack of empathy with Bessie's heartfelt blues. He employs parallel chords and obtrusive chime effects as if in a deliberate attempt to subvert her mood.

Albertson tells us that this was the only session to which Bessie took her niece and companion, Ruby Walker. Ruby had for some time been pressing Bessie to take her along and she now finally succumbed. Whilst they were running through *Honey Man Blues,* Ruby who had been practising Bessie's style, suggested to Frank Walker that he should record her too. Bessie, missing none of this, created a scene and vowed she would never take Ruby to the recording studio again.[11]

[11] 'Bessie, Empress of the Blues', page 98.

From the next day's session, two titles were released, the first of which was *One And Two Blues*. On both, Bessie is accompanied by her 'Blue Boys', Joe Smith, Buster Bailey and Fletcher Henderson. Henderson, under his pseudonym G. Brooks, is credited with this composition which in view of his 'sophisticated' background must have given him a mischievous pleasure – the words tell of a woman whose man has been down on the farm too long, and lost touch with the cost of the city life; she wants 'one and two' dollars instead of small-change.

Bessie keeps her treatment of the common-place words simple, not going beyond short glissandi and two-note ornaments. It is a fine performance in which her only mistake is to run out of breath on her single descent to low G sharp[12] at the end of the verse – an unusual error which stuns the horns into silence, leaving an antiphonal gap. A climax is effected by Bessie's voice over stop-chords in the last 12 bars and by her reshaping of the melody there to attack the upper pitches of her tessitura. It is a climax in which the tension is prolonged by her repeat of the bridge section of the thirty-two bar format.[13]

The backing tends towards a sumptuous legato with both horns making apposite, sometimes pretty, comments. Joe Smith employs a glossy surface-tone which again is often trombone-like. But he and Buster Bailey are not the best matched collaborators in such a small group because of the disparity between their timbres. The sound from Bailey is sometimes so thin as to suggest the pure tones of a piccolo or ocarina. Of course, in a New Orleans style context there must be a clear distinction between the lines of brass and woodwind but between these two here, the discreteness is too marked; it becomes particularly distracting in the eight bars of instrumental chorus.

---

[12] Her rarely used lowest note. Also spelt as Ab, depending upon key.
[13] The choruses are in AABA format.

The other track released from 26th October, 1926 session, *Young Woman's Blues,* is about desertion but ends with a defiant gesture of independence. It has words by Bessie Smith, which refer in the chorus to the caste system based upon shades of skin pigment, endemic to Afro-American society; they hint at her own insecurity.[14] At (probably) over 30, she is no longer a young woman but her considerable acting ability brings authenticity to the performance – her fall-offs from the third-degree of the scale in the verse on 'note', 'Jane' and 'goat' carry great poignancy.

With deep, rich tones, Joe Smith is in splendid form (except for the verse where he is sometimes tentative). As Schuller points out, his 'tone, speed of vibrato, and carefully controlled pitch range provide a perfect matching continuity to Bessie's voice . . . and (he) provides utterly relaxed rococo ornaments'.[15]

Buster Bailey adds little to the quality of the performance – he too often finds himself doubling cornet pitches, seemingly lacking the radar to anticipate Joe Smith's moves. One similarity between Bailey and Joe Smith which has become increasingly apparent during their association with Bessie, is the highly burnished tone they can both impart – but it is not enough in a small group to compensate for their timbral incongruity.

The recording quality is first class with Henderson's bass chords being heard to advantage and matching the sombre mood perfectly.

[14] The lighter the colour, the higher the status. Bessie's skin was deep brown.
[15] 'Early Jazz', page 235.

FIFTEEN

February and March, 1927

Bessie Smith's first session of 1927 found her with a new pianist of sovereign ability. On 17th February she cut *Preachin' The Blues* with James P. Johnson. In the form of a mock-sermon in gospel style on how a woman can keep her man, it looses some credibility when the 'preacher' admits that she is having trouble in that area herself.[1]

James P. Johnson is known as the 'father of jazz piano' and this is no overstatement. It is true that his taste was not always above reproach – his flashy glissandi after Bessie's first words 'Down in Atlanta G.a.' sound very commercial for instance – but he was the most technically accomplished of all the piano men who recorded with her as well as being the one who took ragtime the farthest along the evolutionary road towards jazz. Improvisation is not an element to be found in ragtime but it figures large in Johnson's work. And ragtime borrows little from the blues – Johnson's motifs are full of the pianist's nearest equivalent to the blue-note, the simultaneous (or nearly simultaneous) depression of adjoining semitones. But above all, and that is why I refer to 'motif', his

---

[1] Her early reference to drinking with the down and outs 'under the viaduct' might be seen as a consequence of her problems, but an unsigned review in the 'Melody Maker' for 22nd December, 1951, holds that having met Johnson in 1919 in Atlanta when she was a member of a vocal trio, 'The Liberty Belles' Bessie is here recounting the atmosphere of that meeting.

work stresses rhythm, rather than the melody which is foremost in ragtime.[2] He plays in the so-called 'Harlem stride' piano style,[3] with small rhythmic right-hand motifs substituted for melody. His orchestral texture is not unyielding though, but constantly varying; Schuller points out the felicitous 'low-register chromatic figures' behind Bessie's 'Moanin' Blues, holler them blues' starting in the twenty-seventh bar[4] and a strand of melody does occur at the end of his 8 bar solo, a beautiful ragtime-like right-hand phrase. Three other features amongst his seemingly endless pianistic attributes must be mentioned; his superb dynamic control, one moment pounding away triple forte and the next fingering a delicate trill pianissimo (occasionally doing both simultaneously); the fact that he rarely plays exactly on the pulse and the exceptional independence of his two hands.

It is occasionally argued that less consummate pianists than Johnson provided better accompaniments for Bessie Smith to exercise her skill over and without necessarily going too far along that road, it does seem that sometimes their collaborations consist of two considerable egos competing for supremacy. It is hard then to assert that Bessie is inspired to greater heights by this assuredly superior accompaniment. It is a good performance[5] but she has sung as well and better with lesser pianists. Perhaps too the unusual material restrained her — seven repetitions of virtually the same four bars in the middle of the piece certainly has the effect of creating monotony instead of the cumulative tension which was presumably their purpose.

[2] As well as motifs exploiting adjoining semitones, Johnson's chords display a crunchy dissonance, often being constructed out of seconds, major and minor. This in itself sharpens attack, thus aiding rhythm rather than melody.

[3] Stride piano. At its simplest, left-hand figures like those of ragtime, formed from alternating single bass notes and mid-register chords in 2/4 and 4/4 time. Unlike ragtime they swing.

[4] 'Early Jazz', page 223.

[5] She is perfectly at home again incidentally, at a fast tempo ($\quarternote = 104$).

Backwater Blues, Bessie Smith's most famous collaboration with James P. Johnson was the only other title cut on 17th February, 1927. The words are a personal narrative of the distress caused by seasonal Mississippi floods. Backwaters are areas considered expendable even though often inhabited, and are flooded to relieve pressure on the levees[6] which might otherwise collapse, causing much greater damage.

Bessie here is fully confident at the fast tempo ($\downarrow = 108$) no longer attempting to reduce the pace as she once did. Using mostly unornamented portamento with little dynamic variation, she imparts a sombre despair to the words which she wrote herself. This contrasts well with Johnson's crisp piano. What is less agreeable is his compulsion to provide musical metaphors of the scenes conjured up by Bessie's narrative. Her images are sufficient in themselves, and his rain-like tremolos after her first and second lines and splashing effects of the third chorus for instance, adroitly executed though they are, entirely redundant. On the other hand, his beat is a rock-steady amalgam of boogie and stride piano, he plays with an accuracy (derived from an early 'classical' training) and swing unsurpassed by Bessie's other piano men and as Schuller says 'In the strictly accompanimental segments, Johnson is relaxed and frequently complements Bessie beautifully'.[7]

History provided a footnote to this performance; its sales were greatly assisted by the coincidence of its release in 1927 with the worst Mississippi floods remembered.

Unusually, at the session on 2nd March, 1927, four popular songs of the day were cut. In the first of these, *After You've Gone,* Bessie Smith shows how well she was able to sing a jazz standard, transmuting banal words[8] into pure

---

[6] Levee. Embankment of a river.   [7] 'Early Jazz', page 223.

[8] Bessie's version differs from that copyrighted in 1918 by the Broadway Music Corporation (words and music by Creamer and Layton) in having only one verse whereas words were provided for two; furthermore, she sings two choruses but with words provided for only one, she has to repeat them.

expressionism. With the band intoning opulent, legato organ-like chords behind her, she rearranges words, pitches and especially rhythmic phrasing to produce an excitingly contrasting vocal. Her portamento is set aside to be replaced with a sharp consonantal and glottal attack fashioned into sometimes quite complex ornaments – the brash confidence of her 'gone' in the first and third bars of the first chorus (after the 16 bar verse) is breathtaking in the way in which she initially arches her melisma, and then on the repeat, describes a descending figure.

The band is superb (except in the second chorus where the slack habanera rhythm causes a collapse of tension) and so rich are its lower harmonies that it would be easy to believe a brass bass was present (as it was in the similar group of 5th May, 1925), an illusion which is mainly the work of Henderson's left-hand. They avoid the flashy, technically brilliant, and concentrate on doing simple things well. Jimmy Harrison's circus-like trombone glissandi could hardly be more elementary in concept but his timing is perfect, setting up a delicious anticipation of the passages he preceedes with a richly mellow tone. Harrison was the first trombonist to give indications that his instrument might be played with something approaching the flexibility of the trumpet but here his role is purely harmonic. Sadly he died when only thirty (in 1931) – his development would have been interesting to observe but at least his influence lived on vicariously in the work of others, notably Jack Teagarden and Dickie Wells. Buster Bailey, now in a larger group where his thin tone adds seasoning rather than being a main flavour, is in his true element. He contributes a necessary filament of astringency to the counterpoint.

Alexander's Ragtime Band, the second title from this session, is Irving Berlin's late (1911) but successful attempt to cash in on the ragtime craze. It actually bears little relation to ragtime but has proved a popular jazz vehicle over the years.

Bessie Smith at this, her fastest tempo so far ($\downarrow = 160$), has

to rely upon smears and short slides, and apart from any
natural inclination she might have, is forced to smooth out
the melodic line⁹ for sheer survival; the original melody in
this key (C sharp) for instance, calls for a middle C and a low
G sharp but she does not once descend to these notes. Whilst
her performance generates a genuine excitement, Bessie does
not really sound comfortable. It is not just the synthetic
material – after all she has, in the past, appropriated much
material of similar quality and turned it into gold – but
largely the tempo, which with many quavers to sing pushes
her towards the outer limits of her technique. At times she is
reminiscent of a large mammal attempting to negotiate a ski
slalom – before she has overcome one tricky turn she is into
the next.

Joe Smith plays a pungent and dominating lead at some
remove from his lyrical style. His imaginative bugle call of
the last chorus is glorious. Jimmy Harrison again plays
satisfying harmonies and short, gently propulsive glissandi
but the New Orleans discipline allows him little opportunity
to exhibit his advanced soloistic technique and high register
ability. Coleman Hawkins on clarinet, whose previous work
with Bessie has been less than auspicious (the rejected *Any
Woman's Blues* of 16th October, 1923, and a reticent *Cake
Walkin' Babies* and *Yellow Dog Blues* of 5th May, 1925), again
fails to give warning that he will soon be the first jazz tenor
saxophone of note and Fletcher Henderson's major soloist. It
is in fact, very difficult to comment upon his contribution to
this performance as he stays too close to the cornet line and is
often inaudible.

Nevertheless, a fine, dense, New Orleans polyphony is
produced (although Buster Bailey is missed), with again,
more than a hint of the non-existent brass bass.

⁹ Although the original melody is quite free-ranging, as William H.
Austin points out in 'Music in the Twentieth Century' (page 191), it has a
main motif that 'is an imitation of the blue third, detached from any
melodic continuity'.

The lyrics of *Muddy Water* (*A Mississippi Moan*), (Matrix 143569–1), the next title cut on the 2nd March, 1927, express nostalgia for an idealised South which would cause little serious objection if they did not also sentimentalise the recurrent Mississippi floods. Bessie presumably still had little control over her recording material otherwise it is hard to explain why, having dealt with the theme sincerely in *Back-water Blues,* a fortnight earlier, she now risks casting doubt upon this sincerity by entertaining such ludicrous, Tin Pan Alley words.

Although the pace is slow ($\downarrow = 72$), she uses portamento without complex ornament with the notable exception of her melisma on 'way' in the twenty-sixth bar of the chorus,[10] which she forms into an elaborate flourish. She compensates for the simplicity of her line though, and in spite of the repugnant words, by imparting to many of her higher pitches, a timbre of white-hot intensity.

This time the New Orleans formula is largely discarded, with the brass[11] playing low-register harmonic glissandi for most of the number, only the cornet freeing itself from arrangement once in the verse (a glorious blue-third) and in the coda. Having two clarinets, someone felt impelled to restrict them mostly to arranged upper-register 'stabs' on the weak (second and fourth) beats. And although no doubt thickening the texture, neither the piano nor banjo distinguish themselves.

The second take of *Muddy Water* (*A Mississippi Moan*) Matrix 143569–2,ꞏ was issued by Columbia and under the same record number (14197–D), when damage to the master of

---

[10] The number is constructed from a 4 bar instrumental introduction, a 16 bar verse and a thirty-two bar chorus (in modified AABA format). It finishes with a 4 bar instrumental coda.

[11] The accoustical clarity of this recording is particularly kind to the trombone and allows the suspicion that Harrison is using the bass or tenor-bass instrument, not the normal tenor at this session.

the first occurred after some pressings from it had been released.[12]

Bessie Smith, on this second take is more reflective in mood, her performance not so stirring; it is the only one of her alternates dealt with where there is a significant change of mood. This change results from her more seamless portamento combined with the fact that she slightly restricts her range at the top end and employs lower notes rather more.[13] And symptomatic of her new mood, the marvellous melisma on 'way' in the twenty-sixth bar of the first take chorus has been simplified – the arrogant flourish is missing.

The band sounds much as before except for Joe Smith, who, responds to Bessie's more thoughtful mood whenever he can escape from the arrangement. Although his blue-third in the verse is missing, he substitutes an even more disconsolate blue-seventh in this take. It is not that he plays better this time, only differently.[14]

Unusually for early jazz, *There'll Be A Hot Time In The Old Town Tonight,* the last title from the 2nd March, 1927 session, modulates back and forth between two keys.[15] A sort of proto-sonata principle, the classic European model for contrasting tonal tension with relaxation, it was no doubt adopted here to maintain the listener's interest because of the extreme simplicity of the chord progressions; the number is based entirely upon tonic and dominant harmony. The words were written to advertise the McIntyre and Heath Minstrel Show in Old Town, Louisiana in 1896 and the number was

[12] According to George Avakian in the sleeve notes to Volume 3 of 'The Bessie Smith Story', reissues of the early 1950's.
[13] The key is Bb and on the first take Bessie's range is from the Bb below to the C natural an octave above middle C. On the second take her range is restricted to the octave from the Bb below middle C.
[14] Joe Smith's first note is a useful rapid aid to the identification of these takes. On the first take he splits the note, initially hitting the eighth harmonic instead of the tenth which he is aiming for. On the second take, he aims for the eighth harmonic and locates it accurately.
[15] F major and Eb major.

also adopted as a rallying song by the American forces in the Spanish-American War of 1898; in further confirmation of its persuasive puissance, Theodore Roosevelt, who played a leading role in the war, took it over for his political rallies.

Bessie belts out her vocal in infectious style, full of the sense of a good time, with ornaments kept simple and to a minimum, a simplicity which is the result of the pace and which here, with few quavers to cope with, gives her no problems; at $\quarternote = 168$ it is her fastest on a released recording.[16] The performance contains an interesting confirmation of her natural musicianship; her handling of the two modulations which occur whilst she is singing is immaculate – it is not merely that she does not make mistakes in picking up the new key, but that she actually prepares the band with her two-note decorations on the words just prior to the changes, 'do' and 'said' at the end of verses[17] one and two respectively.

The band is back to an enthusiastic New Orleans style, especially in the two instrumental choruses. Henderson is at his best, rattling along with a fine swing and for once able to display a talent taken for granted in a 'classically' trained musician but not normally called for in early jazz – in his prefatory solo to the first instrumental chorus, he modulates from Eb major to F major in expert fashion. Joe Smith, on the other hand, overlooks the modulation and continues momentarily in Eb, hitting the fifth and third degrees of that scale before rapidly recovering on to the third degree of the F major scale. But it is the only time he falters, otherwise playing a firm lead in the instrumental choruses and intricate figures behind the vocal.

Jimmy Harrison again combines unobtrusive low harmonies with gently thrusting glissandi and Buster Bailey displays his skill with New Orleans clarinet figures – his break

---

[16] *On Revival Day* of 9th June, 1930 is her only other released recording at this tempo.
[17] The number consists of a 4 bar instrumental introduction, a 16 bar verse, two 16 bar choruses, two instrumental choruses, another verse, two more choruses and finally a 4 bar instrumental coda.

between the two instrumental choruses is especially good, a perfectly timed and satisfying cadenza. Charlie Dixon's banjo is the only instrument which tends to detract from the band's performance; his strumming seems anxious to anchor them to the ground when everyone else wants to swing.

Trombone Cholly, cut the next day, 3rd March, 1927 with a smaller group, is virtually a duet between Bessie Smith and Charlie Green. The lyrics tell of a charismatic trombone player actually personified as Charlie Green (which makes the reference to him having come from 'way down South' inaccurate — Omaha, his home town is near the centre of America). The 'Cholly' of the title may therefore result from a mishearing of Bessie's 'Charlie', although Paul Oliver suggests also, that the word being Negro slang for a hobo or tramp, may reflect an in-joke amongst the group.[18]

Bessie applies a variety of decoration to the pentatonically based melody with note fall-offs abounding, mainly as a simple slur but sometimes constituting an articulated glissando. The verse in particular is peppered with unarticulated phrase-end fall-offs, many intended as a challenge to Charlie Green, a challenge he takes up enthusiastically with muted growls and rasps. Humour is there too in some of his satirical rapid-note phrases. His only mistake is in choosing to accompany Bessie's second top C of the last chorus (on 'while') with a long held top C of his own: their timbres, both being emaciated at this altitude, bring an unwelcome, rather rancid sound to the otherwise sunny mood.

In the instrumental chorus Green allows Joe Smith to predominate which he does in thoughtful style, subtly altering the mood with his open cornet describing some rather unjazzy phrases — appoggiaturas constructed out of seconds and fourths, and Bix-like in concept.

As for Fletcher Henderson, one senses his presence, even occasionally hears him.

[18] 'Bessie Smith', page 49.

The second release from 3rd March, 1927, was *Send Me To The 'Lectric Chair*. In relating her confession and death-wish following her murder of her lover, Bessie uses the word 'judge' twenty-eight times, on half of these occasions singing it squarely on the beat and in identical fashion; as Schuller says, '. . . the repetition becomes painful – indeed, one of her few errors of judgement'.[19] Unfortunately, not being of the evanescent kind, her error assumes the nature of a Chinese water-torture, the listener ignoring an otherwise good performance whilst waiting for the inevitable reiteration.

Joe Smith produces tones so broad and notes so unarticulated in the introduction that it sounds as if two trombones, instead of a cornet and trombone are present. Afterwards he stays in the background leaving Charlie Green the main rôle.

The lyrics of *Them's Graveyard Words*, the third release from the 3rd March, 1927 session, a threat of retribution following desertion, could be the prelude to the events described in the last release. Bessie delivers her threats in sombre tones and in a style reminiscent of Green's trombone.

A fine but short performance (2 minutes, 49 seconds), leaving the suspicion that an instrumental chorus was planned – at the end of the first chorus[20] cornet and trombone raise the volume as if to announce this to Bessie but it does not materialise.

The key is Bb major but to underline the grim theme, bars nine to twelve of each chorus temporarily modulate to the relative minor key, G minor; for once this works well but perhaps the funeral march opening and ending, is a little too lugubrious.

The last title from 3rd March, 1927 session, *Hot Springs*

[19] 'Early Jazz' page 240.
[20] The number is constructed from a 2 bar funeral march quotation (Chopin) by brass only, a 4 bar instrumental introduction, a 16 bar verse and two 16 bar choruses in a popular song form. The performance is completed by a further 2 bar funeral march quotation.

Blues, is simply five choruses of twelve-bar blues with a rudimentary melodic line to match — Bessie restricts her compass to mostly the minor-third, F natural to Ab with only occasional descents to middle C. She wrote the piece to commemorate a trip she made to Hot Springs, Arkansas to visit Jack Gee, her second husband, who was recuperating after an alleged nervous breakdown. Recuperations became a recurring feature of Jack's life-style but Bessie showed genuine concern with what everyone else believed to be hypochondria.[21]

Whilst she balances the simplicity of her melodic line with finely controlled microtonal shading, sadly this is not one of her best sides. For a start, some of her pitch control is obscured because of Green's tendency towards stretto;[22] it has always been part of his technique but here he not only shares the same pitches as Bessie more than is usual but the recording balance fails to differentiate their timbre as efficiently as in the previous sides from this session. More importantly the performance disappoints because such simplicity of material requires a theme to which Bessie can fully commit herself — this series of comments upon the therapeutic effects of the waters is just too impersonal and trivial for that.

Whereas in the previous releases from this session, Charlie Green has dominated, this time the contributions of the two horns are democratically arranged. Green and Joe Smith restrict their comments to antiphonal lines and in the first and third choruses the cornet plays, whilst in the second and fourth the trombone takes over. In the last chorus we hear first cornet, and then trombone and finally, for the first time in the piece, both playing together. This segregation of the horn lines allows us to judge the margin of superiority enjoyed by Joe Smith over Charlie Green. Green is consistently reliable but less often inspired. Joe Smith, and

[21] 'Bessie, Empress of the Blues', page 111.
[22] Stretto. Overlapping. In fugal writing, where one voice begins the subject before the preceding voice has finished uttering it.

certainly in the third chorus, is often just that. And this disparity is not only evident in quality of invention, but also in technique where Joe Smith is plainly the more finished.

SIXTEEN

April, 1927 –
to the end of the year

James P. Johnson is back with Bessie at the session held on
1st April, 1927. *Sweet Mistreater*, the first title cut, is a
popular song in thirty-two bar, AABA format by Creamer
and Johnson. It is a lover's complaint but this time from a
man about his fickle girl.

The mood is generally buoyant but Bessie will not be tied
down to a specific interpretation; sometimes she is full of
tongue-in-cheek humour but at others more than a hint of
pain escapes. In the last chorus[1] she suits the lightness of
mood with a fragile, more plaintive timbre and superb
control of dynamics, often shading away to silence. To match
her ambivalent treatment of the lyrics, she slips and slides
around the pitches aimed for, seeking to keep her intentions
uncertain, as if to settle anywhere for long would crystallise
them. In the first chorus however, an opinion does form briefly
in her delivery of 'when you're easin' home to me'[2] – with her
pitch drifting all around the leading-note on 'easin'' she
provides a vivid image of a cringing, returning delinquent.

The commercial elements in Johnson's playing sit more
easily with the mood here, but even so, he completely misses
the poignancy which often breaks through Bessie's voice,
continuing with his clever but uncommited antiphony. And

[1] The number is constructed from a 4 bar introduction and two, 2 bar verse
anticipations by piano, followed by a 16 bar verse and two thirty-two bar
choruses.
[2] This phrase occurs in the bridge section of the first chorus.

as in his first session with Bessie (17th February, 1927), the dichotomy between his accompaniment and his antiphony is disturbing. On the other hand, it is refreshing to hear how his flowing stride (and occasional 'walking') left-hand and his 'rhythmicization of melodic ideas'[3] inspire Bessie to forget her previous antipathy to fast tempos[4] – she often seems to be floating independently of Johnson, with only occasional coincidence with the beat. Johnson, in his obsession with rhythm, parallels the early views of Stravinsky – both (Stravinsky notably in *Le Sacre du printemps* (1913)) will employ notes in rhythmic groupings without too much regard for specific pitches, and both are noted for using extended passages of polyrhythm.[5] This is not to suggest that they were influenced by, or even aware of each other's existence, only that one of the new musical ideas of the time, that rhythm was worth listening to for its own sake, interested them both.

Lock and Key, the second title from 1st April 1927 is faster ($\jmath = 140$) and more humorous than the first and these factors have a noticeable effect upon Bessie's style. Decoration is largely discarded in favour of short slides, sometimes semi-speech, and in particular, she adopts a rhythmic approach based upon consonantal and glottal attacks. This time instead of floating above Johnson's beat, she steps all around it and sometimes squarely on it: often an exciting polyrhythm of three strands is produced by Johnson's two hands and Bessie's voice. With essentially crotchets to cope with she is quite comfortable at the fast tempo: she only once falters – on the first glissando to top Bb on 'change' in the last chorus;[6] she

[3] Gunther Schuller's phrase. See 'Early Jazz', page 217.
[4] The tempo here is $\jmath = 120$.
[5] See Johnson's various performances of *Carolina Shout,* he first recorded it in 1921 but wrote it earlier; here in *Sweet Mistreater,* he employs polyrhythm only in short bursts.
[6] The number is constructed from an 8 bar piano introduction, a 16 bar verse, a 32 bar chorus, a 16 bar interlude and a final 32 bar chorus. The choruses are split into 4 bar sections, AABAABA but with the first B section being of 8 bars.

makes the decision to ascend that high a little late and is almost left behind.

Johnson is in magnificent form, playing fast, accurate, two-handed stride piano (with hints of boogie-woogie) behind Bessie and with an antiphony which sounds much better — the previous disparity between acompaniment and antiphony has almost disappeared.

A fine performance, the best since Bessie last sang with Louis Armstrong.

The words of *Mean Old Bedbug Blues* cut on 27th September, 1927, anthropomorphise the eponymous parasite and present it as an unbeatable adversary. A metaphor for the troubles afflicting Black America.

It has been six months since Bessie's last recording session and now there is a noticeably rougher edge to her voice[7] (in the last full chorus[8] she makes the grain even coarser for climactic purposes). In spite of this however, she still manages to incorporate frequent dynamic reductions at the end of phrases, often down to a whisper.

Porter Grainger's first released accompaniment for Bessie[9] goes by largely unheard, not so much because he is smothered by the country guitar of Lincoln M. Conaway, but because he does little to assert himself. This is a pity because the guitar has little to offer except repetitive phrases, and even, in the third chorus, sinking to a ludicrous zither impression.

This recording quickly became a hit in spite of its deficiencies. Bessie's performance is majestic it is true but no doubt a lot of the reason lies in the psychological message buried in the words.

[7] Although both titles from this session evidence this deterioration, it does not seem to be a permanent feature of her singing. The next day the roughness had largely disappeared.
[8] The number is constructed from a 4 bar guitar introduction, four twelve-bar blues choruses and a final 8 bar chorus.
[9] Porter Grainger previously recorded with Bessie on 23rd April, 1924, (*Banjo Blues* and *Four Flushin' Papa*) but the three takes of each title were rejected.

On *A Good Man Is Hard To Find*, her second title from the 27th September, 1927, Bessie again combines a coarsely textured timbre with controlled dynamic gradation. But she also includes another item from her 'bag'. Both choruses[10] are based upon the same words and as a means of differentiation she uses contrasts of volume in the first (and in the verse) whilst employing phrase manipulation for the second. A comparison of the lines;

A good man, is hard to find.
You always get, the other kind.

at the beginning of each chorus highlights her separate treatments. In the first chorus these phrases are unusually symmetrical and at the end of each phrase, the pitch fall-off rapidly reduces in volume. Her treatment in the second chorus however, is radically different (she changes the words a little too). She soon discards dynamic gradation and roots her interpretation in syllabic contractions and elongations and unorthodox pauses for breath.[11]

When improvising musicians reach maturity in their art there is a tendency for some aspects of it to become simpler. Louis Armstrong offers a particularly striking example with his rapid climb to joint peaks of technical ability and aesthetic integrity being followed by a conscious shift towards a more economical language and commercial outlook. In Bessie's case, complex ornaments are now becoming rarer. Louis's change of direction took the form of an almost clean break in early 1929; Bessie's change was less conscious and abrupt, and any leanings towards commerce more apparent in the titles of her songs than in the reality of their treatment.

[10] The number is constructed from a 4 bar instrumental introduction and 2 bar verse anticipation, a 12 bar verse and two, 22 bar choruses.

[11] It is instructive, to compare Bessie's version with that of Lizzie Miles, recorded many years later. Lizzie Miles is a singer with a style superficially similar to that of Bessie Smith but apart from them both having a broad tone and being sexually assertive, even a cursory comparison reveals that here the similarities end. In Lizzie Miles' interpretation, there is no subtlety of dynamics and her phrase manipulation is naïve.

This time the balance between accompanists is better, although the guitar still tends towards repetition and the piano surfaces too infrequently for any evaluation of its quality to be made.

The theme of *Homeless Blues* cut the next day, 28th September, 1927 is, like that of *Backwater Blues,* the suffering caused by the Mississippi floods. As with that earlier and better treatment, this is basically a twelve-bar blues and the mood is serious, Bessie evoking a deep misery mainly with timbre and vibrato. She adds interest to the elementary structure by phrase manipulation and some half-spoken passages.

But in spite of her sincerity, the performance is blighted by the all pervading non-jazz alto saxophone. Ernest Elliott's lack of empathy is epitomised by his quotations from *Home, Sweet Home* which in this context are an affront to Bessie's veracity. Porter Grainger withers in the enervating atmosphere.

Bessie's technique on *Looking For My Man Blues,* the second title from the 28th September, 1927 is pared down to the bone but her parsimony originates from ennui rather than a desire for economy. A cloud of weariness hangs over the proceedings as for once she gives up the struggle against an unsympathetic accompanist.

It is a performance which should not have been released and the cause of its failure is Ernest Elliott. His etiolated alto noises infect, and eventually subvert the work of the others. [12]

At her final session in 1927 Bessie Smith cut her only two titles with Tommy Ladnier. On 27th October, the first of these was *Dyin' By The Hour.* Bessie responds to the superior accompaniment with a fine performance of wide compass, anchored on her third-seeker (see Ex. 1) but with ornamentation otherwise simple.

[12] Perhaps it is not coincidental that no one has claimed composer credit for the number.

The session provides a tantalising glimpse of what could undoubtedly have grown into a stimulating partnership[13] *Dyin' By The Hour* enchants within the first few bars. It is the third of Bessie's performances to quote from Chopin's funeral march but here it is no longer a cliché: in the introduction the four-note chromatic modulation to the relative major key is elementary but of indescribable beauty.[14] In the choruses, Ladnier politely reserves his pensive muted comments for the gaps between the vocal lines. He was influenced most by King Oliver and Louis Armstrong; here he leans towards Oliver's dignified expressiveness rather than the frontier-nudging energy of the Armstrong of that time.

June Cole[15] was also a fine musician as his harmonies and rhythm on this piece show. Whilst he also played string bass, at this pace ($\downarrow = 80$) and in this company his brass bass is the ideal instrument. He can easily articulate a continuous four crotchets to the bar and when appropriate, running semi-quavers present no problem: in addition, as has been evident before, some of Bessie Smith's best performances occur when she is backed by opulent harmonies and here they form a satisfying contrast to Ladnier's dry blueness as well.

Presumably Frank Walker was happy about the sound as only one take was considered necessary.

The words of *Foolish Man Blues,* the other title from 27th October, 1927, written by Bessie herself, express dislike for effeminate men. Possibly they were prompted by her professional association with Porter Grainger, a homosexual,

[13] This could have come about had not Ladnier left the next year with Sam Wooding's Band to play in Europe. He stayed, playing with various bands for over three years by which time Bessie's recording career was almost over.

[14] The number is constructed from a 4 bar instrumental introduction, four choruses of twelve-bar blues and a 4 bar instrumental coda. The introduction and coda are in F sharp minor and the choruses in A major.

[15] June Cole, like Ladnier was a member of Fletcher Henderson's band at this time and in a year he too was to leave for Europe. Unlike Ladnier however, he stayed until 1941.

according to Albertson.[16] Whatever the inspiration though she is guilty of some hypocrisy since, again relying upon Albertson, she was bisexual herself.[17]

Bessie's style here is again economical. There is some evidence building-up however, that as she approaches the latter stages of her career, she has sometimes less inclination to restrict her range, even in twelve-bar blues. In this number she ranges freely over an octave and on the previous release, a major-ninth.[18]

Two elements of Ladnier's blues playing are note-worthy, a love for short chromatic phrases and considerable reliance upon the pitches of the triad. Bessie's line, particularly in *Foolish Man Blues,* is also based upon triadic pitches and the cornet antiphony is therefore particularly congruous. His reverence for Louis Armstrong is shown by his cadence immediately following Bessie's last line of the piece, a direct quotation of one of his mentor's favourites.

Whilst June Cole produced occasional triplets in the previous number, here he manages some quite extended triplet-runs, demonstrating an agility not usually associated with his instrument.

[16] 'Bessie, Empress of the Blues', page 124.
[17] 'Bessie, Empress of the Blues', page 108.
[18] Both are basically twelve-bar blues.

SEVENTEEN

February and
March, 1928

Thinking Blues, from 9th February, 1928 is a pre-echo of
Bessie Smith's later triumph, *Empty Bed Blues* (20th March,
1928). The tempo ($\quarternote = 84$) and key are the same, and in both
she uses the full tessitura in every chorus, similar glissandi
and is accompanied by the same trombone, Charlie Green. In
addition, the melodic lines are very similar and both deal
with rejected love[1] (although *Empty Bed Blues* is much more
salacious).

Whilst Bessie's line is simple, in this performance she
manipulates timbre more than usual. Many words are given
an expressive distortion but 'me' in the third line of the third
chorus and 'don't' and 'reap' in the fourth chorus are especially noteworthy; the long 'e' sound has become her
favourite vehicle for this treatment.

Demus Dean produces interesting ideas on cornet but
unfortunately they are not consonant with those of Bessie or
the other instrumentalists. He phrases stiffly with a sour,
rather legitimate tone and tends to weld on his throat growls
instead presenting them as an integral part of his technique.
He often sounds very modern (by the standards of the time) —
for example his antiphony in the first chorus is reminiscent of
some of Poulenc's compositions for wind. In the fifth chorus,

[1] The composer credit is different however. *Thinking Blues* is by Bessie
Smith and *Empty Bed Blues* by J. C. Johnson.

133

it is particularly noticeable that whilst Charlie Green's response to Bessie's first line follows her phrasing, Dean's answer to her second line is quite at variance with her mood. At his best he is detached and at worst antagonistic.

Fred Longshaw's piano though is full of interesting things. Especially enlightened is his use of piano harmonies below those ·of the trombone, substituting in less ponderous fashion, for a brass bass.

The second title from 9th February, 1928, *Pickpocket Blues,* might have been culled from some white country blues singer's repertoire: Bessie treats it with respect but her mood is not profound. She constructs her lines about the penalties for peddling gin and pickpocketing, from notes either hit cleanly or with a simple acciaccatura added.

Cornet (more closely muted) and trombone spend much of the time playing somewhat arch, arranged wa-wa comments which whilst not unsympathetic, can hardly be called inventive. Longshaw plays well but less outstandingly than on the last release.

Bessie clearly enormously enjoys the third and last title from the 9th February, 1928 session, *I Used To Be Your Sweet Mama.* The lyrics are a defiant repudiation of an unfaithful man but throughout, humour is not far below the surface. She prepares the way to the climax[2] of the last 8 bars particularly effectively by half-speaking over horn riffs in the interlude.[3]

The accompaniment is in some ways more sympathetic and integrated this time and it often relaxes into an effective polyphony. Dean's phrasing however, as on the previous two

[2] Produced by Bessie's increased use of the top of the pitch compass.
[3] The number is constructed from a 4 bar instrumental introduction, a 16 bar verse, a 16 bar chorus in a popular song form, a 16 bar interlude and the final 8 bars of chorus to finish. The last two bars are rallentando, an end-signalling device which has become fashionable in Bessie's current performances.

titles from this session, tends towards stiffness.

On 16th February, 1928, Bessie was joined by the clarinets of Ernest Elliott and Bob Fuller, and the piano of Porter Grainger, but only one title escaped from the session, *I'd Rather Be Dead And Buried In My Grave.*

Bessie's treatment of the lyrics about the pointlessness of life after rejection by a lover, generates a real despair. Articulated ornaments are rather more to the fore than of late although few are as extravagant as her four note melisma on 'in' at the end of the first chorus.[4] This is another of those days when her voice is pervaded with a coarseness; it is most noticeable in but not limited to, the B sections (where it may have some climactic purpose).

The construction of the vocal line is particularly interesting. The key is Eb major and Bessie's overall range is from the Bb below to the Bb next above middle C. However, in the first 4 bars of each A section, she restricts her range to the minor-third, Eb to Gb: in the second 4 bars she extends it to the perfect-fifth, C natural to G natural and only in the B sections of each chorus does she open up to span the full octave. This gradual dilation makes for a satisfying development of melodic line.

Presumably the dire high-register yelpings of the clarinets in the introduction are intended as references to Bessie's early 'fox' and 'dog' similes but they do not augur well and true to form, Elliott and Fuller proceed to trot out a pack of enervating harmonic clichés. Luckily however, after the introduction, they confine themselves to background noises in the chalumeau register.

For once, in the double-time passage towards the end of the record, Porter Grainger's piano comes to life but unfortunately, many of his ideas are obscured by the reeds.

[4] The number is constructed from a 4 bar instrumental introduction and two 24 bar choruses in a popular song form, each chorus being in three sections of 8 bars each, AAB.

The lyrics of *Standin' In The Rain Blues*, cut on 21st February, 1928 are a sometimes nonsensical[5] hotchpotch written by Bessie herself. It invites comparison with *Backwater Blues* but unlike that earlier recording which deals with real catastrophe, here we are offered a loosely connected series of choruses about the inconvenience of rain. The aimlessness of the lyrics is compounded by the melodic lines of the choruses, each one of which is different, the third incidentally, containing a direct crib from *Backwater Blues*. Bessie's technique is kept suitably simple but her total commitment seems hardly justified by the slight lyrics.

With the two horns providing antiphony alternatively, the aesthetic difference between them becomes more noticeable. Green although technically limited, is closely attuned to Bessie's mood: Dean, more accomplished technically, never approaches it. The cornet growl and triple-tonguing in the middle of the third chorus are blatant examples of insensitivity; like so many of Dean's effects, they are merely tacked on to his stilted phrases without thought.

Longshaw's accompaniment is agreeably varied although the comparison he invites with James P. Johnson by his meteorological images, is not to his advantage.

Encouraged by a pleasing chord progression, Bessie, on *It Won't Be You*, the other release from 21st February, 1928, builds her performance from a mixture of cleanly hit notes, two-note melisma and a few finely shaded and extended microtonal pitch variations. A delightful example of the latter is her prolonged blueing around the major- and minor-third on 'all' in the eleventh bar of the verse.[6] Towards the end of the piece she offers an interesting and abrupt variation in timbre too; after a pure, flute-like 'lose' on top D natural, she imparts a roughness, reinforcing her determination to find a kinder lover.

[5] The words of the second chorus for example.
[6] The number is constructed from a 4 bar instrumental introduction, a 16 bar verse and two 16 bar choruses in a popular song form.

Demas Dean, in the instrumental introduction, plays with his expected gracelessness but his work in the verse and choruses does show some improvement; staying in the middle of his register and avoiding displays of technique, he gets as near as he has ever done to the mood of Bessie and Charlie Green. Unfortunately, this still leaves something of an expressive gulf. Green does not assert himself this time, limiting his role to harmonic support during the antiphony, a support which no doubt accounts for Dean's improvement.

Bessie treats the strange words[7] of *Spider Man Blues* from 19th March, 1928, with a simple technique but also, and unpredictably, introduces a new ornament showing that the development of her style has not yet quite ended. In places where she might previously have used her favourite third-seeker of Ex. 1, she substitutes a slide from the first to the major-third degree of the scale. The example below occurs across the second and third bars of the first chorus:

Ex. 15

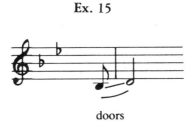

doors

Not much can be said about the arranged wailing of the reeds except that it makes for painful listening. Whilst Bessie gamely tries to counter their subversion with commitment, Porter Grainger seeks to distance himself from the misadventure with detached right-hand phrases made up from quaver triplets.

[7] Seemingly about a suffocatingly possessive lover.

The 20th March, 1928 saw Bessie Smith, Charlie Green and Porter Grainger at their best. The first title cut at that session, *Empty Bed Blues* – Parts 1 and 2, was originally released on the two sides of a 10 inch 78 rpm record[8] and had the effect of reviving Bessie's waning career although probably not entirely because of the artistry of the performance. Albertson reports Lovie Austin as saying 'You could hear that record all over the South Side'.[9]

The lyrics by J. C. Johnson, advise discretion in discussing a satisfactory lover but mainly consist of a salacious catalogue of his skills. Although veiled by double-entendre, the veil is gossamer thin and the performance, in quality and quantity the most blatantly pornographic of Bessie's career so far. As mentioned before, whether this type of material was customary in her stage shows, or whether she really disapproved of prurient lyrics and only sang them to boost sales particularly amongst whites, and on Frank Walker's instructions when her popularity was fading, is not clear. Whatever the truth, she treats the raunchy material honestly, often tempering her earnestness with a palliative humour; see for example the last lines of the first side;

> He's got that sweet somethin', and I tol' my gal friend Lou,
> For the way she's ravin', she must have gone and tried it too.

Technically, she keeps her line simple with a mixture of cleanly hit notes, short slides and a few simple ornaments. Sometimes she uses her newly discovered tonic to major-third slide of Ex. 15; here she uses it in imitation of Green's trombone glissando. Her old third-seeker of Ex. 1 is not found at all in this performance. And although in her last two

---

[8] The purpose of the exercise was presumably to try to overcome the (approximately) three minute limitation of one side of a 10 inch disc, but in that case it is hard to see why an introduction was felt necessary for the second side.

[9] 'Bessie, Empress of the Blues', page 129.

twelve-bar blues, she has restricted her range mostly to a perfect-fifth, in this one she ranges freely again over an octave.[10]

Whether or not a climax is included in Bessie's performances seems to be a quite arbitrary decision although twelve-bar blues have less of them than do her popular songs. Whilst basically a twelve bar blues[11] there is a climax to this performance however, one that is quite carefully prepared. In the last chorus of Part 1, she avoids the top Bb she has hit at least once in each of the previous four choruses, thus providing a sort of anti-climax. Then in the fourth chorus of Part 2 she goes no higher than Ab, in the fifth she hits Bb once and in the last chorus of 8 bars, she hits Bb five times.

Evaluation of Charlie Green's contribution has perhaps been too uncritical in the past. Much of his time is spent providing rather obvious reflections of Bessie's words. One soon tires of his 'grinding' response to 'coffee grinder' in the first chorus and his low growls after 'deep sea diver' in the second. But when he sticks to 'absolute' music, he is first class, especially on the muted second side. For example, in the second and fourth choruses of this side his perfectly timed, driving riff-like antiphony produces emotional jolts that stay longer in the memory than anything even Bessie does.

Grainger is happy here too and this is the first time that he has been sufficiently audible to make some evaluation of his work possible. His accompaniment is satisfyingly varied and through most of the piece a proto-Errol Garner left-hand sets

[10]   This previously noted tendency of this period in her career is presumably a result of the omnipotent popular song.
[11]   The number is constructed as follows: Part 1; a 4 bar instrumental introduction followed by five choruses of twelve-bar blues. Part 2; a 2 bar instrumental introduction, five choruses of twelve-bar blues and a final 8 bars consisting of a twelve-bar chorus with the middle 4 bars omitted. Bessie's only real mistake occurs at the start of Part 2; she starts to take the truncated route of the final 8 bars to come; Grainger and Green follow, undismayed, then provide suitable harmony and antiphony to bring her back on course.

up a rocking rhythm which plainly inspires the other two. Bessie particularly is stimulated towards a freer than usual across-the-beat rhythm.

Put It Right Here (Or Keep It Out There), the other title cut on 20th March, 1928 has its theme summed up in the first few lines;

> I've had a man for fifteen year,
> give him his room and board:
> Once he was like a Cadillac,
> now he's like an old worn-out Ford;
> He never brought me a lousy dime,
> and put it in my hand:
> So there'll be some changes from now on,
> accordin' to my plan.

Although the complaint is ostensibly an economic one, sexual parallels are never far away. Blesh says;

> This type of humor is often found in the blues and it relates closely to the African *songs of derision* which are used to intimidate and enforce social conformity. Put it Right Here also has definite affinities with the animal fables of West Africa, many of which survived in the Uncle Remus stories and in many Afro-American songs. [12]

The large number of (mainly single syllable) words encourages Bessie to adopt a more declamatory style than usual (although it is still some way from her half-speech used on some releases). With the possibilities for melodic subtleties therefore reduced, she decides to give even more attention than usual to rhythmic opportunities and at this medium pace ($\downarrow$ = 92), the result is an arrangement of percussive rhythmic patterns across the main beat, continually creating and then resolving tensions. Unusually, for a

---

[12] 'Shining Trumpets', page 133. His second sentence refers to the interlude which is full of animal analogies.

popular song[13] most of her melodic line devolves around the major-third, Eb to G natural, especially emphasising the blue-third.[14]

Charlie Green shuns imagery this time, even when animals are mentioned, and matches the implied humour with mocking muted replies in the manner of a circus trombone commenting upon the antics of a clown. Porter Grainger contributes reliable progressions and varied patterns and textures; he too avoids obvious imagery although he must have been very tempted behind Bessie's reference to the Chinese laundryman in the last chorus. The exercise of restraint is a significant element in the success of this performance.

[13] The number is constructed from a 4 bar instrumental introduction, a 16 bar verse, a 16 bar chorus, a 16 bar interlude and another 16 bar chorus. The choruses are in AABA format but with only 4 bars to each section.
[14] The key is Eb.

EIGHTEEN
August, 1928

Yes Indeed He Do! cut on 24th August, 1928 and credited to Porter Grainger, has words and music which are above the average for a vaudeville song. Bessie's syncopated first line, 'I don't know what makes it rain', arching up easily near the top of her range, produces an acute frisson and is one of her best openings. No doubt Grainger's chord progressions inspire her because in spite of the inferior reeds, she is coaxed into an excitingly rhythmic performance based upon a simple surging portamento alternating with notes cleanly hit. Her ability with between-the-beat rhythm is heard for example in the line, 'I ask myself this question', at the end of the verse.[1]

The lyrics consist of a series of ironic comments upon an unfaithful man. The first lines of the first chorus give the flavour;

> Oh, do my sweet, sweet Daddy love me?
> Yes indeed he do.
> Is he true as stars above me?
> What kind of fool is you?
> He don't stay from home all night,
> More'n six times a week;
> No, I know that I'm his Sheba;
> An' I know that he's my sheik.

[1] The number is constructed from a 4 bar instrumental introduction, a 16 bar verse, a 32 bar chorus, 16 bars of instrumental chorus and a final 32 bar chorus. The choruses are in two sections of 16 bars each.

Bessie delivers the song with growling gusto, as if it were really a panegyric to an exemplary lover; she relates his wrongs with the approval of virtues and it comes as a jolt when the exultation in her voice is compared with her actual words.

The trouble with the reeds is that although aiming for a New Orleans style polyphony, they can manage only a chaotic, pitch-doubling heterophony. The instrumental chorus is typical – they not only get in each other's way but sound alike too, in spite of the alternative instruments available at the session. And Grainger, although playing his own tune, seems diffident. None of it matters though, Bessie's high spirits are enough to carry them all.

The second title from the 24th August, 1928 session, *Devil's Gonna Get You* is also credited to Porter Grainger but the composition is not of the same quality as the previous one in spite of a modulation from the C minor of the introduction and verse to the relative major, Eb, of the two thirty-two bar choruses.[2]

Bessie tries to redeem the performance with a simple vocal line that sometimes anticipates the beat and is full of her 'hot' growl but unfortunately leaves the impression that she is trying too hard. Too much is against her. The words are commonplace and the chord progressions hackneyed; she has to contend with a 'pretty' piano and reeds pouring out insipid harmony lacking the richness to arouse her.

The discographies show Bob Fuller playing clarinet and alto saxophone and Ernest Elliott clarinet, alto and tenor saxophones at this session; it is a reflection of their lack-lustre performance that no one has bothered to identify which instruments are used on which sides.

You Ought To Be Ashamed, (another Porter Grainger composition) from the 24th August, 1928 session, has lyrics based

[2] The choruses are in AABA format.

upon a set of reproaches to a 'mistreatin' man' and from Bessie's past handling of such themes of deep unhappiness, we might have expected a superlative performance. But this one is leaden — there is even more amiss than with the previous one. The chord sequence is uninspiring, the words and Bessie's line not varied enough, the reeds[3] sound muddy with the tenor saxophone often out of tune and the piano languishes.

Although at $\sance = 68$ one of Bessie's slowest performances and therefore one in which a decorated melodic line and rhythmic manipulation of phrase could once almost have been counted upon, she instead offers cleanly hit notes alternating with portamento packaged into neatly symmetrical phrases. She seems to realise it is a performance beyond redemption and with her simulation of misery falling far short of the transcendental, lapses into a dispiriting monotony.

The words of *Washwoman's Blues*[4] the fourth title from 24th August, 1928, comprise a mild social protest against the type of work Blacks are forced into. Spencer Williams who was responsible for many fine tunes (*I Ain't Got Nobody, Basin Street Blues, I Found A New Baby* and others) is credited with the composition but this is one of his less successful efforts. The lyrics are jejune and lack authenticity with their use of such cultural anachronisms as 'duds', 'livelihood' and the archaic 'scullion'. As has been mentioned before, it is unusual for Bessie to use her songs as vehicles for social protest and here in the fourth chorus, the already innocuous remonstration is further weakened by sycophantic gestures towards those against whom it should be directed:

[3] Here with the oily timbre of the clarinet absent, it takes little effort to identify the reeds as tenor (Ernest Elliott) and alto (Bob Fuller) saxophones.
[4] This is not the same composition as *Wash Woman Blues* sung by Hociel Thomas with Louis Armstrong and his Hot Four on 11th November, 1925.

Rather be a scullion,
cooking in some white folk's yard; (twice)
I could eat up plenty,
wouldn't have to work so hard.

This time however, in spite of its drawbacks, Bessie treats
the material seriously applying some articulated ornament as
well as using unarticulated slides. And for the first time she
employs her original third-seeker of Ex. 1 (for example on
'suds' twice in the first chorus) in the same composition as her
tonic-to-third ornament of Ex. 15 (for example on 'livelihood' in the second line of the third chorus[5]).

Whilst Bessie varies the phrasing of similar lines and
generally makes sober observations upon the disagreeable life
of a drudge, the reeds take an unsympathetically Olympian
view, the most offensive expression of which is the jeering
'laugh' at the end of the third chorus.

On the next title from the 24th August, 1928 session, *Slow
And Easy Man,* Bessie gains further strength in her battle
against the reeds. She growls in spirited fashion, refusing to
be submerged and of course the tempo helps her here
($\rfloor = 124$). Manipulating a riff basically constructed from F
natural, G natural and Ab (and sometimes including A
natural too) into countless variations of pitch, rhythm and
timbre, she manages to rise above the obtuse accompaniment. But nothing she can do in any way influences the reeds
to abandon their worn-out phrases full of pitch and timbre
collisions. It is true that in the instrumental chorus, the
arranged lines prevent pitch collision but there it is their
rapid vibratos and considerable imprecision which offends.

Porter Grainger seems to have moved to another room.

Albertson states that *Poor Man's Blues,* the final side from the
24th August, 1928 session is 'considered by some to be the

[5] The number is constructed from a 4 bar instrumental introduction
followed by five choruses of twelve-bar blues.

finest record she (Bessie Smith) ever made'.[6] Although I do
not rank the performance that high, (neither presumably
does Albertson) it is certainly one of her best and a considerable amount of the credit must go to Joe Williams whose fine
trombone has the vital effect of pushing the reeds into a
subordinate role, one they are capable of coping with.

After a 4 bar instrumental introduction the number comprises five choruses of twelve-bar blues but with subdominant
and dominant harmony introduced into the first 4 bars of
each chorus. Many of Bessie Smith's twelve-bar blues are
modified from the basic format outlined in the Introduction
to this book but this one is unusual in having only the first 4
bars amended: it is the sequence of chords in this first 4 bars
which is largely responsible for the particularly attractive
melodic line and together they coax from the musicians a
superior performance.

The theme is again a protest against social conditions[7] but
this time making more pointed accusations. The Wall Street
Crash was still over a year ahead but poverty was endemic in
American Black society and whilst it was ironic that soon the
rich man would know 'what hard time mean' too, this would
be of little consolation to the Black, since his lot would
become even harsher. As Albertson points out, for 'poor man'
read 'Black man'[8] and by inference the 'rich man' is the white
man. In view of her forcible character it is, on the surface,
strange that Bessie should always be so careful to avoid direct
criticism of whites on record but presumably the white
shareholding and management of Columbia Records, the
only company she recorded for, was responsible; significantly, her stage shows in which Albertson says 'she frequently alluded to the subject'[9] were produced by Blacks in
theatres owned by Blacks. Here her meaning becomes clear

[6] 'Bessie, Empress of the Blues', page 131.
[7] The second from this session but almost non-existent in the rest of Bessie
Smith's recorded work.
[8] 'Bessie, Empress of the Blues', page 132.
[9] The sleeve notes to the early 1970's Columbia complete reissues.

from her references to the rewards due to the poor man following his war service, plainly a complaint over broken promises to Blacks. The history of Black American participation in the fighting, from at least the time of the Civil War, is littered with promises of freedom made by whites, which turned out to be largely worthless. Even when a political freedom was granted, the cruder forms of slavery were often replaced by an economic slavery. The current perfidy followed the First World War, in which Blacks participated – it had been over for ten years but their circumstances had changed hardly at all.

Bessie herself was hardly poor, at least during the eleven years of her recording career but she knew that most of her audience were and the knowledge helps her towards a performance of complete honesty. Her ornamentation is plain and not especially subtle; she occasionally employs the tonic-to-third ornament of Ex. 15 but not her earlier favourite of Ex. 1. On the other hand she does indulge in some rather sophisticated phrase manipulation and although her contractions and elongations of syllables are quite small, she manages never to sing the same words twice in exactly the same way.

It is interesting to compare Bessie's version with that of her latter-day white copyist, Ottilie Patterson. The Patterson version with Chris Barber's Jazz Band dating from many years later carries, on the surface, much of Bessie's conviction. But her melodic line depends more upon portamento than does Bessie's although at the same time she does use the third-seeker of Ex. 1 which is absent from Bessie's version. This is not the reason she is less persuasive than Bessie however – the reason lies in her lack of the original environmental stimulus out of which Bessie's performances grew naturally and which Miss Patterson can approach only as an informed stranger.

Joe William's trombone fits in better with Bessie's style here than even Charlie Green's would. At first hearing they sound similar but as Schuller says, Williams' observations have 'an extra touch of tension and nastiness'.[10] Above all though, Williams is technically more proficient and subtle. His antiphony to Bessie's first line of the second chorus, 'While you livin' in your mansion, you don't know what hard time mean', is a good example. Charlie Green's reply would no doubt have been stimulating but rough hewn, and would never have tailed away in telling understatement as William's does.

Even the reeds, relieved of their melodic and antiphonal duties are not unpleasing; their organ-like harmony, richer now, hangs as a stable backdrop in front of which Bessie and Joe Williams display their art. Williams can now be seen to be the flux necessary to join effectively the disparate talents of Bessie and the reeds. Not that the reeds are blameless – that the performance falls short of the highest quality is due entirely to the saxophone's uncertain harmonies behind Bessie's first words and the obtrusive tonguing of both reeds in the second chorus.

It is not important that Porter Grainger's contribution is often unheard in a performance of this rich texture. Like the harpsichordist in a concerto grosso he acts as harmonic pilot, audible to his fellow performers if not always to the audience.

The next day, Bessie, shedding the reeds, is left with only the trombone and piano from the previous session. The first title cut was *Please Help Me Get Him Off My Mind,* a plea to a gypsy that is summed up in the title. The words are by Bessie herself and Albertson considers they reflect the inner conflict she was experiencing at the time over Jack Gee, her second husband;[11] the pain in her voice inclines one to believe it. Her melodic line is very simple carrying few noteworthy ornaments; an exception is her 'sagging' tonic-to-third slide on 'groaned' in the first line. Instead she relies upon shading away the volume on words at the end of phrases for poignant

[10] 'Early Jazz', page 236.
[11] 'Bessie, Empress of the Blues', page 132.

effect and in the last chorus, to reinforce her demands upon the gypsy, an extra rasp in her timbre.

Joe Williams' lighter textured sound is perhaps not quite so appropriate this time as Charlie Green's broader brush strokes would have been, in another piece somewhat reminiscent of *Empty Bed Blues*, especially the fourth chorus.[12] Of course, to some extent this is carping — without the memory of Green's performance at that earlier session, Williams would have been hard to fault. But it does seem that his acerbic style is best applied to less personal material such as *Poor Man's Blues* than more introverted themes. His phrasing and dynamics, alternatively open and muted, sound a shade too precise and buoyant here, but it is undoubtedly his control of dynamics that inspires Bessie's end of phrase shading.[13] And there cannot really be much wrong with a performance which includes his exquisite overlapping arpeggios after Bessie's repeat of the line 'Beggin' on my bended knees' in the third chorus.

Porter Grainger provides adequate packing for the melodic interstices but sometimes his ideas take on disturbing shapes, his gauche cadence of the last few bars for instance.

The lyrics of the other title cut on 25th August, 1928, *Me And My Gin,* celebrate Bessie Smith's (real) addiction to gin.[14] She takes keen delight in her revelations and is in more buoyant mood than when making her earlier disclosures in *The Gin House Blues* which was one of her most deeply felt performances. Then the addiction was attributed to emotional insecurity but here it has become habit.

This number is very similar to the other release from this session and it is presumably for this reason that Columbia

[12] The number is constructed from a 4 bar instrumental introduction followed by five choruses of twelve-bar blues. The first chorus however is twelve-and-a-half bars long due to some rather lanquid phrasing by Bessie.

[13] Of the three titles she shared with Joe Williams, this is the only one on which he had a significant influence upon her approach.

[14] Although the number was actually written by H. Burke.

pressed these adjoining masters on separate discs.[15] Bessie differentiates between the two however — two note decorations are frequent here, including both her third-seeker of Ex. 1 and the tonic-to-third ornament of Ex. 15, with dynamic gradation being neglected.

Although Joe Williams sometimes plays phrases identical to those in the previous number, he sounds more at home with this lighter-weight material. And for the first time he has the chance to show us if he has a sense of humour. The lyrics allow Bessie to take a detached view of her problem: they contain an element of self-awareness sometimes bordering upon farce. But whilst Williams' work here is fine and congruous with much of Bessie's mood, he does not respond to the admittedly few opportunities for humour given to him. His reply to Bessie's 'I'll fight the Army, Navy, just me and my gin' at the end of the second chorus makes no reference to the hyperbole.

Much of the literature mentions Porter Grainger in propitious terms and he was certainly a particular favourite of Bessie's. By far the greater number of their collaborations would have taken place on stage it is true but from recordings alone it is hard to be wholeheartedly enthusiastic. He exhibits a retiring musical personality resulting in much of his work being obscured by other musicians and with the notable exception of *Empty Bed Blues,* what we do hear is not outstanding. Now, on his final title with her, he is briefly allowed the limelight. In the penultimate chorus, Williams stays silent during the antiphony to the first two lines as part of the preparation for a last chorus climax. This leaves Grainger to respond alone and the result, confirming a previous suspicion of stiff right-hand phrasing, is disappointing.

[15] The key (Bb) and tempo ($\quad = 92$) are identical: the structure and melodic line very similar.

NINETEEN

1929 – The first half

After a gap of eight months, the longest since she started to record with Columbia, Bessie is back in the studio, this time with Clarence Williams and Eddie Lang. On 8th May, 1929 they successfully recorded three titles, the first of which, *I'm Wild About That Thing,* is a twelve-bar blues[1] the words consisting of a series of salacious statements without narrative continuity, and of such transparency as to deprive them of the dignity even of double-entendres. But the main offence is not the pruriency but the total lack of wit.

Although a twelve-bar blues, the performance has the air of a popular song due to the free ranging melody, the fast tempo ($\lrcorner = 140/150$) the fragility of the accompaniment and the nugatory words. The pace encourages Bessie to phrase across the beat and eschew embellishment. Taken alone, this record suggests a definite deterioration in her voice. In the last chorus particularly, it carries a very rough edge, her growl at times seeming almost out of control. But on the last title from this session, *Kitchen Man,* she shows that its use is still largely at her discretion.

Eddie Lang died at the age of 30 (in 1933) but during his short life came to be the first real jazz guitar soloist. When he cut these sides he was about to join the Paul Whiteman

---

[1] The number is constructed from eight choruses of twelve-bar blues with 2 bar instrumental coda. Almost uniquely in Bessie Smith's oeuvre, the first chorus is instrumental.

Orchestra where a brilliant musician could get overlooked but in spite of this he survived aesthetically, becoming an inspiration to the following generation of guitar players, including Django Reinhardt.[2] He was also a link between Bessie Smith and the popular singers of the 1930's – for a year at the end of his life he was accompanist to Bing Crosby. Both he and Bing were able to flourish because of the invention of the electric microphone which allowed their quieter voices to be heard. This record is in fact so well recorded that the squeaks caused by Lang's fingers moving along the frets are plainly audible.

He treats the guitar quite differently from his contemporaries, rather as a melodic instrument than a harmonic or rhythmic one, although both harmony and rhythm are highly developed facets of his work. On this record his first chorus, antiphony and accompaniment behind Bessie is precise but sensitive, a combination of chordal and single string work (as with the 'classical' guitar). His blue notes and smears particularly are a delight; the first chorus is full of them.

Clarence Williams, back with Bessie after three years is sensitive enough to allow her and Lang to play the main roles and the result, in spite of the lyrics, is a stimulating performance of superior quality.

You've Got To Give Me Some, the second title from 8th May, 1929 session is, except for different words,[3] the same number as *I'm Wild About That Thing.*[4] Moreover, the words are of the same degraded quality as before and were obviously considered the main selling point as both tracks were released on the same 78 rpm 10 inch record.

Bessie uses a similar technique to that on the previous track but this time her growl permeates the whole per-

[2] Although it must be admitted that compared to his successors, Lang's phrasing sometimes sounds a little awkward.
[3] The structure is marginally different too.
[4] Both are by Spencer Williams.

formance more evenly, avoiding the excesses of the previous last chorus. She still does not appear to be entirely in control though, her first note for instance seems to filter through a frog in her throat. On the other hand, there are some good moments, her 'please' on high Bb in several of the choruses for example – it rises briefly out of a fog, to illuminate the proceedings.

Lang's performance though is clearly worse; he rushes his 12 bars of solo and a proportion of his notes have poor intonation. It is hard to account for these lapses unless by now he was losing interest – it was, after all, effectively a fifth take of a twelve-bar blues.[5]

The last title from 8th May, 1929 session *Kitchen Man*, is undoubtedly the best. It is again a vehicle for tired sexual metaphors but the lack of wit is less noticeable because this time the lyrics, about a lady who has lost her favourite servant, have some narrative flow.

Bessie is quietly relaxed, singing in her simplest manner with hardly an articulated ornament to be heard. Her timbre too, is largely free from the forced growl of the earlier releases from this session and she phrases across the beat with nice understatement. No doubt the agreeable balance of tension and release created by the chord progressions[6] was a considerable factor in this fine performance.

With all trace of stiffness gone, Eddie Lang is at his best. His liquid phrases ring out in limpid timbre, evidence of his respect for Andres Segovia. The descending phrase full of 'ghosted' notes behind Bessie's '. . quite deluxe' in the second bar of the verse and again his chromatic chain of lower mordents behind 'likes the way he warms my chop' in the second A section of the first chorus, are breathtaking. He is noted too for his guitar textures; here his chords double much

[5] Three takes of *I'm Wild About That Thing* and two of *You'v e Got To Give Me Some* were cut.
[6] The number is constructed from a 4 bar instrumental introduction, a 16 bar verse and two thirty-two bar choruses in AABA format.

of what the piano is doing but at the same time add necessary swing.

It is perhaps unfair to compare Lang with Bessie's earlier guitar accompanists on record as they were all 'country' musicians achieving their effects through expressiveness rather than technique. Nevertheless, to refresh the memory with the sides on which she was joined by Harry Reser, John Griffin and Lincoln Conaway is to appreciate the measure of Lang's considerable superiority both in technique and sincerity of feeling. His single-string counter-melodies behind the voice, with their 12/8 thinking, are prophetic of countless jazz guitar solos of the 1930's and 1940's.[7]

A week later, on 15th May, 1929, Bessie is accompanied by a band producing the rich organ-like texture above which she sings so well. The first title *I've Got What It Takes (But It Breaks My Heart To Give It Away),* has lyrics, virtually the same in both choruses,[8] ostensibly about a woman careful with money; but full of irony, they actually refer to her favours which are only venally bestowed.

Bessie's delivery is energetic and exciting with a hard rasping edge (except when she descends to low G natural, her lowest note on record, and which is outside her comfortable range). Simple therefore but not as simple as on the last release; here she decorates her line with many two-note melisma, and almost single-handedly propels the piece forward with her phrase contractions and elongations. Strangely, her 'go' and 'dough' in the verse come out as 'gore' and 'door'; not part of her normal accent, it is hard to explain this affectation.

The band sounds larger than it is as a result of the broad-toned saxophones and brass bass. Ed Allen's cornet is

---

[7] Eddie Lang is most famous for his series of guitar duets with Lonnie Johnson and in fact he cut a piece called *Blue Guitars* with Johnson on the same date as this session with Bessie Smith.

[8] The number is constructed from a 4 bar instrumental introduction, a 16 bar verse and two 32 bar choruses in a popular song form (not AABA).

trombone-like in the opening bars but he soon fits a mute and moves to a higher octave. With the exception of a few short breaks his is a subdued performance. The saxophones occasionally contribute a short break too but mainly serve to produce a mid-register mud. The low pitches of the brass bass however, whilst contributing to the turbid texture have a timbre sufficiently burnished to surface more consistently than any other instrument except the cornet. The piano gets lost in the fog, rarely do we hear more than two consecutive chords from it. A negative set of traits, then, but as could confidently have been predicted from listening to the instrumental introduction, they gell to form the perfect matrix for a Bessie Smith performance.

'Once'st I lived a life of a millionaire' says Bessie on *Nobody Knows You When You're Down And Out,* the other release from the 15th May, 1929 session. She goes on to tell of the friendless times she suffers now she has no money: cynical words which she sings without self-pity. Her technique is a mixture of the simple and more complex incorporating precise microtonal and dynamic shading. Occasionally her voice threatens to break free from control as her growl frays at the edges but for most of the time she is in perfect command dominating with a sheer weight of melancholy, far transcending the superficial lyrics.

It is a performance full of subtleties. On 'time' in the sixth bar of her first chorus,[9] she changes gear, moving into half-speech for the 'buyin' bootleg liquor' which follows; she seems at this point to have wandered into introspection over the injustice of it all. Then there is her manipulation of 'Nobody' at the start of the second chorus. The long vowel of 'No' is drawn through every graduation of pitch between major-and minor-third, achieving an effect of great deso-

[9] The number is constructed from a 4 bar instrumental introduction, two 16 bar choruses, the second of which carries a 2 bar codetta, an instrumental 8 bars of chorus with 2 bar codetta and a final 16 bar chorus with a 2 bar coda.

lation. Humphrey Lyttelton has produced an excellent analysis [10] of this, one of the best things Bessie Smith ever did on record, and, whilst further detailed discussion of her performance would merely duplicate the points he makes, one final refinement must be mentioned. It is the contrast in the last chorus between the simplicity of her humming passages almost entirely on one note over changing harmonies below, with the subtle complexity of her slightly articulated four-pitch melisma on 'doubt' just before the end.

Some commentators have linked Bessie's mood at this session with her disastrous Broadway debut of the night before in 'Pansy'. The reviews of this musical were sufficiently scathing to the show as a whole to have caused her deep misery and perhaps there is a connection – but it does not explain her buoyancy on *I've Got What It Takes,* the immediately preceding number. However, apart from melancholy she suggests another quality in this performance which may have some roots in the fiasco of the previous evening; rebelliousness – it is implicit that she will never surrender.

Of the instrumentalists, Cyrus St Clair underpins Bessie's dark mood more than anyone else. He phrases in an austere legato (like a bowed bass) far below the rest but with consummate pitch production; unlike some brass bass players, he is able to distinguish clearly between even the lowest pitches. Somehow his aureate timbre and the inevitability of his progress result in a sense of ineffable sadness.

Ed Allen starts with open cornet but then fits a mute and in his fine and thoughtful solo produces some felicitious 'oo-ah' effects. Some liken him to Joe Smith but in this solo at least, he keeps closer to the melody than would his contemporary. The piano and saxophones are hard to isolate for most of the time but their contributions are vital to this superb recording none the less.

The record was released in September, 1929, coinciding with the start of America's depression. In 1966 Gunther

[10] 'The Best of Jazz', pages 80/84.

Schuller integrated this piece into his Kafka opera 'The Visitation'.

Although by 1929, Bessie Smith's record sales were falling, there was a contrary tide flowing as well. In May she made her Broadway debut (admittedly a flop but contemporary sources do not suggest that this was Bessie's fault), and towards the end of June she appeared in a film.

St Louis Blues, a short (seventeen minute) film with slender plot is a vehicle purely for Bessie's singing, and overcoming the susurrations of half a century she shines through using both the simple and complex elements of her technique including much expressive growl. A superb performance. In parts the film is considerably more exuberant than the earlier recording of the piece with Louis Armstrong and Fred Longshaw.

The film titles are accompanied by a 'jungle' version of Handy's tune by the band alone. Then we see a crap game being played in the hallway of a Black apartment block. The janitor appears and a Hollywood version of a negro argument complete with eye-rolling follows; over the talk, a blues harmonica plays pensively. Albertson claims that in 1950 a group of white liberals tried to get the NAACP to buy and destroy what appeared to be the only copy of this film. They took offence over the film's portrayal of dice-shooting, Uncle Tomish Blacks. As he points out however, they seemed to lose sight of the fact that every ethnic group became a stereotype in Hollywood but more importantly that this film represents the only visual performance of Bessie's art.[11]

Jimmy, Bessie's lover in the film (played by Jimmy Mordecai) appears and joins the game. Soon his new girlfriend (played by Isabel Washington) arrives; his reply to her worried enquiry about Bessie sums up his character, 'don't pay Bessie no mind . . . no, this is my room, Bessie just pays for it'. A guitar joins the harmonica and Jimmy and his new

[11] 'Bessie, Empress of the Blues', page 142. It is also the first time we have heard her accompanied by drums.

girlfriend go into his room, then as the game is breaking up Bessie arrives in the hall, having heard her name mentioned. She bursts into the room catching the lovers in an embrace. She throws the girl out whereupon Jimmy knocks Bessie down, leaving the room to Bessie's cries of 'Jimmy, don't leave me'.

On the floor of the room with a bottle in her hand, Bessie starts to sing unaccompanied, 'My man, my man'. A cut to a gloomy dive finds Bessie leaning on the bar; she starts her song again a tone higher and is joined by the choir and shortly afterwards by James P. Johnson's piano a fourth higher again.[12] Johnson's introduction leads into *The St Louis Blues* with Bessie singing over the choir and with the band playing quietly in the background. The choir is typical of the period's Europeanised spiritual singing – only Bessie imparts genuine blues feeling. But as with all her efforts over rich backgrounds, however unimaginative they may be, it works beautifully.

Jimmy Mordecai performs an athletic solo dance now, observing the convention of the time by keeping his hat on. An instrumental interlude at a faster pace and a tone higher follows (sounding rather like the swing music of the next decade) and on film we see a view of the band, dancing customers, and waiters performing dextrous tricks with trays. Jimmy reappears and there is a reconciliation. While he and Bessie slowly dance, he steals a wad of notes from her stocking. There is a quote from Gershwin's *Rhapsody in Blue* and then money in hand, he departs triumphantly, leaving Bessie to sing out the film.

The poor quality of the soundtrack makes dogmatic comment upon the music unwise but as a visual document it is valuable and unique and one which certainly confirms the extraordinary mobility of Bessie's features hinted at by Van Vechten's later photographs.[13]

---

[12] Because of the uncertainty over the correctness of recording speeds in transcribing from film to record, one cannot be specific about keys.

[13] Photographs taken in 1936 by Carl Van Vechten.

TWENTY

1929 – The second half

Ten choruses in an 8 bar popular song form are squeezed into Bessie's recording of *Take It Right Back ('Cause I Don't Want It Here)* cut on 25th July, 1929; another on the theme of infidelity.

Although the harmonic rhythm is quite fast, the 8 bar format is too short to allow for a really satisfying chord sequence and the result is a constant flirtation with monotony. Bessie recognises this and gradually changes the simple pitch decorations and between-the-beat accentuation of the first chorus into something more varied by the end but this relatively small development is not enough to keep tedium from encroaching.

Clarence Williams provides a pleasant accompaniment, enough of which can be heard to indicate that his touch has improved since his early days with Bessie. But unfortunately the similarity of his choruses can also be heard, emphasising their short-winded structure.

At her next session, on 20th August, 1929, James P. Johnson is back on the piano and the first successful title cut was *He's Got Me Goin'* a popular song on the theme of a less than rapturous infatuation. Bessie keeps her technique simple – at this pace ($\dotted = 144$) she has no option – using mainly timbre to suggest deep pain, a mood she fosters by leeching her delivery of all humour.

Gunther Schuller considers this to be Johnson's best accompaniment for Bessie[1] and certainly he avoids the sometimes jarring disparity between his passages behind the voice and his antiphony. But superb though his performance would be as a solo, in mood it is quite at odds with what Bessie is doing; while she suffers, 'Johnson's happily romping piano'[2] displays a heedless joy. Two first-class performances unfortunately tendered as one.

There is much more agreement between Bessie and James P. Johnson on the other release from the 20th August, 1929 session, *It Makes My Love Come Down*. This is partly because Johnson plays more quietly, drawing less attention to himself but mainly because the lyrics forming a blissful declaration of love are largely free from the misery which in Bessie Smith's world usually accompanies that emotion.

The melody (and tempo) is very similar to that of *I'm Wild About That Thing* and *You've Got To Give Me Some*[3] cut earlier in the year but this time Bessie has difficulty in fitting the omnipresent title words into the available space. The problem seems to stem from the hard consonantal ending to the first word and the necessity to emphasise 'love' which falls on a weak beat — the earlier titles do not call for the emphasis of any particular word. She sounds hurried, not completely in control of the material; it is therefore not surprising that her technique is pared to the bone, shunning articulated ornament almost completely.

Wasted Life Blues from the session on 1st October, 1929 is unusual in being constructed from chord sequences only 4 bars in length[4] whilst at the same time sounding entirely

[1] 'Early Jazz', page 241.
[2] Schuller's words from 'Early Jazz', page 241.
[3] Both written by Spencer Williams: here Bessie Smith is given composer credit and it is interesting to note that these words are much less salacious.
[4] The number is constructed from a 4 bar piano introduction and four 16 bar choruses in a popular song form divided after two choruses by an 8 bar piano interlude. Each chorus is formed from four similar 4 bar units.

satisfying to the ear. The despairing lyrics written by Bessie herself tell of an afflicting sea of troubles the causes of which remain undefined. Shortly after this session considerable doubts about the future of the stock-market were being voiced following a decline in the value of many kinds of equity. Whilst this is unlikely to have had any direct effect upon Bessie Smith, the uncertainties expressed in the words may have been picked up from the growing hysteria of that materialist society.

Her technique, as so often now, consists of juxtaposing short slides with cleanly hit notes; and she particularly emphasises the blue third. In the penultimate four bars of each chorus however she does set off the basic simplicity of her line with a ravishing snake-like melisma on 'end'. Generally she sounds relaxed and comfortable but on the debit side there is some evidence that her voice is growing less reliable; her 'what' in the last line for instance is of very unsettled pitch and gravelly timbre.

Although Johnson is still not perfectly attuned to Bessie's mood, some rapport is evident. He plays quietly with a gently rocking rhythm and whilst his textures range from single bass notes to high-register tremolos they are almost always felicitous (the elements in his style which impressed Fats Waller can clearly be heard).

The other side cut at the 1st October, 1929 session, *Dirty No-Gooder's Blues* carries one of Bessie's favourite themes, the mistreatin' man. At this performance a simple technique is spiced with a revival of her now rare third-seeker of Ex. 1; it occurs just once on the second of the four 'through's in the second chorus.

James P. Johnson reverts to his dichotic approach this time. Some of his antiphony is unobjectionable it is true, but some, like the cascading quadruplet responses of the first chorus is superficial in the extreme. At best his piano is too polite for Bessie's cathartic narrative; at worst meretricious.

But, as so often, he fails to corrode her total commitment to the material.

The lyrics of *Blue Spirit Blues,* the first of four releases from the 11th October, 1929, tell of a dream of hell. An obsessive Gothic twilight, they are reminiscent of some of the poems by Giraud used by Schoenberg in his song-cycle Pierrot lunaire. Bessie sings them simply and with a fierce intensity.

After a 4 bar piano introduction the number comprises five choruses of 8 bar blues which, minor-key inflected, build up a quite considerable tension. It is completed by two choruses in twelve-bar blues form, the first of which has the effect of releasing the tension: the rather rushed piano double-time passages of the last chorus as well as referring to the words, are presumably intended to culminate in a climax again but if so, they fail because of the too rapid alternations with normal time.

And James P. Johnson is back to providing pictures at the very time they are not wanted — the words and Bessie's delivery conjure up all the atmosphere required, and he diminishes the performance with his 'running' double-time and waggish 'silent-cinema' passages.

Bessie's voice on *Worn Out Papa Blues,* the second release from the 11th October, 1929 has a hard, intractable edge to it matching the cruel lyrics, a series of casually dismissive statements to her 'worn out papa'. Her technique is kept at an elementary level but with just a suggestion of articulation to some of the portamento. Once again she employs her third-seeker of Ex. 1 on a single occasion (on 'way' in the third bar of the first chorus) only to reject it for the rest of the performance:[5] perhaps a tacit recognition that further use of this sorrow-intensifying device would be wasted in the company of such a detached piano.

[5] She did this previously on her *Dirty No-Gooder's Blues* of 1st October, 1929, also with James P. Johnson.

She is in an intransigent cast of mind but predictably, Johnson's artistry runs in more buoyant directions, his oriental-sounding parallel chords for example have not the slightest relevance to the words or mood. Johnson was the brilliant jazz musician who felt he would only be taken seriously if he moved to a more respectable music and this resulted in a life-long schizophrenic approach to jazz. By the late 1920's he was engaged in writing symphonic poems, symphonies and even an 'opera'[6] but whilst his popular song compositions[7] met with great success, his 'serious' work did not.

You Don't Understand, the third release from 11th October, 1929 session is perhaps the most 'commercial' number tackled by Bessie so far. Leaping all over the tune's compass in a dilute timbre, touches of growl contrasting with dynamic fade-away, she is joyously inspired. The fast tempo ($\downarrow = 140$) ensures that articulated ornaments are rare but the vocal line is not exactly simple; some of her glissandi for instance move in more than one direction.[8] It is an angular melody that demands agility, often octave leaps, but she manages it all with an unhurried ease which belies the tempo.

Bessie and James P. Johnson get near to an aesthetically symbiotic relationship in the lighter-weight materials of this side and for that reason it is probably their best collaboration. Johnson eschews prettiness, concentrating on solid rocking walking and stride basses in a performance of considerable integrity. Almost everything he does has musical meaning uncluttered by the plethora of extra-musical images he often

[6] De Organizer in collaboration with Langston Hughes.
[7] For example, *If I Could Be with You, Old Fashioned Love* and *Runnin' Wild.*
[8] Bessie never uses her third-seeker, of Ex. 1 in numbers with a popular song construction, only in blues, but here she gets near to it. In Ex. 1 the third of the scale is sought from the fifth; in the middle verse here on 'aroun'' she starts the ornament on the sixth. The number is constructed from an 8 bar piano introduction, a 16 bar verse, a thirty-two bar chorus, another 16 bar verse and a final thirty-two bar chorus. (The choruses are in AABA format).

incorporates. In the second bar of the introduction incidentally, he indulges in one of his favourite devices, a temporary change of key; it has not been conspicuous in his work with Bessie — behind the singer it would be inappropriate, tending to unsettle her.

Bessie's efforts to come to terms with the fashionable requirements of the popular song are meeting with some success but however much she increases her agility and lightens her timbre, she still exudes traces of an elemental misery quite redundant to Tin Pan Alley.

Don't Cry Baby, another Tin Pan Alley vehicle, was the fourth title released from the 11th October, 1929 session. Its melody is even more 'Europeanised' (for example it is more chromatic) than the previous number and perhaps because of this Bessie's voice sometimes fails her; on 'me' in the second line of the verse[9] for instance — she seems uncertain whether to pitch it on the first or third degree of the scale. Then on 'cry', the second word of the first chorus, her glissando fails to climb quite high enough.

Johnson of course is perfectly at home with the material. A 'society' piano with an automated blandness about it, favourite phrases trotted out at appropriate places. But as in all his work his sense of form is immaculate — no superfluous bars, lost beats or wayward progressions sully his playing.

[9] The number is constructed from an 8 bar introduction, a 16 bar verse and two thirty-two bar choruses in AABA format.

TWENTY-ONE

The year 1930

On *Keep It To Yourself,* the first title from the 27th March, 1930 session, Bessie shows us a new facet of her personality in taking portamento almost to the point of caricature. But with adenoidal tones[1] and tongue-in-cheek phrasing she is evidently enjoying herself.

The band exhibits little trace of New Orleans style, providing mostly a harmonic backdrop to the melodic line of one of the instruments or Bessie's vocal but since it has to rely for its rythmic base solely upon Clarence Williams it has equally little in common with the new swing bands just beginning to appear. Louis Bacon's trumpet is strongly Armstrong influenced but refers to his new 'commercial' style rather than the earlier innovatory period. Some of his phrasing is uncannily like that of his mentor, for example the first notes of his solo in the instrumental chorus.[2] But the resemblance is of course superficial, otherwise going little further than a similar timbre and the occasional terminal vibrato. And whenever he decides to display his technical facility the deception is exposed. Bacon worked with the Luis Russell/ Louis Armstrong band in the mid-thirties and this session

[1] At times reminiscent of Howard da Silva the film actor.
[2] The number is constructed from an 8 bar instrumental introduction, a thirty-two bar chorus, a thirty-two bar instrumental chorus and a final thirty-two bar chorus. The choruses are in AABA format.

suggests that even now he was busy training himself to impress his future employers.

Charlie Green's broad, slippery tones are as solid harmonically as we have come to expect but also as usual, without a lot of melodic invention. As for Garvin Bushell, in accompaniment he is excellent, producing his best performance with Bessie. Although exposed to real blues influence relatively late in his career, he was the type of classically trained musician she liked to have with her. But his solo is a disappointment; heat and invention are negligible and the tension drops like a stone even though, as the dynamically weakest horn, he is allowed the harmonically stimulating bridge. Interestingly, Louis Bacon was playing in Garvin Bushell's band as late as 1960.

Bessie is far from her best on the other title from 27th March, 1930, *New Orleans Hop Scop Blues.* She is reduced to shouting her way through the number in a defiant, even forced manner, whilst the band provides a rather loose harmony as before.

Louis Bacon contributes an interesting solo but overall reveals serious deficiencies when compared with his mentor, Louis Armstrong. One area of short-fall is exemplified in his antiphonal phrase at the end of the first chorus: part of Armstrong's greatness stems from his superior choice of notes, always avoiding the commonplace — Bacon provides us with a cliché cloaked in Armstrongesque surface gloss.

Green and Bushell play soundly and safely within their limitations and Clarence Williams although more extrovert than usual still tends to leave everyone to generate their own swing.

On 12th April, 1930, Charlie Green and Clarence Williams came together for the first time to accompany Bessie Smith in *See If I'll Care,* a popular song with choruses in AABA format.[3] Using a few more articulated ornaments than of late

[3] The number is constructed from an 8 bar instrumental introduction, a 16 bar verse and two thirty-two bar choruses.

in this warning to a departing lover, she gives a piquant performance with ironically, some of its appeal the consequence of her failing abilities – her strain in each of the bridge sections up to top C on 'com(in')' is quite exquisite.

Charlie Green takes up the role he often adopts when he is the only horn, commenting continually and appositely upon Bessie's phrases. It is a fine, restrained performance although one which adds little new to our knowledge of his work.[4] But one or two graceful and gentle right-hand figures do escape from the piano providing a welcome diversion from Williams' accurate but enervating pulse.

The two sides from this session were not released until 1947[5] possibly, as Albertson suggests, because of their doleful nature[6] at a time when the Nation's economic problems were calling for happier fare. It needed the New Orleans revival movement of the 1940's to make their release economic.

The chord sequence of *Baby Have Pity On Me*,[7] the other release from 12th April, 1930 session is particularly attractive and examination reveals it to be relatively complex for a Bessie Smith vehicle. The verse is in Bb major but when it comes to the chorus, over half of each A section is in the relative minor key (G minor) building up a tension which is not released until the modulation back to Bb is reached just before the end. More tonal tension/relaxation is created in the bridge since whilst it starts in Bb, it modulates briefly and unexpectedly to the subdominant key (on 'riding on a rainbow').

Bessie gives this plea for affection her full commitment

[4] However Charlie Green has clearly been listening to Louis Armstrong – note his chromatic cadence at the end of the instrumental introduction.
[5] Columbia's 1947 release was in fact a dubbing.
[6] 'Bessie, Empress of the Blues', page 152.
[7] The composer credit is given to B. Moll and C. Williams. It is constructed from a 4 bar instrumental introduction, and two, thirty-two bar choruses, the first 16 bars of the second chorus being instrumental. The choruses are in AABA format.

relying mainly upon timbral contrasts which range from growls to a lyric clarity. Although her advisers often find for her material of a less elemental nature now, she still has difficulty in distancing herself from it as demanded by the new fashion. We are fortunate that this is so but in her lifetime it was a main factor contributing to the declining sales of her records.

Charlie Green, unusually as the only horn, restricts himself to a mainly harmonic/rhythmic supportive rôle. Except for his 16 bars of solo that is, and there, some of his melodic phrases, again unusually, sound decidedly tongue-in-cheek and at variance with the general mood. Clarence Williams not only tells us nothing new but even reverts to an earlier device,[8] his upper mordent based riff of Ex. 2 (at the end of the second A section of the first chorus).

On 9th June, 1930, Bessie Smith's recording career took a new turn (although in the event it led nowhere); *On Revival Day (A Rhythmic Spiritual)* is pure hot gospel. Backed by James P. Johnson's piano and a male vocal quartet, she gives one of her very best jazz performances. At this fast pace[9] and with such a fine rhythmic pianist, she is able to exploit her own rhythmic improvisatory ability to the full. At times she sounds like a driving lead trumpet, setting up complex systems of polyrhythm against piano and chorus. Again she achieves variation through timbral contrast — her freely used growl with rich vibrato forms one end of the spectrum but it is deployed for rhythmic effect too. She has never been more inspired and this enables her to touch her highest note on record (in her normal voice), top Eb, without a trace of strain (on 'day' in the last 8 bars).[10] One of the reasons for her in-

[8] Last used on record with Bessie Smith four-and-a-half years previously on *New Gulf Coast Blues* and *Florida Bound Blues* but first used on her second release, *Gulf Coast Blues*.

[9] $\downharpoonleft = 168$. This is the fastest tempo used by Bessie on record with only *There'll Be A Hot Time In The Old Town Tonight* of 2nd March, 1927 as quick.

[10] Top Eb is also touched on *Gimme A Pigfoot* of 24th November, 1933. It

spiration is no doubt the presence of those ostensibly unsuitable collaborators, the Bessemer Singers. This 'Europeanised' quartet mainly humming barber-shop chords, lays down the rich, pliant base which invariably excites Bessie to give one of her better performances.

James P. Johnson is also at his very best. The fast pace suits him and there is no doubt that he too uses the quartet as a matrix from which to create a superb performance in which melodic ideas are subordinated to rhythmic energy.[11] His is 'absolute' music without a trace of the disturbing antiphonal/accompanimental dichotomy of some earlier collaborations.

The other title cut on the 9th June, 1930, *Moan, You Mourners,* is artistically less successful. Its links with the hot gospel style are more tenuous and Tin Pan Alley influences stronger. But at least Bessie acknowledges the lack of veracity by effecting a rather tongue-in-cheek delivery. Her technique otherwise carries less subtlety and swing. And the vocal quartet do this time anchor the performance to the ground mainly through their deadly, on-the-beat articulation. In the previous number they at least restricted themselves to mainly legato chords, a device which is not detrimental to the rhythm and which as we have seen, usually has the effect of positively encouraging Bessie towards inspiration. Here their sustained chords are missing, replaced with coy antiphony.

James P. Johnson fights hard to overcome the quartet's sogginess but to little avail.

Hustlin' Dan, the first release from the session on 22nd July 1930, is a folk-like eulogy to a gambler so perfect, that the narrator contemplates suicide when he dies. The sombre

---

is unusual for a singer to extend her range at this late stage of her career – usually the reverse occurs. Note also *I've Got What It Takes* of 15th May, 1929 where she descends to low G for the first time.

[11] Of course we cannot overlook either, the charismatic quality of Bessie's singing as a cause of his fine performance.

lyrics are matched by the music of this twelve-bar blues in having the first 8 bars of each chorus in a minor key.[12]

Bessie's technique is generally kept quite simple but does include some lightly articulated ornaments and one which is heavily articulated. The latter is her melisma on 'Dan' in the last 4 bars of each chorus which, although it alternates in each chorus from the upper to lower areas of her range and each one varies in detail, is sufficiently striking as to form a structurally unifying device.

Ed Allen's work here is quite different from that on *Nobody Knows You When You're Down And Out* of the previous year. There he was lyrical but here his Charlie Green-like muted responses to Bessie's lines are sharply realistic. Between them they produce a disciplined performance heavily informed with sorrow.

Steve Stevens, a new pianist for Bessie, gives an undistinguished and repetitive performance mostly in the lower register.

The other title cut on 22nd July, 1930 session, *Black Mountain Blues,* also has folk-like lyrics, this time caricaturing a tough, anti-social mountain community. Bessie carries the sometimes witty words upon a very economical melodic line in a voice of hard edged intensity. But Schuller is surely too premature when, inter alia referring to this number, he says '. . . her voice was worn out by excessive drinking, (and) sometimes there was only spirit (left)'.[13] Of course she is now less good than five years earlier but still a consummate artist.

Ed Allen assumes largely the same role as that on *Hustlin' Dan,* responding inventively to Bessie's lines. But here he shows us more of his technique – his fast chromatic run in the seventh bar of the first chorus (after the instrumental intro-

---

[12] C minor. The last 4 bars are in C major.
[13] 'Early Jazz', page 240.

duction) for instance, is quite masterly in its timing.

Albertson tells us that this title (with *Hustlin' Dan* on the reverse) was released in October 1930 and only 2095 pressings were made. He remarks that not many years before her records had often sold more in a single day.[14]

[14] 'Bessie, Empress of the Blues', page 156.

TWENTY-TWO

The year 1931

On 11th June, 1931, eleven months after her last session, Bessie returns to the recording studio to cut four titles with an unusual sounding band led by Clarence Williams. On the first release, *In The House Blues,* her voice is at its roughest as she turns the words about an enervating grief for her lover taken by the police, into one of her most whole-hearted and direct statements of anguish. She achieves this in particular by ambiguous note-end fall-offs for example her 'house' in the first bar of the first chorus which descends to an undefined pitch, and her moan at the start of the last chorus where the glissando suggests a drop to the tonic although it is hard to be sure that it quite reaches it. She also enlivens what would otherwise be a melodic line of rather limited interest with a phrase manipulation more extreme than any she has employed for some time, every chorus exhibiting a different set of variations.

The band produces the wildest sound yet to accompany Bessie. The horns playing only antiphony yield a welter of pitch collisions and to add to the confusion, their higher harmonics are similar (they appear to be using matching mutes). At times chaos threatens as the cornet vibrato seeks to emulate that of the voice. But apart from some fast stamping chords at the very beginning, Clarence Williams stands apart from the turbulence; a wise decision in view of his role as timekeeper and director of harmonic progressions –

some solid foundation being necessary to prevent a complete disintegration. For most of the performance he plays away blithely at his quasi-swinging ragtime although in the last chorus he does introduce some particularly apposite tuba-like single notes from his middle register.

Paul Oliver[1] and Albertson[2] consider the cornet (or trumpet) to be played by Louis Bacon but aural evidence tends to refute this; certainly there is little trace of his penchant for Armstrong's phrases. As it is being played in a deliberately affected, 'novelty' manner, it could be by one of a number of players[3]

Bessie was said to dislike drums in her groups and the fact that this is the only recording session at which they are included tends to support this (only in her film, *St Louis Blues,* have we heard them with her before). Moreover Floyd Casey is restricted to instrumental passages and mainly wood blocks and cymbals.

Long Old Road, the second title from 11th June, 1931, has pensive lyrics telling of the search for a lover whose affection turns out to be worthless. As with the other titles from this session, the mood is mostly sombre.[4]

Bessie's voice is even coarser than on the previous title — evidence of textural disintegration.[5] On the other hand, from the third chorus on, her ornaments become more complex than of late; in the last one for instance her old third-seeker of Ex. 1 makes a solitary appearance (on 'alone' in the first line).

Both cornet and trombone display the same muted timbre as before and at the beginning their work (mainly antiphonal) is quite appropriate to Bessie's melancholy mood but from

---

[1] 'Bessie Smith', page 66.
[2] 'Bessie, Empress of the Blues', page 159.
[3] Rust in 'Jazz Records 1897–1942', page 1532 says Bacon denies it is him, but for a less negative identification of the cornet, see *Blue Blue* also from this session.
[4] All four titles are credited to Bessie Smith.
[5] Fine control of dynamics has been a thing of the past for some time.

their facetious 'crying' in the third chorus, traces of levity
creep in to undermine it. It may be therefore that her striving
for a more complex, committed line from the third chorus on
is an unconscious response to their flippancy.[6]

Piano and drums are much as before with Floyd Casey's
wood blocks and cymbals making the most positive contribution of the two to the 'jungle ' atmosphere: in the 4 bar
coda, the bass drum is heard for the first time.

On the third title from the 11th June, 1931 session, *Blue
Blue,* Bessie's voice is often on the brink of collapse as she
delivers the cheerless lyrics about deserted love. But relying
upon note-end fall-offs to imbue her words with a deep
poignancy her intentions triumph over failing technique;
particularly moving are her powerful wails of 'Blue, blue' at
the beginning of the first and last verses[7]

The band is full of 'jungle' sounds again with satire never
far below the surface. It may be that the curious sounds at this
session were produced by the musicians to distance themselves from their star's imperfections, ridiculing her roughness to make it clear that their involvement was not to be
taken seriously.

Interestingly this release does provide valuable evidence of
the identity of the cornet player at the session. In the ninth
bar of the first instrumental chorus he plays a nimble
descending chromatic run so similar to the one mentioned
under *Black Mountain Blues,* as to leave little doubt that he is
Ed Allen. It is a conclusion that does not have to rely entirely
upon the similarity of two phrases; it also follows from the
fact that it is not a phrase to be found in the 'bag' of other
cornettists of the time.

[6] It is noticeable that in the line immediately after the horns' first 'cries' of
the third chorus, Bessie reacts with a four-note melisma on 'cryin'.
[7] The number is constructed from an 8 bar instrumental introduction, a 12
bar verse, a 16 bar interlude, a twelve-bar blues chorus, two instrumental
twelve-bar blues choruses and finally a 12 bar verse.

On *Shipwreck Blues,* the last title from the 11th June, 1931 session, Bessie elaborates her technique a little, including some two-note decorations along with her basic slides. And her third-seeker of Ex. 1 makes two appearances; on 'board' and 'do' in the third bars of the first and third choruses [8] respectively.[9] The performance is notable however for the fact that Bessie leaves her last line in each of the first two choruses for the band to complete. Paul Oliver suggests that this was because of a 'tiring Bessie'[10] and her apparent carelessness in the fifth chorus where words seem to be missing from the first two lines tends to support this. On the other hand the band's promptness in filling the gaps at the end of the first two choruses might indicate some degree of premeditation.

The band plays much as on the previous tracks from this session but with Green's trombone more outspoken. It is hard to agree entirely with Albertson about this session; he says that it was 'flawed by poor balance; Bacon's trumpet sounds as if it is coming from another room, Green's trombone appears to be swallowing the microphone, and Bessie's voice has a shrill sound to it . . . Columbia's usual technical excellence is not in evidence.'[11] Certainly the sound is quite different from anything that has gone before but this is mainly the result of the deliberately perverse tone-colours generated by the horns and the plangent sounds produced by the drummer[12] rather than technical recording deficiencies.

[8] The number is constructed from an 8 bar instrumental introduction, three twelve-bar blues choruses, an instrumental twelve-bar blues chorus, another with voice, a second instrumental chorus and a final one with voice.

[9] The slide from the first to the third degrees of the scale which she first introduced in *Spider Man Blues* of 19th March, 1928 (see Ex. 15) and which seemed destined to replace the ornament of Ex. 1 appears to have been lost without trace.

[10] 'Bessie Smith', page 67.

[11] 'Bessie, Empress of the Blues', page 159. Albertson incidentally considers that Bessie is singing extremely well at this session.

[12] In the fifth chorus the bass drum, hardly heard before, makes a tentative appearance which rapidly leads to the self-assertive storm impressions of the last chorus. Floyd Casey had presumably become immune to Bessie's disapproval by now.

As Humphrey Lyttelton says about another of Bessie Smith's performances, even her double-entendres have a 'certain melancholy dignity'.[13] This also sums up perfectly the mood of *Need A Little Sugar In My Bowl*, the first title cut on 20th November, 1931. The words are about the physical aspects of loneliness and Bessie's despondency is enhanced by a sparing use of note-end fall-offs, for example on 'sugar' and 'bowl' in the first line of each chorus.[14] Whilst less raucous than at the last session, the deterioration in her voice is quite apparent — the fibres of her texture are often quite exposed but as we have seen before, rather than detracting from the performance, it heightens the pathos.

Although the melodic line is quite free-ranging Bessie tends to build a lot of phrases around one note: for example she operates around C natural in the fifth bar of the first chorus ('can stand a bit of lovin'') and around D natural in bars 10/12 of this chorus ('On my floor — maybe I can fix things up — so they'll go, what's the matter...'). Phrasal manipulation is well in evidence too. She brings words forward as in bar 12 of the first chorus where 'what's the matter' strictly belongs to the next bar; and 'wrong' breathing pauses are used extensively to underline the meaning of words (and of course to avoid symmetry). At the end of the first chorus for instance she takes a breath before 'sugar'; conventional phrasing would require a breath earlier — perhaps before 'I' or maybe later, before the blued 'in'. Certainly not in the middle of a phrase. But by breaking the phrase at this point, Bessie isolates this important word very effectively. See Ex. 16 below.

The number has a delicious chord sequence with fast harmonic rhythm and gives much evidence of having been quite carefully constructed.[15] The climax for instance is

[13] 'The Best of Jazz', page 81.
[14] The number is constructed from a 4 bar piano introduction, a 12 bar verse, and two 16 bar choruses in a popular song form, the first with a 2 bar codetta and the second a 2 bar coda.
[15] The composer credit is given to C. Williams, D. Small and J. Brymn.

prepared towards the end of the second chorus by Bessie reverting to speech and arrives with her flight up to top A natural on 'stop your fool(in)'. The words spoken by Bessie are the most salacious of the whole number and have the effect incidentally, of providing a separate climax of less aesthetic content.

Ex. 16

bowl dog-gone it, I need some   sugar–   in my   bowl

The identity of the pianist has been something of a mystery. Albertson in his book[16] assumes Fred Longshaw. Oliver admits the mystery and favours Joe Turner.[17] Rust, on the other hand suggests Fred Longshaw or Clarence Williams.[18] I think Longshaw can be eliminated since he tends to make much use of short glissandi, often in places where Williams for example, would use an appoggiatura or an acciaccatura. Here there are plenty of the latter ornaments but only one short glissando (underneath Bessie's 'blue' in the fourth bar of the verse). But more positively, the piece is full of Clarence Williams' trade marks. Two should be sufficient to confirm his presence at this session. In the seventh bar of the verse he plays some middle-register tuba-like notes below Bessie's 'to tell my troubles', reminiscent for example, of his work at the end of *In The House Blues*. More significantly the upper mordent based riff of the next bar recollects the one outlined in Ex. 2 from *Gulf Coast Blues* and used by him in other performances too.

It is a subtle, understated performance in which Williams demonstrates a vastly improved touch since his early days

[16] 'Bessie, Empress of the Blues', page 160.
[17] 'Bessie Smith', page 67.
[18] 'Jazz Records 1897–1942', page 1532.

with Bessie, and in which there is little duplication of material between choruses. Moreover he captures the listener's attention with his first note quite remarkably. He holds this isolated G natural long enough to make us think it is to be the only note of the anacrusis then at the last moment squeezes in a perfectly chosen D natural before the bar ends.

It was at this session that Frank Walker told Bessie that Columbia would be dropping her.[19] She had been overtaken by events both artistic and economic. But perhaps she was not too far off course, at least regarding the quality of her material here – this number was successfully taken up again by Nina Simone in the late 1960's.

The other side released from the 20th November, 1931 session, *Safety Mama,* was Bessie's last on the Columbia label. It is of poorer quality than the first mainly because she has a problem with her breathing. She takes breaths much more frequently and patently not for artistic purposes. She is also less vigorous than usual, leaving the impression that she is not giving everything to the performance. It may not be too fanciful to imagine that Frank Walker's bad news had just been imparted.[20]

Evidence of Clarence Williams' presence at this session is even stronger on this release; note for example his upper mordent based riff of which there is a suggestion at the end of the introduction,[21] a definite pronouncement at the end of the first chorus and another at the very end of the performance.

Few pressings of these sides were released in 1931. This was probably expected by the production team and it may be a reflection of their apathy that only one take of each selection was cut.

[19] 'Bessie, Empress of the Blues', page 160.
[20] See the previous release.
[21] The number is constructed from a 4 bar piano introduction, a 16 bar verse and two, 20 bar choruses in a popular song form. The piece is completed by an 8 bar coda.

TWENTY-THREE

November, 1933

Two years have elapsed since Bessie Smith was last in the recording studio and a lot has changed in the entertainment world. The session on 24th November, 1933 was arranged for her by John Hammond, a wealthy music critic, but since Columbia was now in financial difficulties it is astonishing that he was able to persuade them to record a singer generally considered a has-been. But agree they did although their cheap label, Okeh, was used for the pressings and they were scheduled for European consumption only. It is the first time we have heard Bessie in a modern setting and also with a deliberately racially integrated group. She insisted that she would not sing blues and chose four songs with vaudeville overtones written by Coot Grant and Kid Wilson.

On the first side *Do Your Duty,* she delivers the mildly salacious words in a forthright, rather strident manner. Her voice does not seem to have deteriorated any more; it is still a little shredded at its margins but that merely adds to her luminous aura. Her attack and swing are powerful, spurning the subtlety of which she was capable. She seems invigorated by the fresh sound of the backing, her voice revived from the dilute delivery of *Safety Mama,* her previous pressing. A wonderful performance wholly informed with the cut and thrust of Northern life.

Frankie Newton's muted trumpet is intense behind Bessie and in his open solo he reveals a considerable technique.

Whereas most of his contemporaries would content themselves with vibrato on the longer notes, Newton often applies an incandescent fast shake, an extreme contrast with the mellow pitches at the beginning of his solo. Considered by many admirers to be one of the foremost swing trumpeters, this side shows why.

The white 28-year-old Jack Teagarden's smooth and flexible trombone reveals clearly the influence of the already dead Jimmy Harrison. Although, like the tenor saxophone, he is often difficult to isolate behind Bessie's voice, in his solo he shows up as prosaic the styles of most other trombonists of the time. It is an agile solo played trumpet-like and with a sleek timbre offset by across-the-beat phrasing.

Bessie has been unfortunate with her saxophonists; at best they were unnecesary and at worst downright bad. It is true that some of them became fine players later but when they were with Bessie, in the words of Chris Albertson, they sounded like refugees from a dance hall.[1] For the first time on record she now has one who plays fine jazz. Chu Berry's technique is such that even at this pace ($\quarternote = 120$) he can play in semiquavers and still swing. And his subtlety is shown in the 'ghosted' notes which pepper his solo.

The Earl Hines-inspired pianist leader, Buck Washington (of Buck and Bubbles fame) does not play with quite the crispness of his slightly younger mentor but he does provide a rich harmonic texture guiding the horns surely through the changes. His solo unfortunately is the weakest part of the whole performance, allowing the tension to sag badly.[2]

The real powerhouse of the band is the string bass assisted by rhythm guitar. This is the first time that a string bass has been used on record with Bessie and it illustrates perfectly the way the instrument, well-played, can weld a band into a surging unit, relieving voice and horns of some of the

[1] 'Bessie, Empress of the Blues', page 168.
[2] It is felicitious that Buck Washington should emulate the Hine's 'trumpet' style of piano playing since he was himself a trumpeter too.

responsibility for swing. Brass basses have a certain nostalgic appeal (Billy Taylor originally played one incidentally), but they cannot make a band swing. Taylor achieves his lift by plucking his crotchet and occasional quaver beats like all good string bass players, sometimes a little before and sometimes a little after the implied pulse.

Strangely, Hammond later said that the sides from this session did not equal those using Bessie's own material of the twenties. Few would now agree with him.

The second side from what turned out to be Bessie's last session, *Gimme A Pigfoot,* is an enthusiastic celebration of a legendary speak-easy.[3] Using a little more growl than on the last track, she confirms once more her liking for legato chordal backgrounds, touching her highest note (excluding falsetto pitches) on a recording, top Eb,[4] arching up to it twice on the words 'give the piano player a drink'.

Frankie Newton, in his solo[5] does not sound as comfortable as previously but his cadential chromatic scale at the very end of the performance carrying more than a suggestion of Armstrong, is sheer delight.

This time trombone and tenor saxophone are almost completely submerged in the harmony but the pianist romps away, sprinkling Hines-like tremolos about and much happier at this pace ($\quarternote = 108$). He makes another obeisance to Hines behind Bessie's twice occurring line 'give the piano player a drink, because he's bringin' me down'; his right -hand octaves was a trick adopted by Hines early in his career to make himself heard through the band.

The string bass lays down a fine, resilient pulse as before and this time the guitar manages to surface through the

[3] Speak-easy. Illicit liquor shop. Prohibition was abolished on 5th December, 1933.

[4] Only touched once before and on another number with a legato chordal background, *On Revival Day* of 9th June, 1930.

[5] A solo in which he uses the buzz mute for which he was later to become famous.

chordal mud occasionally – Bobby Johnson's ascending run towards the end of the verse after Bessie's 'just at the break of day' is a deliciously timed filament.

The 24-year-old Benny Goodman's appearance arose by chance. He was recording in a nearby studio with Adrian Rollini's Orchestra and dropped in to hear Bessie. In this, his only appearance with her, his clarinet, later to rule the Swing Era, is under-recorded and although he emerges once or twice towards the end, not enough notes are heard to make any meaningful assessment possible.

Like *Need A Little Sugar In My Bowl,* this number too was recorded by Nina Simone in the 1960's.

On *Take Me For A Buggy Ride,* the third selection from the 24th November, 1933 session, Bessie employs more phrase-end note fall-offs than in the previous two releases but to match the mildly humorous lyrics, a eulogy to a lover synthesised from automotive metaphors, she often turns them into less weighty two-note ornaments. Perhaps her sense of swing has less resilience than usual but still a diverting example of her late style we could not be without.

The band lay aside their proto-swing mode in favour of the looser Chicago style, the slacker discipline propagating a rash of colliding pitches not helped by the presence of the tenor saxophone, the timbre and register of which overlap those of trumpet and trombone. Although a pertinent choice to thicken the legato chords of the two previous releases, here a clarinet would have provided some much needed aural perspective. Instrumentally flawed too then, but only in comparison with the high standards set at this session.

I'm Down In The Dumps, Bessie Smith's last recording is the most serious in mood of the four sides from 24th November, 1933. On the theme of a wretched infatuation, the lyrics end with hope as Bessie promises to pull herself together (her simile for resolution, 'Andy Gump' in the fourth chorus[6]

[6] The number is constructed from a 4 bar instrumental introduction and five 16 bar choruses in a popular song form.

refers to the comic strip, The Gumps, a set of absurdly rigid figures). She shows us that her over-used voice is still capable of subtlety when occasion demands, as she manipulates pitch especially around the third degree of the scale (G natural) the fulcrum for her limited compass.[7] But the words are sometimes so contrived that even Bessie is unable completely to disguise their awkwardness,[8] nevertheless, helped by the rhythm section's richly propulsive harmony she does not allow them to subvert her commitment.

The band produce more variations in texture. The first four choruses have trombone, tenor saxophone, piano and trumpet respectively 'soloing' over the rhythm section and behind Bessie, with the whole band playing in Chicago style behind her in the last chorus. Newton in his 'solo' is inventive, keeping mainly to the middle of his register without mute and incidentally sounding strangely like a saxophone for the first few notes. He leaves the middle register twice, once towards the end of his 'solo' displaying his skill with the 'squeeze'[9] and again in the last few bars where his high notes help to effect a satisfying climax.

Teagarden gives his best performance of the session. After a shaky start to the first chorus when invention seems to desert him, he goes on to play a melodically impeccable line, the only objection to which is that it is just a shade too 'international' for Bessie's still vernacular style. Chu Berry also has trouble with his first 'solo' phrase — he soon forgets the cliché however and puts his semiquavered arabesques to stimulating use. Buck Washington also turns in a fine performance, calling Earl Hines to mind even more strongly

[7] The key is Eb major and her range is limited almost entirely to the perfect fifth, Eb to Bb next above middle C.

[8] The worst example is her line in the second chorus 'I'm goin' down to the river; into it I'm goin' to jump'.

[9] Squeeze. An upward glissando of cloudy timbre, breaking into a clear high note at the end. It is effected by depressing the valves half-way and gradually tightening the lips.

than before — blander than Hines perhaps but achieving a remarkably similar timbre.

Sometimes at this session, the band has shown a paralysing over-reverence towards Bessie but at this last opportunity they throw off their inhibitions to show how exciting they can be.

TWENTY-FOUR

26th September, 1937

Bessie Smith died on 26 September, 1937 near Clarksdale Mississippi, following the injuries she suffered in a motor accident which occurred in the early hours of that morning. She was being driven in a car which ran into the back of a stationary truck.

At the time, it was widely rumoured that her death was the result of the blood she lost after she was refused treatment at a white hospital. This is probably incorrect and what evidence[1] there is suggests that she was taken directly to the Black hospital in Clarksdale where she died later in the day. On the other hand, the white surgeon who found her in the road may have been guilty of some negligence in waiting for an ambulance instead of taking her to the hospital in his car. Whatever the facts really were, Bessie's death attracted more space in the white press than anything she ever did during life.

[1] See Chapter Eleven of Chris Albertson's 'Bessie, Empress of the Blues' for a collation of the evidence.

Selected Bibliography

Bessie, Empress of the Blues. Chris Albertson. Sphere/Abacus, 1975.
Bessie Smith, Kings of Jazz Series. Paul Oliver. Cassell, 1959.
The Best of Jazz. Humphrey Lyttelton. Robson Books, 1978.
Early Jazz. Gunther Schuller. Oxford University Press Inc., 1968.
Expressionism. John Willett. Weidenfelt and Nicholson, 1970.
Harvard Dictionary of Music. Willi Apel. Heinemann, 1976.
Hear Me Talkin' To Ya. Shapiro and Hentoff, Eds. Dover, 1966.
Jazz, Hot and Hybrid. Winthrop Sargeant. Da Capo Press, 1975.
Jazz in Perspective. Charles Fox. BBC Publications, 1969.
Jazz Masters of the Twenties. Richard Hadlock. Collier Books, 1974.
Jazz Records 1897–1942. Brian Rust. Storyville Publications, 1975.
Louis, The Louis Armstrong Story 1900–1971. Max Jones and John Chilton. Mayflower Books, 1975.
Man and His Music, Part Four. Wilfred Mellers. Barrie and Jenkins, 1977.
Ma Rainey and the Classic Blues Singers. Derrick Stewart-Baxter. Studio Vista, 1970.
Mister Jelly Roll. Alan Lomax. Cassell, 1952.
Music in the Twentieth Century. W. W. Austin. Dent, 1977.
The Rise of Modernism in Music. 1890–1935, Course A 308, Units 25–27. Richard Middleton. Open University Press, 1979.
Shining Trumpets. Rudi Blesh. Da Capo Press, 1976.
The Story of the Blues. Paul Oliver. Penguin, 1978.
The Trumpet and Trombone. Philip Bate. Ernest Benn, 1978.

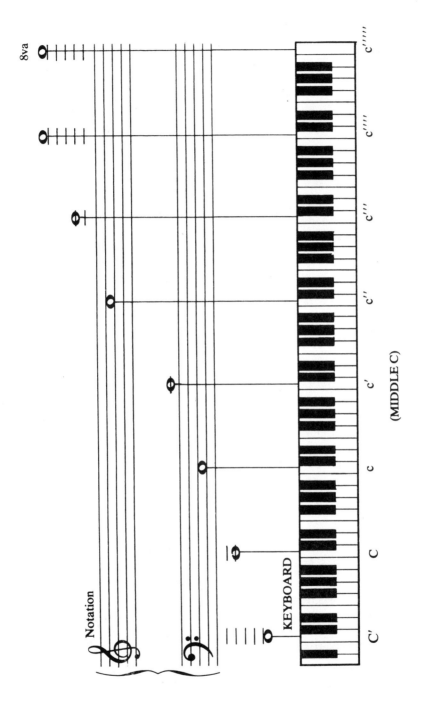

AMERICAN PRACTICE

English		*American*
bar		measure
time		meter
note (the sound of a definite pitch, as distinct from 'noise')		tone
semibreve	𝅝	whole-note
minim	𝅗𝅥	half-note
crotchet	𝅘𝅥	quarter-note
quaver	𝅘𝅥𝅮	eighth-note
semiquaver	𝅘𝅥𝅯	sixteenth-note
demisemiquaver	𝅘𝅥𝅰	thirty-second-note
hemidemisemiquaver	𝅘𝅥𝅱	sixty-fourth-note

DISCOGRAPHY

of

Reviewed Titles

(All recordings were cut in New York)

16th February, 1923
Down-Hearted Blues   Matrix 80863–5   Columbia A–3844
Composers: Alberta Hunter and Lovie Austin
                              (Lawrence Wright Music Ltd)
Voice Compass: c′ to b′
Tempo: ♩ = 80
Essential Form: twelve-bar blues
Accompanied by: Clarence Williams, piano

16th February, 1923
Gulf Coast Blues   Matrix 80864–3   Columbia A–3844
Composer: Clarence Williams (Pickwick Music Ltd)
Voice Compass: Octave up from b flat
Tempo: ♩ = 96
Essential Form: twelve-bar blues
Accompanied by: Clarence Williams, piano

11th April, 1923
Aggravatin' Papa   Matrix 80949–3   Columbia A–3877
Composers: R. Turk, J. R. Robinson and A. Britt
                              (B. Feldman and Co. Ltd)
Voice Compass: b flat to c″
Tempo: ♩ = 104
Essential Form: popular song
Accompanied by: her Down Home Boys;
                              Ernest Elliott, (probably), clarinet;
                              Clarence Williams, piano;
                              Buddy Christian, banjo

11th April, 1923
Beale Street Mama   Matrix 80950–2   Columbia A–3877
Composers: R. Turk and J. R. Robinson
                                    (B. Feldman and Co. Ltd)
Voice Compass: c′ to d″
Tempo: ♩ = 92
Essential Form: popular song
Accompanied by: her Down Home Boys;
                                    Ernest Elliott,(probably), clarinet;
                                    Clarence Williams, piano;
                                    Buddy Christian, banjo

11th April, 1923
Baby Won't You Please
Come Home   Matrix 80952–3   Columbia A–3888
Composer: Clarence Williams (Pickwick Music Ltd)
Voice Compass: d′ to c″
Tempo: ♩ = 82
Essential Form: popular song
Accompanied by: Clarence Williams, piano

11th April, 1923
Oh Daddy Blues   Matrix 80953–2   Columbia A–3888
Composers: E. Herbert and W. Russell
                                    (Pickwick Music Ltd)
Voice Compass: a to b′
Tempo: ♩ = 96
Essential Form: popular song
Accompanied by: Clarence Williams, piano

11th April, 1923
'Tain't Nobody's
Biz'ness If I Do   Matrix 80862–10   Columbia A–3898
Composers: Porter Grainger and E. Robbins
                                    (Lawrence Wright Music Ltd)
Voice Compass: b flat to a′ flat
Tempo: ♩ = 82
Essential Form: popular song
Accompanied by: Clarence Williams, piano

26th April, 1923
Keeps On A-Rainin'   Matrix 80865–10   Columbia A–3898
Composers: Spencer Williams and M. Kortlander
                                    (B Feldman and Co. Ltd)
Voice Compass: octave up from a

Tempo: ♩ = 72
Essential Form: popular song
Accompanied by: Clarence Williams, piano

30th April, 1923
Mama's Got The Blues   Matrix 80995–2   Columbia A–3900
Composers: S. Martin and Clarence Williams
                          (Pickwick Music Ltd)
Voice Compass: octave up from b flat
Tempo: ♩ = 78
Essential Form: twelve-bar blues
Accompanied by: Fletcher Henderson, piano

30th April, 1923
Outside Of That   Matrix 80996–1   Columbia A–3900
Composers: Clarence Williams and J. H. Trent
                          (Pickwick Music Ltd)
Voice Compass: octave up from b flat
Tempo: ♩ = 76
Essential Form: popular song
Accompanied by: Fletcher Henderson, piano

14th June, 1923
Bleeding Hearted Blues Matrix 81075–3   Columbia A–3936
Composer: Lovie Austin (Cop. Con.)
Voice Compass: c to b' flat
Tempo: ♩ = 66+
Essential Form: twelve-bar blues
Accompanied by: Fletcher Henderson, piano

14th June, 1923
Lady Luck Blues   Matrix 81078–3   Columbia A–3939
Composers: W. Weber and Clarence Williams
                          (B. Feldman and Co. Ltd)
Voice Compass: a to c''
Tempo: ♩ = 80
Essential Form: popular song
Accompanied by: Fletcher Henderson, piano

14th June, 1923
Yodling Blues   Matrix 81079–3   Columbia A–3939
Composers: Clarence Williams and A. Hill
                          (Lawrence Wright Music Ltd)
Voice Compass: b flat to c''
Tempo: ♩ = 72

Essential Form:	twelve-bar blues
Accompanied by:	Fletcher Henderson, piano

15th June, 1923
Midnight Blues

	Matrix 81080–3 Columbia A–3936
Composers:	B. Thompson and Spencer Williams (Cop. Con.)
Voice Compass:	octave up from b flat
Tempo:	♩ = 72
Essential Form:	twelve-bar blues
Accompanied by:	Fletcher Henderson, piano

21st June, 1923
If You Don't I Know Who Will

	Matrix 81092–A Columbia A–3942
Composers:	Clarence Williams, S. Smith and T. Brymn (Pickwick Music Ltd)
Voice Compass:	octave up from a
Tempo:	♩ = 80
Essential Form:	popular song
Accompanied by:	Fletcher Henderson, piano

22nd June, 1923
Nobody In Town Can Bake A Sweet Jelly Roll Like Mine

	Matrix 81095–2 Columbia A–3942
Composers:	Clarence Williams and Spencer Williams (B. Feldman and Co. Ltd)
Voice Compass:	octave up from b flat
Tempo:	♩ = 80
Essential Form:	popular song
Accompanied by:	Fletcher Henderson, piano

21st September 1923
Jail House Blues

	Matrix 81226–2 Columbia A–4001
Composers:	Bessie Smith and Clarence Williams (B. Feldman and Co. Ltd)
Voice Compass:	b flat to g′
Tempo:	♩ = 80
Essential Form:	twelve-bar blues
Accompanied by:	Irving Johns, piano

24th September, 1923
St. Louis Gal

	Matrix 81231–3 Columbia 13005–D
Composer:	J. R. Robinson (MCPS)

Voice Compass: octave up from b
Tempo: ♩ = 76
Essential Form: popular song
Accompanied by: Irving Johns and Jimmy Jones, pianos

24th September, 1923
Sam Jones Blues   Matrix 81232–2   Columbia 13005–D
Composers: A. Bernard, R. Turk and J. R. Robinson
                            (B. Feldman and Co. Ltd)
Voice Compass: c' to a'
Tempo: ♩ = 88
Essential Form: popular song
Accompanied by: Irving Johns, piano

26th September, 1923
Graveyard Dream Blues   Matrix 81237–3   Columbia A–4001
Composer: I. Cox (Lawrence Wright Music Ltd)
Voice Compass: b flat to a' flat
Tempo: ♩ = 76
Essential Form: twelve-bar blues
Accompanied by: Jimmy Jones, piano

26th September, 1923
Cemetery Blues   Matrix 81241–2   Columbia 13001–D
Composers: S. Laney and Spencer Williams (MCPS)
Voice Compass: b flat to c''
Tempo: ♩ = 68+
Essential Form: twelve-bar blues
Accompanied by: Jimmy Jones, piano

4th October, 1923
Far Away Blues   Matrix 81261–3   Columbia 13007–D
Composer: G. Brooks (Fletcher Henderson) (Cop. Con.)
Voice Compass: e' flat to b' (Bessie Smith)
Tempo: ♩ = 72
Essential Form: popular song
Accompanied by: Clara Smith, vocal and
                            Fletcher Henderson, piano

4th October, 1923
*I'm Going Back To My
Used To Be*   Matrix 81262–2   Columbia 13007–D
Composer: J. Cox (MCPS)
Voice Compass: octave up from a (Bessie Smith)
Tempo: ♩ = 66

Essential Form:	popular song
Accompanied by:	Clara Smith, vocal and
	Fletcher Henderson, piano

15th October, 1923
Whoa, Tillie,
Take Your Time   Matrix 81244–7   Columbia 13000–D
Composers: T. Layton and H. Creamer (Leeds Music Ltd)
Voice Compass: octave up from a
Tempo: ♩ = 100+
Essential Form: popular song
Accompanied by: Ernest Elliott or George Baquet, clarinet and
Fletcher Henderson or Jimmy Jones, piano

15th October, 1923
My Sweetie Went Away   Matrix 81245–6   Columbia 13000–D
Composers: L. Handman and R. Turk
(B. Feldman and Co. Ltd.)
Voice Compass: octave up from b flat
Tempo: ♩ = 96
Essential Form: popular song
Accompanied by: Ernest Elliott or George Baquet, clarinet and
Fletcher Henderson or Jimmy Jones, piano

16th October, 1923
Any Woman's Blues   Matrix 81283–3   Columbia 13001–D
Composer: Lovie Austin (Mills Music Ltd)
Voice Compass: b to a′
Tempo: ♩ = 72
Essential Form: twelve-bar blues
Accompanied by: Fletcher Henderson, piano

4th December, 1923
Chicago Bound Blues   Matrix 81391–3   Columbia 14000–D
Composer: Lovie Austin (Mills Music Ltd)
Voice Compass: octave up from a
Tempo: ♩ = 72
Essential Form: twelve-bar blues
Accompanied by: Don Redman, clarinet and
Fletcher Henderson, piano

4th December, 1923
Mistreatin' Daddy   Matrix 81392–3   Columbia 14000–D
Composers: Porter Grainger and B. Ricketts
(Bourne Music Ltd)

Voice Compass: b to b' flat
Tempo: ♩ = 80
Essential Form: popular song
Accompanied by: Don Redman, clarinet
                         and Fletcher Henderson, piano

8th January, 1924
Frosty Mornin' Blues   Matrix 81464–4   Columbia 14005–D
Composer: E. Brown (Cop. Con.)
Voice Compass: octave up from a flat
Tempo: ♩ = 72
Essential Form: twelve-bar blues
Accompanied by: Jimmy Jones, piano and Harry Reser, guitar

9th January, 1924
Haunted House Blues   Matrix 81466–1   Columbia 14010–D
Composer: J. C. Johnson (MCPS)
Voice Compass: octave up from b flat
Tempo: ♩ = 96
Essential Form: thirteen-bar blues
Accompanied by: Don Redman, clarinet and
                         Fletcher Henderson, piano

9th January, 1924
Eavesdropper's Blues   Matrix 81469–2   Columbia 14010–D
Composer: J. C. Johnson (MCPS)
Voice Compass: a flat to b'
Tempo: ♩ = 88
Essential Form: twelve-bar blues
Accompanied by: Don Redman, clarinet and
                         Fletcher Henderson, piano

10th January, 1924
Easy Come, Easy Go Blues   Matrix 81470–4   Columbia 14005–D
Composers: W. Jackson and E. Brown (Cop. Con.)
Voice Compass: octave up from a
Tempo: ♩ = 76
Essential Form: popular song
Accompanied by: Jimmy Jones, piano and Harry Reser, guitar

4th April, 1924
Sorrowful Blues   Matrix 81664–1   Columbia 14020–D
Composers: Bessie Smith and Irving Johns
                         (Frank Music Ltd)
Voice Compass: c' to b'

Tempo: ♩ = 80
Essential Form: twelve-bar blues
Accompanied by: Robert Robbins, violin and
John Griffin, guitar

4th April, 1924
Pinchbacks,
Take 'Em Away   Matrix 81668–3   Columbia 14025–D
Composers: Bessie Smith and Irving Johns
                        (Frank Music Ltd)
Voice Compass: c′ to b′ flat
Tempo: ♩ = 120+
Essential Form: popular song
Accompanied by: Irving Johns, piano

4th April, 1924
Rocking Chair Blues   Matrix 81669–2   Columbia 14020–D
Composers: Bessie Smith and Irving Johns
                        (Frank Music Ltd)
Voice Compass: octave up from c′
Tempo: ♩ = 84
Essential Form: twelve-bar blues
Accompanied by: Robert Robbins, violin and
Irving Johns, piano

5th April, 1924
Ticket Agent, Ease Your
Window Down   Matrix 81670–2   Columbia 14025–D
Composer: Spencer Williams
                        (Campbell Connelly and Co. Ltd)
Voice Compass: octave up from b flat
Tempo: ♩ = 88
Essential Form: twelve-bar blues
Accompanied by: Robert Robbins, violin and
Irving Johns, piano

7th April, 1924
Boweavil Blues   Matrix 81671–3   Columbia 14018–D
Composers: G. Rainey and Lovie Austin
                        (Campbell Connelly and Co. Ltd)
Voice Compass: c′ to g′
Tempo: ♩ = 76
Essential Form: twelve-bar blues
Accompanied by: Irving Johns, piano

8th April, 1924
Hateful Blues
Composer: Matrix 81672–2   Columbia 14023–D
Voice Compass: E. Johnson (Cop. Con.)
Tempo: a flat to c''
Essential Form: ♩ = 72
Accompanied by: twelve-bar blues/popular song
                         Robert Robbins, violin and
                         Irving Johns, piano

8th April, 1924
Frankie Blues
Composer: Matrix 81675–2   Columbia 14023–D
Voice Compass: E. Johnson (Cop. Con.)
Tempo: octave up from b flat
Essential Form: ♩ = 76
Accompanied by: twelve-bar blues/popular song
                         Robert Robbins, violin and
                         Irving Johns, piano

9th April, 1924
Moonshine Blues
Composer: Matrix 81676–1   Columbia 14018–D
Voice Compass: G. Rainey (Leeds Music Ltd)
Tempo: octave up from b flat
Essential Form: ♩ = 80
Accompanied by: twelve-bar blues/popular song
                         Irving Johns, piano

22nd July, 1924
Lou'siana Low Down Blues
Composer: Matrix 81881–1   Columbia 14031–D
Voice Compass: Spencer Williams (B. Feldman and Co. Ltd)
Tempo: b flat to g'
Essential Form: ♩ = 72
Accompanied by: twelve-bar blues
                         Don Redman, alto saxophone and
                         Fletcher Henderson, piano

22nd July, 1924
Mountain Top Blues
Composer: Matrix 81882–1   Columbia 14031–D
Voice Compass: Spencer Williams (Leeds Music Ltd)
Tempo: b flat to g'
Essential Form: ♩ = 80
Accompanied by: twelve-bar blues
                         Don Redman, alto saxophone and
                         Fletcher Henderson, piano

23rd July, 1924
Work House Blues   Matrix 81883–2   Columbia 14032–D
Composer: T. Wallace (Cop. Con.)
Voice Compass: octave up from c′
Tempo: ♩ = 80
Essential Form: twelve-bar blues
Accompanied by: Charlie Green, trombone and
                               Fletcher Henderson, piano

23rd July, 1924
House Rent Blues   Matrix 81884–4   Columbia 14032–D
Composer: T. Wallace (C. R. Publishing Co/MCPS)
Voice Compass: octave up from b flat
Tempo: ♩ = 80
Essential Form: twelve-bar blues
Accompanied by: Charlie Green, trombone and
                               Fletcher Henderson, piano

31st July, 1924
Salt Water Blues   Matrix 81893–2   Columbia 14037–D
Composer: G. Brooks (Fletcher Henderson) (Cop. Con.)
Voice Compass: octave up from a flat
Tempo: ♩ = 80
Essential Form: twelve-bar blues
Accompanied by: Charlie Green, trombone and
                               Fletcher Henderson, piano

8th August, 1924
Rainy Weather Blues   Matrix 81907–1   Columbia 14037–D
Composer: G. Brooks (Fletcher Henderson) (Cop. Con.)
Voice Compass: octave up from b flat
Tempo: *♩ = 80*
Essential Form: *twelve-bar blues*
Accompanied by: *Charlie Green, trombone and*
                               Fletcher Henderson, piano

26th September, 1924
Weeping Willow Blues   Matrix 140062–2   Columbia 14042–D
Composer: P. Carter (C. R. Publishing Co/MCPS)
Voice Compass: c′ to b′ flat
Tempo: ♩ = 88
Essential Form: popular song
Accompanied by: Joe Smith, cornet; Charlie Green, trombone
                               Fletcher Henderson, piano

26th September, 1924

The Bye Bye Blues	Matrix 140063–3 Columbia 14042–D
Composer:	P. Carter (C. R. Publishing Co/MCPS)
Voice Compass:	c' to a'
Tempo:	♩ = 72
Essential Form:	popular song
Accompanied by:	Joe Smith, cornet; Charlie Green, trombone; Fletcher Henderson, piano

6th December, 1924

Sing Sing Prison Blues	Matrix 140170–4 Columbia 14051–D
Composers:	Porter Grainger and F. Johnson (Leeds Music Ltd)
Voice Compass:	c' to g'
Tempo:	♩ = 80
Essential Form:	twelve-bar blues
Accompanied by:	Buster Bailey and Don Redman, clarinets; Fred Longshaw, piano

11th December, 1924

Follow The Deal On Down	Matrix 140161–5 Columbia 14052–D
Composer:	T. Delaney (Cop. Con.)
Voice Compass:	octave up from b flat
Tempo:	♩ = 80
Essential Form:	popular song
Accompanied by:	Fred Longshaw, piano

11th December, 1924

Sinful Blues	Matrix 140162–5 Columbia 14052–D
Composer:	Perry Bradford (Cop. Con.)
Voice Compass:	octave up from b flat
Tempo:	♩ = 108
Essential Form:	popular song
Accompanied by:	Fred Longshaw, piano; Bessie Smith also plays kazoo

12th December, 1924

Woman's Trouble Blues	Matrix 140166–6 Columbia 14060–D
Composer:	Jack Gee (but probably Bessie Smith) (Cop. Con.)
Voice Compass:	c' to g'
Tempo:	♩ = 84
Essential Form:	twelve-bar blues
Accompanied by:	Buster Bailey and Don Redman, clarinets; Fred Longshaw, piano

12th December, 1924

Love Me Daddy Blues	Matrix 140167–5 Columbia 14060–D
Composer:	Fred Longshaw (Cop. Con.)
Voice Compass:	octave up from b flat
Tempo:	♩ = 80
Essential Form:	popular song
Accompanied by:	Buster Bailey and Don Redman, clarinets; Fred Longshaw, piano

12th December, 1924

Dying Gambler's Blues	Matrix 140176–2 Columbia 14051–D
Composer:	Jack Gee (but probably Bessie Smith) (Cop. Con.)
Voice Compass:	c′ to b′ flat
Tempo:	♩ = 84
Essential Form:	popular song
Accompanied by:	Charlie Green, trombone and Fred Longshaw, piano

14th January, 1925

The St. Louis Blues	Matrix 140241–1 Columbia 14064–D
Composer:	W. C. Handy (Francis, Day and Hunter Ltd)
Voice Compass:	c′ to b′ flat
Tempo:	♩ = 70
Essential Form:	twelve-bar blues/popular song
Accompanied by:	Louis Armstrong, cornet and Fred Longshaw, reed organ

14th January, 1925

Reckless Blues	Matrix 140242–1 Columbia 14056–D
Composer:	Fred Longshaw (C. R. Publishing Co/MCPS)
Voice Compass:	octave up from b flat
Tempo:	♩ = 76
Essential Form:	twelve-bar blues
Accompanied by:	Louis Armstrong, cornet and Fred Longshaw, reed organ

14th January, 1925

Sobbin' Hearted Blues	Matrix 140249 Columbia 14056–D
Composers:	Bradford, Layer, Davis(Cop. Con.)
Voice Compass:	c′ to b′ flat
Tempo:	♩ = 76
Essential Form:	twelve-bar blues
Accompanied by:	Louis Armstrong, cornet and Fred Longshaw, piano

14th January, 1925
Cold In Hand Blues
Composers:

Voice Compass:
Tempo:
Essential Form:
Accompanied by:

Matrix 140250–2   Columbia 14064–D
Jack Gee (but probably Bessie Smith) and
Fred Longshaw (C. R. Publishing Co/MCPS)
c′ to a′ flat
♩ = 80
twelve-bar blues
Louis Armstrong, cornet and
Fred Longshaw, piano

14th January, 1925
*You've Been A Good
Ole Wagon*
Composer:
Voice Compass:
Tempo:
Essential Form:
Accompanied by:

Matrix 140251–1   Columbia 14079–D
J. Henry (Cop. Con.)
c′ to a′
♩ = 80
popular song
Louis Armstrong, cornet and
Fred Longshaw, piano

5th May, 1925
Cake Walkin' Babies
Composers:

Voice Compass:
Tempo:
Essential Form:
Accompanied by:

Matrix 140585–2   Columbia 35673
Bessie Smith, A. Troy and Clarence Williams
(B. Feldman and Co. Ltd)
d′ to b′
♩ = 96
popular song
Henderson's Hot Six: Joe Smith, cornet;
Charlie Green, trombone; Buster Bailey,
clarinet; Coleman Hawkins, tenor saxophone;
Fletcher Henderson, piano; Charlie Dixon,
banjo; Ralph Escudero, brass bass

5th May, 1925
The Yellow Dog Blues
Composer:
Voice Compass:
Tempo:
Essential Form:
Accompanied by:

Matrix 140586–2   Columbia 14075–D
W. C. Handy (Francis, Day and Hunter Ltd)
b to b′ flat
♩ = 92
twelve-bar blues
Henderson's Hot Six; Joe Smith, cornet
Charlie Green, trombone; Buster Bailey,
clarinet; Coleman Hawkins, tenor saxophone
Fletcher Henderson, piano; Charlie Dixon,
banjo; Ralph Escudero, brass bass

5th May, 1925
The Yellow Dog Blues   Matrix 140586–1   Columbia 14075–D
Composer: W. C. Handy (Francis, Day and Hunter Ltd)
Voice Compass: d′ to b′ flat
Tempo: ♩ = 84
Essential Form: twelve-bar blues
Accompanied by: Henderson's Hot Six: Joe Smith, cornet;
                                Charlie Green, trombone; Buster Bailey,
                                clarinet; Coleman Hawkins,
                                tenor saxophone; Fletcher Henderson, piano;
                                Charlie Dixon, banjo; Ralph Escudero,
                                brass bass

14th May, 1925
Soft Pedal Blues   Matrix 140601–2   Columbia 14075–D
Composer: Bessie Smith (C. R. Publishing Co/MCPS)
Voice Compass: octave up from c′ in normal voice but on up to
                                a″ in falsetto
Tempo: ♩ = 80
Essential Form: popular song
Accompanied by: Charlie Green, trombone and
                                Fletcher Henderson, piano

14th May, 1925
Soft Pedal Blues   Matrix 140601–1   Columbia 14075–D
Composer: Bessie Smith (C. R. Publishing Co/MCPS)
Voice Compass: octave up from c′ in normal voice but on up to
                                a″ in falsetto
Tempo: ♩ = 76
Essential Form: popular song
Accompanied by: Charlie Green, trombone and
                                Fletcher Henderson, piano

15th May, 1925
Dixie Flyer Blues   Matrix 140607–1   Columbia 14079–D
Composer: Bessie Smith (Cop. Con.)
Voice Compass: c′ to a′
Tempo: ♩ = 80
Essential Form: twelve-bar blues
Accompanied by: Charlie Green, trombone; Buster Bailey,
                                clarinet; Fletcher Henderson, piano;
                                James T. Wilson, miscellaneous sound effects

26th May, 1925
Nashville Woman's Blues
Composer:
Voice Compass:
Tempo:
Essential Form:
Accompanied by:

Matrix 140625–2   Columbia 14090–D
Fred Longshaw (B. Feldman and Co. Ltd)
b flat to c″ sharp
♩ = 68
twelve-bar blues
Louis Armstrong, cornet; Charlie Green,
trombone; Fletcher Henderson, piano

26th May, 1925
Nashville Woman's Blues
Composer:
Voice Compass:
Tempo:
Essential Form
Accompanied by:

Matrix 140625–3   Columbia 14090–D
Fred Longshaw (B. Feldman and Co. Ltd)
b flat to c″ sharp
♩ = 76
twelve-bar blues
Louis Armstrong, cornet;
Charlie Green, trombone;
Fletcher Henderson, piano

26th May, 1925
Careless Love Blues
Composer:
Voice Compass:
Tempo:
Essential Form:
Accompanied by:

Matrix 140626–1   Columbia 14083–D
W. C. Handy (Francis, Day and Hunter Ltd)
c′ sharp to b′
♩ = 100
?
Louis Armstrong, cornet;
Charlie Green, trombone;
Fletcher Henderson, piano

26th May, 1925
Careless Love Blues
Composer:
Voice Compass:
Tempo:
Essential Form:
Accompanied by:

Matrix 140626–2   Columbia 14083–D
W. C. Handy (Francis, Day and Hunter Ltd)
d′ to b′
♩ = 100
?
Louis Armstrong, cornet;
Charlie Green, trombone,
Fletcher Henderson, piano

27th May, 1925
J. C. Holmes Blues
Composer:
Voice Compass:
Tempo:
Essential Form:

Matrix 140629–2   Columbia 14095–D
G. Horsley (Leeds Music Ltd)
c′ to d″
♩ = 72
eight-bar blues

Accompanied by: Louis Armstrong, cornet;
                           Charlie Green, trombone;
                           Fletcher Henderson, piano

27th May, 1925
I Ain't Goin' To Play
No Second Fiddle   Matrix 140630–1   Columbia 14090–D
Composer: Perry Bradford (B. Feldman and Co. Ltd)
Voice Compass: octave up from c′
Tempo: ♩ = 84
Essential Form: popular song
Accompanied by: Louis Armstrong, cornet;
                         Charlie Green, trombone;
                         Fletcher Henderson, piano

23rd June, 1925
He's Gone Blues   Matrix 140717–3   Columbia 14083–D
Composer: Bessie Smith (Frank Music Co. Ltd)
Voice Compass: c′ sharp to b′
Tempo: ♩ = 72
Essential Form: popular song
Accompanied by: Fred Longshaw, piano

19th August, 1925
Nobody's Blues But Mine Matrix 140857–3   Columbia 14098–D
Composer: Clarence Williams (Leeds Music Ltd)
Voice Compass: octave up from c′ sharp
Tempo: ♩ = 80
Essential Form: popular song
Accompanied by: her band: Bob Fuller, clarinet;
                         Isadore Myers, piano; Elmer Snowden, banjo.

19th August, 1925
I Ain't Got Nobody   Matrix 140858–3   Columbia 14095–D
Composers: R. Graham and Spencer Williams
                         (Campbell, Connelly and Co. Ltd)
Voice Compass: octave up from b
Tempo: ♩ = 120
Essential Form: popular song
Accompanied by: her band: Bob Fuller, alto saxophone;
                         Isadore Myers, piano; Elmer Snowden, banjo

1st September, 1925
My Man Blues   Matrix 140890–2   Columbia 14098–D
Composer: Bessie Smith (Frank Music Co. Ltd)

Voice Compass:	octave up from c′ (Bessie Smith)
Tempo:	♩ = 72
Essential Form:	eight-bar blues
Accompanied by:	Clara Smith, vocal; Stanley Miller piano. (Miller probably also plays the part of Charlie Grey)

17th November, 1925

New Gulf Coast Blues	Matrix 141276–3 Columbia 14109–D
Composer:	Clarence Williams (Leeds Music Ltd)
Voice Compass:	octave up from b
Tempo:	♩ = 72
Essential Form:	twelve-bar blues
Accompanied by:	Clarence Williams, piano

17th November, 1925

Florida Bound Blues	Matrix 141277–3 Columbia 14109–D
Composer:	Clarence Williams (B. Feldman and Co. Ltd)
Voice Compass:	octave up from b
Tempo:	♩ = 80
Essential Form:	twelve-bar blues
Accompanied by:	Clarence Williams, piano

18th November, 1925

At The Christmas Ball	Matrix 141283–1 Columbia 35842
Composer:	Fred Longshaw (Cop. Con.)
Voice Compass:	a to b′
Tempo:	♩ = 88
Essential Form:	popular song
Accompanied by:	Joe Smith, cornet; Charlie Green, trombone; Fletcher Henderson, piano

18th November, 1925

I've Been Mistreated And I Don't Like It	Matrix 141285–3 Columbia 14115–D
Composer:	Fred Longshaw (Cop. Con.)
Voice Compass:	d′ to b′
Tempo:	♩ = 84
Essential Form:	popular song
Accompanied by:	Joe Smith, cornet; Charlie Green, trombone Fletcher Henderson, piano

20th November, 1925

Red Mountain Blues	Matrix 141293–2 Columbia 14115–D
Composer:	H. Troy (Cop. Con.)

Voice Compass: a to b′
Tempo: ♩ = 88
Essential Form: sixteen-bar blues
Accompanied by: Don Redman, clarinet;
                             Fletcher Henderson, piano

20th November, 1925·
Golden Rule Blues   Matrix 141294–2   Columbia 14123–D
Composer: Bessie Smith (Frank Music Co. Ltd)
Voice Compass: c′ to a′
Tempo: ♩ = 80
Essential Form: twelve-bar blues
Accompanied by: Don Redman, alto saxophone;
                             Fletcher Henderson, piano

9th December, 1925
Lonesome Desert Blues   Matrix 141370–3   Columbia 14123–D
Composer: Bessie Smith (Frank Music Co. Ltd)
Voice Compass: c′ sharp to b′
Tempo: ♩ = 68
Essential Form: popular song
Accompanied by: Shelton Hemphill, cornet;
                             Fred Longshaw, piano

5th March, 1926
Them 'Has Been' Blues   Matrix 141767–2   Columbia 14147–D
Composers: W. E. Skidmore and M. Walker
                             (Leeds Music Ltd)
Voice Compass: octave up from b flat
Tempo: ♩ = 80
Essential Form: popular song
Accompanied by: Clarence Williams, piano

5th March, 1926
Squeeze Me   Matrix 141768–3   Columbia 14133–D
Composers: Clarence Williams and Thomas 'Fats' Waller
                             (Leeds Music Ltd)
Voice Compass: c′ to b′ flat
Tempo: ♩ = 76
Essential Form: popular song
Accompanied by: Clarence Williams, piano

5th March, 1926
What's The Matter Now?   Matrix 141769–2   Columbia 14129–D
Composers: Clarence Williams and Spencer Williams
                                (B. Feldman and Co. Ltd)

Voice Compass: octave up from b flat
Tempo: $\quad$ = 120
Essential Form: popular song
Accompanied by: Clarence Williams, piano

5th March, 1926
I Want Ev'ry Bit Of It   Matrix 141770–2   Columbia 14129–D
Composers: Clarence Williams and Spencer Williams
                                (Leeds Music Ltd)

Voice Compass: b flat to c''
Tempo: $\quad$ = 84
Essential Form: popular song
Accompanied by: Clarence Williams, piano

18th March, 1926
Jazzbo Brown From
Memphis Town   Matrix 141819–2   Columbia 14133–D
Composer: G. Brooks (Fletcher Henderson)
                                (Leeds Music Ltd)

Voice Compass: c' to b' flat
Tempo: $\quad$ = 120
Essential Form: popular song
Accompanied by: Buster Bailey, clarinet and
                                Fletcher Henderson, piano

18th March, 1926
The Gin House Blues   Matrix 141820–3   Columbia 14158–D
Composers: H. Troy and Fletcher Henderson
                                (Carlin Music Corp.)

Voice Compass: octave up from b
Tempo: $\quad$ = 76
Essential Form: twelve-bar blues
Accompanied by: Buster Bailey, clarinet and
                                Fletcher Henderson, piano

4th May, 1926
Money Blues   Matrix 142146–3   Columbia 14137–D
Composers: D. K. Leader and H. Eller
                                (Leeds Music Ltd)

Voice Compass: c' sharp to a' sharp
Tempo: $\quad$ = 84

Essential Form:	popular song
Accompanied by:	Joe Smith, cornet and
	Fletcher Henderson, piano

4th May, 1926
Baby Doll   Matrix 142147–2   Columbia 14147–D

Composer:	Bessie Smith (Frank Music Co. Ltd)
Voice Compass:	c′ sharp to a′ sharp
Tempo:	♩ = 80
Essential Form:	popular song
Accompanied by:	Joe Smith, cornet and
	Fletcher Henderson, piano

4th May, 1926
Hard Driving Papa   Matrix 142148–3   Columbia 14137–D

Composer:	G. Brooks (Fletcher Henderson)
	(Cop. Con.)
Voice Compass:	octave up from a flat
Tempo:	♩ = 76
Essential Form:	twelve-bar blues
Accompanied by:	Joe Smith, cornet and
	Fletcher Henderson, piano

4th May, 1926
Lost Your Head Blues   Matrix 142149–1   Columbia 14158–D

Composer:	Bessie Smith (Frank Music Co. Ltd)
Voice Compass:	b flat to c″
Tempo:	♩ = 92
Essential Form:	twelve-bar blues
Accompanied by:	Joe Smith, cornet and
	Fletcher Henderson, piano

25th October, 1926
Hard Time Blues   Matrix 142874–2   Columbia 14179–D

Composer:	Bessie Smith (Frank Music Co. Ltd)
Voice Compass:	b flat to c″
Tempo:	♩ = 72
Essential Form:	popular song/twelve-bar blues
Accompanied by:	Fletcher Henderson, piano

25th October, 1926
Honey Man Blues   Matrix 142875–3   Columbia 14172–D

Composer:	G. Brooks (Fletcher Henderson) (Cop. Con.)
Voice Compass:	octave up from b flat
Tempo:	♩ = 80

Essential Form: twelve-bar blues
Accompanied by: Fletcher Henderson, piano

26th October, 1926
One And Two Blues   Matrix 142876–2   Columbia 14172–D
Composer: G. Brooks (Fletcher Henderson) (Cop. Con)
Voice Compass: g sharp to a$'$ sharp
Tempo: $\bcJ = 84$
Essential Form: popular song
Accompanied by: her Blue Boys: Joe Smith, cornet;
                            Buster Bailey, clarinet;
                            Fletcher Henderson, piano

26th October, 1926
Young Woman's Blues   Matrix 142878–3   Columbia 14179–D
Composer: Bessie Smith (Frank Music Co. Ltd)
Voice Compass: octave up from c$'$
Tempo: $\bcJ = 80$
Essential Form: popular song
Accompanied by: her Blue Boys: Joe Smith, cornet;
                            Buster Bailey, clarinet;
                            Fletcher Henderson, piano

17th February, 1927
Preachin' The Blues   Matrix 143490–2   Columbia 14195–D
Composer: Bessie Smith (Frank Music Co. Ltd)
Voice Compass: octave up from b flat
Tempo: $\bcJ = 104$
Essential Form: popular song
Accompanied by: James P. Johnson, piano

17th February, 1927
Back Water Blues   Matrix 143491–1   Columbia 14195–D
Composer: Bessie Smith (E. H. Morris and Co. Ltd)
Voice Compass: octave up from a
Tempo: $\bcJ = 108$
Essential Form: twelve-bar blues
Accompanied by: James P. Johnson, piano.

2nd March, 1927
After You've Gone   Matrix 143567–2   Columbia 14197–D
Composers: T. Layton and H. Creamer
                            (Francis, Day and Hunter Ltd)

Voice Compass:	c′ to b′ flat
Tempo:	♩ = 96
Essential Form:	popular song
Accompanied by:	her band: Joe Smith, cornet;
	Jimmy Harrison, trombone;
	Buster Bailey, clarinet;
	Fletcher Henderson, piano;
	Charlie Dixon, banjo

2nd March, 1927
Alexander's Ragtime Band

	Matrix 143568–1 Columbia 14219–D
Composer:	Irving Berlin (B. Feldman and Co. Ltd)
Voice Compass:	octave up from c′ sharp
Tempo:	♩ = 160
Essential Form:	popular song
Accompanied by:	her band: Joe Smith, cornet;
	Jimmy Harrison, trombone
	Coleman Hawkins, clarinet;
	Fletcher Henderson, piano;
	Charlie Dixon, banjo

2nd March, 1927
Muddy Water

	Matrix 143569–1 Columbia 14197–D
Composers:	P. De Rose, H. Richman and J. Trent
	(Lawrence Wright Music Co. Ltd)
Voice Compass:	b flat to c″
Tempo:	♩ = 72
Essential Form:	popular song
Accompanied by:	her band: Joe Smith, cornet;
	Jimmy Harrison, trombone;
	Buster Bailey and Coleman Hawkins,
	clarinets; Fletcher Henderson, piano;
	Charlie Dixon, banjo

2nd March, 1927
Muddy Water

	Matrix 143569–2 Columbia 14197–D
Composers:	P. De Rose, H. Richman and J. Trent.
	(Lawrence Wright Music Co. Ltd)
Voice Compass:	octave up from b flat
Tempo:	♩ = 72
Essential Form:	popular song
Accompanied by:	her band: Joe Smith, cornet;
	Jimmy Harrison, trombone; Buster Bailey
	and Coleman Hawkins, clarinets;
	Fletcher Henderson, piano;
	Charlie Dixon, banjo

2nd March, 1927
There'll Be A Hot Time
In The Old Town Tonight   Matrix 143570–2   Columbia 14219–D
Composer: T. Metz (Francis, Day and Hunter Ltd)
Voice Compass: b flat to c''
Tempo: ♩ = 168
Essential Form: popular song
Accompanied by: her band: Joe Smith, cornet;
                              Jimmy Harrison, trombone;
                              Buster Bailey, clarinet;
                              Fletcher Henderson piano;
                              Charlie Dixon, banjo

3rd March, 1927
Trombone Cholly   Matrix 143575–3   Columbia 14232–D
Composers: G. Brooks (Fletcher Henderson) and Johnson
                              (Belwin-Mills Music Ltd)
Voice Compass: octave up from c'
Tempo: ♩ = 108
Essential Form: popular song
Accompanied by: her Blue Boys: Joe Smith, cornet;
                              Charlie Green, trombone;
                              Fletcher Henderson, piano

3rd March, 1927
Send Me To The
'Lectric Chair   Matrix 143576–2   Columbia 14209–D
Composer: G. Brooks (Fletcher Henderson)
                              (Belwin-Mills Music Ltd)
Voice Compass: e' flat to b' flat but with some
                              note-end fall-offs down to c'
Tempo: ♩ = 88
Essential Form: popular song
Accompanied by: her Blue Boys: Joe Smith, cornet;
                              Charlie Green, trombone;
                              Fletcher Henderson, piano

3rd March, 1927
Them's Graveyard Words   Matrix 143583–2   Columbia 14209–D
Composer: G. Brooks (Fletcher Henderson)
                              (Belwin-Mills Music Ltd)
Voice Compass: octave up from b flat
Tempo: ♩ = 80
Essential Form: popular song

Accompanied by: her Blue Boys: Joe Smith, cornet;
                                   Charlie Green, trombone;
                                   Fletcher Henderson, piano

3rd March, 1927
Hot Springs Blues   Matrix 143584–2   Columbia 14569–D
Composer: Bessie Smith (C. R. Publishing Co/MCPS)
Voice Compass: c to a′ flat
Tempo: ♩ = 84
Essential Form: twelve-bar blues
Accompanied by: her Blue Boys: Joe Smith, cornet;
                                   Charlie Green, trombone:
                                   Fletcher Henderson, piano

1st April, 1927
Sweet Mistreater   Matrix 143735–3   Columbia 14260–D
Composers: H. Creamer and J. Johnson (Cop. Con.)
Voice Compass: a to b′
Tempo: ♩ = 120
Essential Form: popular song
Accompanied by: James P. Johnson, piano

1st April, 1927
Lock And Key   Matrix 143736–3   Columbia 14232–D
Composers: H. Creamer and J. Johnson (Cop. Con.)
Voice Compass: octave up from b flat
Tempo: ♩ = 140
Essential Form: popular song
Accompanied by: James P. Johnson, piano

27th September, 1927
Mean Old Bedbug Blues   Matrix 144796–3   Columbia 14250–D
Composer: I. Wood (Cross Music Ltd)
Voice Compass: octave up from a
Tempo: ♩ = 80
Essential Form: twelve-bar blues
Accompanied by: Porter Grainger, piano and
                                   Lincoln M. Conaway, guitar

27th September, 1927
*A Good Man Is Hard
To Find*   Matrix 144797–3   Columbia 14250–D
Composer: E. Green (Francis, Day and Hunter Ltd)
Voice Compass: octave up from b flat
Tempo: ♩ = 88
Essential Form: popular song

Accompanied by: Porter Grainger, piano and
                                Lincoln M. Conaway, guitar

28th September, 1927
Homeless Blues   Matrix 144800–3   Columbia 14260–D
Composer: Porter Grainger (Wabash Music/MCPS)
Voice Compass: octave up from b flat
Tempo: ♩ = 88
Essential Form: twelve-bar blues
Accompanied by: Ernest Elliott, alto saxophone and
                                Porter Grainger, piano

28th September, 1927
Looking For My Man
Blues   Matrix 144801–3   Columbia 14569–D
Composer: Unknown (Cop. Con.)
Voice Compass: b flat to a' flat
Tempo: ♩ = 92
Essential Form: twelve-bar blues
Accompanied by: Ernest Elliott, alto saxophone and
                                Porter Grainger, piano

27th October, 1927
Dyin' By The Hour   Matrix 144918–1   Columbia 14273–D
Composer: G. Brooks (Fletcher Henderson) (Cop. Con.)
Voice Compass: a to b'
Tempo: ♩ = 80
Essential Form: twelve-bar blues
Accompanied by: Tommy Ladnier, cornet;
                                Fletcher Henderson, piano;
                                June Cole, brass bass

27th October, 1927
Foolish Man Blues   Matrix 144919–3   Columbia 14273–D
Composer: Bessie Smith (Cop. Con.)
Voice Compass: octave up from a flat
Tempo: ♩ = 80
Essential Form: twelve-bar blues
Accompanied by: Tommy Ladnier, cornet;
                                Fletcher Henderson, piano;
                                June Cole, brass bass

9th February, 1928
Thinking Blues   Matrix 145626–2   Columbia 14292–D
Composer: Bessie Smith (Cop. Con.)

Voice Compass:	octave up from b flat
Tempo:	♩ = 84
Essential Form:	twelve-bar blues
Accompanied by:	Demas Dean, cornet;
	Charlie Green, trombone;
	Fred Longshaw, piano

9th February, 1928

Pickpocket Blues   Matrix 145627–1 or –2 Columbia 14304–D

Composer:	Bessie Smith (Cop. Con.)
Voice Compass:	octave up from b flat
Tempo:	♩ = 80
Essential Form:	popular song
Accompanied by:	Demas Dean, cornet;
	Charlie Green, trombone;
	Fred Longshaw, piano

9th February, 1928

*I Used To Be Your
Sweet Mama*   Matrix 145628–1   Columbia 14292–D

Composers:	L. Miller and Fred Longshaw
	(E. H. Morris and Co. Ltd)
Voice Compass:	octave up from b flat
Tempo:	♩ = 88
Essential Form:	popular song
Accompanied by:	Demas Dean, cornet;
	Charlie Green, trombone;
	Fred Longshaw, piano

16th February, 1928

*I'd Rather Be Dead And
Buried In My Grave*   Matrix 145650–2   Columbia 14304–D

Composer:	P. Fuller (Cop. Con.)
Voice Compass:	octave up from b flat
Tempo:	♩ = 72
Essential Form:	popular song
Accompanied by:	Ernest Elliott and Bob Fuller, clarinets;
	Porter Grainger, piano

21st February, 1928

Standin' In The Rain Blues   Matrix 145670–1   Columbia 14338–D

Composer:	Bessie Smith (Frank Music Ltd)
Voice Compass:	octave up from c'
Tempo:	♩ = 76
Essential Form:	twelve-bar blues

Accompanied by: Demas Dean, cornet;
                                   Charlie Green trombone;
                                   Fred Longshaw, piano

21st February, 1928
It Won't Be You   Matrix 145671–1   Columbia 14338–D
Composer: Bessie Smith (Frank Music Ltd)
Voice Compass: a to d''
Tempo: ♩ = 76
Essential Form: popular song
Accompanied by: Demas Dean, cornet;
                                   Charlie Green, trombone;
                                   Fred Longshaw, piano

19th March, 1928
Spider Man Blues   Matrix 145783–2   Columbia 14324–D
Composers: Bessie Smith and H. Gray
                                   (Frank Music Ltd)
Voice Compass: octave up from b flat
Tempo: ♩ = 76
Essential Form: twelve-bar blues
Accompanied by: Abraham Wheat, clarinet and soprano
                                   saxophone; Bob Fuller, clarinet;
                                   Porter Grainger, piano

20th March, 1928
Empty Bed Blues   Part One
                                   Matrix 145785–3   Columbia 14312–D
                                   Part Two
                                   Matrix 145786–1   Columbia 14312–D
Composer: J. C. Johnson
                                   (Record Music Publishing Co/MCPS)
Voice Compass: octave up from b flat
Tempo: ♩ = 88
Essential Form: twelve-bar blues
Accompanied by: Charlie Green, trombone;
                                   Porter Grainger, piano

20th March, 1928
Put It Right Here   Matrix 145787–3   Columbia 14324–D
Composer: Porter Grainger (Leeds Music Ltd)
Voice Compass: b flat to c''
Tempo: ♩ = 92
Essential Form: popular song
Accompanied by: Charlie Green, trombone;
                                   Porter Grainger, piano

24th August, 1928
Yes Indeed He Do!   Matrix 146887–2   Columbia 14354–D
Composer: Porter Grainger (Leeds Music Ltd)
Voice Compass: b flat to c''
Tempo: ♩ = 128
Essential Form: popular song
Accompanied by: Bob Fuller, clarinet and alto saxophone; Ernest Elliott, clarinet, alto saxophone and tenor saxophone; Porter Grainger, piano

24th August, 1928
Devil's Gonna Get You   Matrix 146888–2   Columbia 14354–D
Composer: Porter Grainger (Leeds Music Ltd)
Voice Compass: c' to b' flat
Tempo: ♩ = 108
Essential Form: popular song
Accompanied by: Bob fuller, clarinet and alto saxophone; Ernest Elliott, clarinet, alto saxophone and tenor saxophone; Porter Grainger, piano

24th August, 1928
You Ought To Be Ashamed   Matrix 146889–3   Columbia 14399–D
Composer: Porter Grainger (E. H. Morris and Co. Ltd)
Voice Compass: octave up from c'
Tempo: ♩ = 68
Essential Form: popular song
Accompanied by: Bob Fuller, alto saxophone; Ernest Elliott, tenor saxophone; Porter Grainger, piano

24th August, 1928
Washwoman's Blues   Matrix 146893–2   Columbia 14375–D
Composer: Spencer Williams (E. H. Morris and Co. Ltd)
Voice Compass: octave up from b flat
Tempo: ♩ = 84
Essential Form: twelve-bar blues
Accompanied by: Bob Fuller, clarinet and alto saxophone; Ernest Elliott, clarinet, alto saxophone and tenor saxophone; Porter Grainger, piano

24th August, 1928
Slow And Easy Man   Matrix 146894–2   Columbia 14384–D
Composer: S. Red (E. H. Morris and Co. Ltd)
Voice Compass: d' to c'
Tempo: ♩ = 124

| Essential Form: | twelve-bar blues |
| Accompanied by: | Bob Fuller, clarinet and alto saxophone; Ernest Elliott, clarinet, alto saxophone and tenor saxophone; Porter Grainger, piano |

24th August, 1928

Poor Man's Blues	Matrix 146895–1 Columbia 14399–D
Composer:	Bessie Smith (Frank Music Ltd)
Voice Compass:	b to g′
Tempo:	♩ = 80
Essential Form:	twelve-bar blues
Accompanied by:	Joe Williams, trombone; Bob Fuller, clarinet and alto saxophone; Ernest Elliott, clarinet, alto saxophone and tenor saxophone; Porter Grainger, piano

25th August, 1928

Please Help Me Get Him Off My Mind	Matrix 146896–2 Columbia 14375–D
Composer:	Bessie Smith (Frank Music Ltd)
Voice Compass:	octave up from b flat
Tempo:	♩ = 92
Essential Form:	twelve-bar blues
Accompanied by:	Joe Williams, trombone and Porter Grainger, piano

25th August, 1928

Me And My Gin	Matrix 146897–3 Columbia 14384–D
Composer:	H. Burke (Record Music Publishing Co/MCPS)
Voice Compass:	octave up from b flat
Tempo:	♩ = 92
Essential Form:	twelve-bar blues
Accompanied by:	Joe Williams, trombone and Porter Grainger, piano

8th May, 1929

I'm Wild About That Thing	Matrix 148485–3 Columbia 14427–D
Composer:	Spencer Williams (Cop. Con.)
Voice Compass:	octave up from b flat
Tempo:	♩ = 140/150
Essential Form:	twelve-bar blues
Accompanied by:	Clarence Williams, piano and Eddie Lang, guitar

8th May, 1929
You've Got To Give Me
Some   Matrix 148486–2   Columbia 14427–D
Composer: Spencer Williams (Cop. Con.)
Voice Compass: octave up from b flat
Tempo: ♩ = 140
Essential Form: twelve-bar blues
Accompanied by: Clarence Williams, piano and
Eddie Lang, guitar

8th May, 1929
Kitchen Man
Composers: Matrix 148487–4   Columbia 14435–D
                    Andy Razaf and A. Beledna
                    (B. Feldman and Co. Ltd)
Voice Compass: octave up from b flat
Tempo: ♩ = 116
Essential Form: popular song
Accompanied by: Clarence Williams, piano and
Eddie Lang, guitar

15th May, 1929
I've Got What It Takes
Composers: Matrix 148533–2   Columbia 14435–D
                    Clarence Williams and H. Jenkins
                    (B. Feldman and Co. Ltd)
Voice Compass: g to b'
Tempo: ♩ = 108
Essential Form: popular song
Accompanied by: Ed Allen, cornet;
Garvin Bushell, alto saxophone;
Arville Harris, tenor saxophone;
Clarence Williams, piano;
Cyrus St. Clair, brass bass

15th May, 1929
Nobody Knows You When
You're Down And Out
Composer: Matrix 148534–3   Columbia 14451–D
Voice Compass: Jimmy Cox (B. Feldman and Co. Ltd)
                    a to b'
Tempo: ♩ = 92
Essential Form: popular song
Accompanied by: Ed Allen, cornet;
Garvin Bushell, alto saxophone;
Arville Harris, tenor saxophone;
Clarence Williams, piano;
Cyrus St. Clair, brass bass

Circa, 24th June, 1929

Soundtrack Of The Film
St. Louis Blues
Based upon
W. C. Handy's
composition
Accompanied by:

Part 1 NY 39	Circle J–1016
Part 2 NY 40	Circle J–1016
Part 3 NY 41	Circle J–1017
Part 4 NY 42	Circle J–1017

J. Rosamond Johnson and The Hall Johnson Choir (40 mixed voices) and James P. Johnson, piano; director. Joe Smith, cornet; Russell Smith, trumpet; Charlie Green, trombone; Buster Bailey, clarinet; Happy Caldwell, tenor saxophone; Charlie Dixon, banjo; Harry Hull, brass bass; Kaiser Marshall drums; unknown harmonica; possibly also Sidney de Paris, trumpet and Bernard Addison, guitar. (Some sources claim it to be a 42 voice mixed choir with jazz band and strings but strings are not audible).

25th July, 1929

Take It Right Back
Composer:
Voice Compass:
Tempo:
Essential Form:
Accompanied by:

Matrix 148854–3   Columbia 14451–D
H. Gray (Cop. Con.)
octave up from b flat
$\quad = 96$
popular song
Clarence Williams, piano

20th August, 1929

He's Got Me Goin'
Composer:
Voice Compass:
Tempo:
Essential Form:
Accompanied by:

Matrix 148902–2   Columbia 14464–D
H. Gray (MCPS)
b to g' sharp
$\quad = 144$
popular song
James P. Johnson, piano

20th August, 1929

*It Makes My Love
Come Down*
Composer:
Voice Compass:
Tempo:
Essential Form:
Accompanied by:

Matrix 148904–1   Columbia 14464–D
Bessie Smith (Frank Music Ltd)
octave up from a flat
$\quad = 132$
twelve-bar blues
James P. Johnson, piano

1st October, 1929
Wasted Life Blues   Matrix 149074–3   Columbia 14476–D
Composer: Bessie Smith (Frank Music Ltd)
Voice Compass: octave up from c'
Tempo: ♩ = 104
Essential Form: popular song
Accompanied by: James P. Johnson, piano

1st October, 1929
Dirty No-Gooder's Blues   Matrix 149075–1   Columbia 14476–D
Composer: Bessie Smith (Frank Music Ltd)
Voice Compass: octave up from b flat
Tempo: ♩ = 104
Essential Form: twelve-bar blues
Accompanied by: James P. Johnson, piano

11th October, 1929
Blue Spirit Blues   Matrix 149134–3   Columbia 14527–D
Composer: Spencer Williams
                                        (B. Feldman and Co. Ltd)
Voice Compass: octave up from b flat
Tempo: ♩ = 96
Essential Form: eight/twelve-bar blues
Accompanied by: James P. Johnson, piano

11th October, 1929
Worn Out Papa Blues   Matrix 149135–3   Columbia 14527–D
Composer: Spencer Williams (Cop. Con.)
Voice Compass: b flat to a' flat
Tempo: ♩ = 112
Essential Form: twelve-bar blues
Accompanied by: James P. Johnson, piano

11th October, 1929
You Don't Understand   Matrix 149136–2   Columbia 14487–D
Composers: Clarence Williams, Spencer Williams and
                                        J. Johnson (Pickwick International Ltd)
Voice Compass: a to b'
Tempo: ♩ = 140
Essential Form: popular song
Accompanied by: James P. Johnson, piano

11th October, 1929
Don't Cry Baby   Matrix 149137–2   Columbia 14487–D
Composers: S. Unger and S. Bernie (Blossom Music Ltd)

Voice Compass:	octave up from b flat
Tempo:	♩ = 116
Essential Form:	popular song
Accompanied by:	James P. Johnson, piano

27th March, 1930
Keep It To Yourself   Matrix 150131–3   Columbia 14516–D
Composer: Clarence Williams
                          (B. Feldman and Co. Ltd.
Voice Compass: c′ to a′ flat
Tempo: ♩ = 120
Essential Form: popular song
Accompanied by: Louis Bacon, trumpet;
                          Charlie Green, trombone;
                          Garvin Bushell, clarinet and soprano
                          saxophone; Clarence Williams, piano

27th March, 1930
New Orleans Hop Scop Blues   Matrix 150132–2   Columbia 14516–D
Composer: G. W. Thomas (B. Feldman and Co. Ltd)
Voice Compass: octave up from c′
Tempo: ♩ = 120
Essential Form: twelve-bar blues
Accompanied by: Louis Bacon, trumpet;
                                Charlie Green, trombone;
                                Garvin Bushell, clarinet and soprano
                                saxophone; Clarence Williams, piano

12th April, 1930
See If I'll Care   Matrix 150458–3   Columbia 37576
Composers: Clarence Williams and A. Hill (Cop. Con.)
Voice Compass: octave up from c′
Tempo: ♩ = 104
Essential Form: popular song
Accompanied by: Charlie Green, trombone and
                       Clarence Williams, piano

12th April, 1930
Baby Have Pity On Me   Matrix 150459–3   Columbia 37576
Composers: B. Moll and Clarence Williams (Cop. Con.)
Voice Compass: octave up from b flat
Tempo: ♩ = 112
Essential Form: popular song
Accompanied by: Charlie Green, trombone and
                           Clarence Williams, piano

9th June, 1930
On Revival Day   Matrix 150574–4   Columbia 14538–D
Composers: Andy Razaf and K. Macomber
                                          (Lawrence Wright Music Ltd)
Voice Compass: c′ to e″ flat
Tempo: ♩ = 168
Essential Form: popular song
Accompanied by: James P. Johnson, piano and the
                                          Bessemer Singers (a male quartet)

9th June, 1930
Moan, You Mourners   Matrix 150575–4   Columbia 14538–D
Composer: Spencer Williams
                                          (Lawrence Wright Music Ltd)
Voice Compass: a flat to b′
Tempo: ♩ = 120
Essential Form: popular song
Accompanied by: James P. Johnson, piano and the
                                          Bessemer Singers (a male quartet)

22nd July, 1930
Hustlin' Dan   Matrix 150657–1   Columbia 14554–D
Composer: J. Crawford (Cop. Con.)
Voice Compass: a to c″
Tempo: ♩ = 104
Essential Form: twelve-bar blues
Accompanied by: Ed. Allen, cornet and Steve Stevens, piano

22nd July, 1930
Black Mountain Blues   Matrix 150658–2   Columbia 14554–D
Composer: H. Cole (Cop. Con.)
Voice Compass: octave up from c′
Tempo: ♩ = 116
Essential Form: twelve-bar blues
Accompanied by: Ed. Allen, cornet and Steve Stevens, piano

11th June, 1931
In The House Blues   Matrix 151594–1   Columbia 14611–D
Composer: Bessie Smith (Frank Music Ltd)
Voice Compass: c′ to g′
Tempo: ♩ = 112
Essential Form: twelve-bar blues
Accompanied by: Ed. Allen, cornet; Charlie Green, trombone;
                                          Clarence Williams, piano;
                                          Floyd Casey, drums

11th June, 1931
Long Old Road   Matrix 151595–3   Columbia 14663–D
Composer: Bessie Smith (Frank Music Ltd)
Voice Compass: c' to a'
Tempo: $\downarrow = 80$
Essential·Form: twelve-bar blues
Accompanied by: Ed Allen, cornet; Charlie Green, trombone;
                           Clarence Williams, piano;
                           Floyd Casey, drums

11th June, 1931
Blue Blue   Matrix 151596–1   Columbia 14611–D
Composer: Bessie Smith (Frank Music Ltd)
Voice Compass: e' flat to b' flat
Tempo: $\downarrow = 108$
Essential Form: twelve-bar blues/popular song
Accompanied by: Ed Allen, cornet; Charlie Green, trombone;
                           Clarence Williams, piano;
                           Floyd Casey, drums

11th June, 1931
Shipwreck Blues   Matrix 151597–3   Columbia 14663–D
Composer: Bessie Smith (Frank Music Ltd)
Voice Compass: octave up from b flat
Tempo: $\downarrow = 112$
Essential Form: twelve-bar blues
Accompanied by: Ed Allen, cornet; Charlie Green, trombone;
                           Clarence Williams, piano;
                           Floyd Casey, drums

20th November, 1931
Need A Little Sugar
In My Bowl   Matrix 151883–1   Columbia 14634–D
Composers: Clarence Williams, D. Small and J. Brymn
                           (Cop. Con.)
Voice Compass: a flat to a'
Tempo: $\downarrow = 80$
Essential Form: popular song
Accompanied by: Clarence Williams, piano

20th November, 1931
Safety Mama   Matrix 151884–1   Columbia 14634–D
Composer: Bessie Smith (Frank Music Ltd)
Voice Compass: octave up from a flat
Tempo: $\downarrow = 84$

Essential Form: popular song
Accompanied by: Clarence Williams, piano

24th November, 1933

Do Your Duty   Matrix 152577–2   Okeh 8945
Composer: S. Wilson (Leeds Music Ltd)
Voice Compass: c′ to a′
Tempo: ♩ = 120
Essential Form: popular song
Accompanied by: Buck and his Band: Frankie Newton,
                             trumpet; Jack Teagarden, trombone;
                             Chu Berry, tenor saxophone;
                             Buck Washington, piano;
                             Bobby Johnson, guitar;
                             Billy Taylor, string bass

24th November, 1933

Gimme A Pigfoot   Matrix 152578–2   Okeh 8949
Composer: S. Wilson (Peter Maurice Music Co. Ltd)
Voice Compass: c′ to e′′ flat
Tempo: ♩ = 108
Essential Form: popular song
Accompanied by: Buck and his Band: Frankie Newton,
                             trumpet; Jack Teagarden, trombone;
                             Benny Goodman, clarinet
                             Chu Berry, tenor saxophone;
                             Buck Washington, piano;
                             Bobby Johnson, guitar;
                             Billy Taylor, string bass

24th November, 1933

Take Me For A Buggy Ride Matrix 152579–2   Okeh 8949
Composer: S. Wilson (MCPS)
Voice Compass: c′ to a′ flat
Tempo: ♩ = 108
Essential Form: popular song
Accompanied by: Buck and his Band: Frankie Newton,
                             trumpet; Jack Teagarden, trombone;
                             Chu Berry, tenor saxophone;
                             Buck Washington, piano;
                             Bobby Johnson, guitar;
                             Billy Taylor, string bass

24th November, 1933

I'm Down In The Dumps	Matrix 152580–2 Okeh 8945
Composers:	L. Wilson and W. Wilson (Cop. Con.)
Voice Compass:	e′ flat to b′ flat but with some
	note-end fall-offs down to b flat
Tempo:	♩ = 108
Essential Form:	popular song
Accompanied by:	Buck and his Band: Frankie Newton,
	trumpet; Jack Teagarden, trombone;
	Chu Berry, tenor saxophone;
	Buck Washington, piano;
	Bobby Johnson, guitar;
	Billy Taylor, string bass

List of Examples in Notation

Alphabetical List of
Bessie Smith Record Titles

(Italic number refers to Discography section)